THE DYNAMICS OF PUBLIC POLICY:

A Comparative Analysis

CONTRIBUTORS

Tom Bowden *Social Science Department, Manchester Polytechnic, England.*

Jack Brand *Strathclyde Area Survey, University of Strathclyde, Glasgow.*

Ernst Gehmacher *Institute for Empirical Social Research, Vienna.*

Hugh Heclo *Brookings Institution, Washington, DC.*

Arnold J. Heidenheimer *Political Science, Washington University, St. Louis.*

Christopher C. Hood *Politics Department, University of Glasgow.*

Robert Jackson *Political Science, Carleton University, Ottawa.*

B. Guy Peters *University of Delaware, Newark, Delaware.*

Richard Rose *Politics Department, University of Strathclyde, Glasgow.*

THE DYNAMICS OF PUBLIC POLICY:

A Comparative Analysis

Edited by

Richard Rose

Secretary, Committee on Political Sociology, IPSA/ISA

SAGE Publications London and Beverly Hills

For information address

SAGE Publications Ltd. 44 Hatton Garden London EC 1		SAGE Publications Inc 275 South Beverly Drive Beverly Hills, California 90212

International Standard Book Number
0 8039 9965-8 Cloth
0 8039 9966-6 Paper

Library of Congress Catalog Card Number 75-31293

First Printing

Printed in the United States of America

CONTENTS

ACKNOWLEDGMENTS

This book is a product of the Comparative Public Policy work group of the Committee on Political Sociology, a research body of the International Political Science and International Sociological associations. The purpose of the Work Group is to elucidate and test empirically concepts and hypotheses of significance in public policy and to understand similarities and differences in policy processes caused by differences of national boundaries, social structures and the attributes of issues.

This volume follows from a conference of the work group at Cumberland Lodge, Windsor Great Park, England, May 6-10, 1974. The conference concentrated upon a single concept crucial to the understanding of public policy: how major policies of government do and do not change. The topics of case studies were diverse, to see to what extent different models of change are appropriate to contrasting circumstances.

Five of the chapters in this volume were prepared specifically for the Conference, and revised subsequently. The papers by Gehmacher and Heidenheimer were presented at another conference organized by the Committee on Political Sociology, in conjunction with the Polish Academy of Sciences, at Jablonna Palace, Warsaw, later in 1974. The papers benefitted from the criticism of the following confreres: Herman Aquina, Michel Bassand, Rudolf Klein, Leslie Lenkowsky, Gunther Schaefer, Philippe Schmitter and Harold Wilensky.

The conference was made possible by a research grant from the Ford Foundation to the Committee on Political Sociology; their support is gratefully acknowledged. In addition to the hospitality of the Warden and Staff at Cumberland Lodge, the meeting was also made more pleasurable by support from the British Council.

1975

Richard Rose
Politics Department
University of Strathclyde
Glasgow

Chapter I

MODELS OF CHANGE

Richard Rose

Politics Department
University of Strathclyde
Glasgow, Scotland

Change is one of the few certainties of life. The passage of time alters each individual biologically; cumulatively, the processes of birth, reproduction and death change the membership of every society. While the institutions of government are not subject to change as predictably as are biological organisms, the policies of government are continuously subject to demands for alteration. Changes in one part of society can have a catalytic effect throughout it, for example, the articulation of new black demands in America in the 1960s. Political values can change more rapidly than a demographic turnover in the population, e.g., the growing dissatisfaction with governments in all Western nations in the 1970s. The attempt to stand still may even require altered. policies in order to resist pressures for social change. In the words of a character in Lampedusa's *The Leopard,* 'If things are going to stay the same around here, there are going to have to be some changes made'.

The flux of life does not determine whether, when or how governments respond to pressure of change in the society around them. Political optimists assume that governments can adapt to changes in benign ways that increase social satisfaction. Political pessimists tend to assume that government makes conditions worse, responding too slowly or in the wrong way to challenges to action. A very senior British civil

* *The author is indebted* to the John Simon Guggenheim Foundation for the Fellowship which has given him the time to think through a number of the issues described herein.

servant, a spokesman for the 'middle way', responded to the 1974 political crisis in Britain with the thought, reassuring to himself if not to others: 'Thank God we have so little effect'. (Armstrong, 1974).

The object of this book is to identify the different ways in which governments in Western post-industrial societies respond to the fact of change, and to illustrate the extent to which government policies do change. This first chapter defines basic concepts required to understand the dynamics of public policy; it identifies four alternative models of change, and constraints upon as well as pressures to change. In the chapters that follow, case studies illustrate circumstances in which public policies show gradual progress, oscillate cyclically between two horns of a dilemma, keep things as they are, or lead to major discontinuities in the very institution of the state. The final chapter by Hugh Heclo locates persistence and change along a continuum of policy dynamics.

To understand the dynamics of public policy, one must look closely and carefully at what governments do in response to a variety of real problems that confront them. The chapters herein elucidate general concerns of social scientists and citizens by concentrating upon very specific problems: health, education, employment, fishing, public order and, not least, changes in the structure of government itself. In order to see how Western governments differ in responses to a multiplicity of demands, the dynamics of public policy are examined in a variety of national settings: America, Austria, Britain, Canada, France, Germany, Ireland and Sweden. The comparative focus of the volume allows the reader to assess to what extent governments of different countries are similar or dissimilar in their ability to cope with the challenge of change.

I THE BASIC CONCEPTS

The idea of change is familiar in politics from the days of classical philosophers onwards. Like contemporary writers, the ancients disagreed about what they expected from change. Plato described a society in which politics might reach static perfection through the wise education of governors. Polybius described a world in which forms of government altered from monarchy through tyranny to democracy, then the cycle started over again. Heraclitus emphasized, 'All is flux, nothing is stationary'. In this volume, the term *change* is used in a generic sense to refer to any kind of alteration in the world of which government is a part. No assumption is made about the direction or amount of change, or whether change is a good thing in itself.

Dynamics is a term that can be used in more than one sense in the physical and social sciences. In engineering sciences it can refer to forces that set such things as jet propulsion engines in motion. But it can also refer to forces that maintain an equilibrium through tension, e.g. the dynamic equilibrium that holds the structure of a bridge in place. The common factor in both uses of the term is of particular relevance here: it is force or power, as the Greek root makes clear (*dynamis* = power). To investigate the dynamics of public policy is to seek to understand the forces that make for change and the forces that make government hold to a fixed policy — even when the world around it is changing.

In its most familiar form, time is measured by a clock or a calendar. In chronological analysis, all units of time are of equal duration and, prima facie, of equal importance. In politics, some days are more important than others, for example, an election day. Some years are also more important than others: 1914 and 1939 are turning points in time because of the outbreak of world war, and 1848 is famous as the year of revolution. The significance of a given amount of time is relative to the problem at hand. It takes only a few minutes to turn a group of demonstrators into a rioting mob or a peaceful assembly. It takes weeks or months to carry out an election campaign, and years for a newly elected government to realize most of its promises. To change a society by altering its educational system would take generations for the majority of adult citizens to pass through the new educational system.

In colloquial English, we might say that policy is 'what politics is about'. Etymologically, the same Greek root, *polis,* appears in three English words: policy, politics and police. Contemporary political scientists differ in the meaning they give the word. The term policy can be used to refer to the intentions of politicians, e.g., 'We have a policy to deal with this problem', to the actions of government, e.g., 'Our policy is being carried out by the Department of Agriculture'; or to the impact of government, e.g., 'Our policy enables an extra 100,000 young people to go to university this year'.

Anything is potentially the subject of public policy, from far-reaching questions of war and peace or the management of the economy to whether one can paint one's front door purple in a society with detailed regulations for environmental planning. In the non-totalitarian societies of the Western world, there must always be a substantial number of activities, e.g., religious practices or individual diet, that the state does not seek to regulate; intervention would even be considered illegitimate. To speak of *public* policy concentrates attention upon issues that concern government, whether a government is trying to carry out a program, e.g. to reduce poverty, or trying to ignore demands for action, e.g., the studied avoidance of charges of religious discrimination in Northern Ireland by successive British governments. The agenda of issues that a government can consider at any one moment is limited by the time available to policy-makers. The more pluralistic the political and social institutions of a country the greater the potential for issues being forced upon the attention of government, whether it wishes to respond to them or not.

The *impact* of a government program can be very different from intentions stated by policy-makers, for the desires of governors are not automatically realized by the programs that they introduce. The environment that creates pressures for change may simultaneously present obstacles to the satisfaction of popular demands. For example, in every Western country, citizens want an end to rising prices and full employment; many economists argue that actions taken to attain one of these objectives will deny citizens the other. The War on Poverty launched by Washington in the 1960s demonstrated that government programs designed to provide more services to the poor did not have benefits proportionate to resources invested. (Ginzberg and Solow, 1974). In every Western nation, governments concerned with reducing poverty have found they lack the understanding and/or the ability to eliminate contemporary hardcore poverty. The economic problems of Western nations in the 1970s emphasize that many problems are insoluble within the confines of a single land, because of the interdependence of national economies.

Public policy is best conceived in terms of a *process,* rather than in terms of policy-making. A policy-making framework is narrow; it concentrates attention upon the decision-making stage of the policy process, and perhaps the steps leading up to a government decision as well. The choice of a particular program to realize a government's goal is the half-way point, rather than the end of the policy process. If citizens are to feel the impact of a politician's decision, much else must be done. The model of the policy process that follows (Rose, 1973) makes clear what the steps are in a lengthy, complex and often recursive series of political interactions between those within and those outside government.

1) *The initial state:* Analysis of the causation of events can be extended

back indefinitely in time. For example, a researcher studying govern-ment pension policies could start at any point from the 19th century pre-welfare state to the latest proposal for major change. (Heclo, 1974). A decision about when the process starts will be determined by the interests of a researcher. The study of the policy process logically commences with a consideration of society prior to the first stirrings of demands for change. The initial state is best conceived as a social condition, rather than as evidence of social need. Poverty existed for centuries in Western societies without stimulating a positive demand for government action.

2) *Placing a condition on the agenda of political controversy:* This represents a crucial translation from social system analysis to matters within the political system. The rapid rise within many nations of issues such as environmental pollution and moral permissiveness shows that entry to the agenda of controversy can be easier than students of mass political behaviour might expect. Comparative analysis is particularly useful to identify what is unusual or unique in the agenda of issues of a country. A particular national government may be found to ignore problems that are a subject of concern elsewhere, e.g., the absence of regional policy in the United States, or to attend to matters not an issue elsewhere, e.g., the debate about whether contraception should be legalized in Ireland.

3) *The advancement of demands:* Organized group action is required to advance political demands, or to oppose demands advanced by others. Unfortunately, the vast literature about political parties concentrates more attention upon the way in which parties conduct election cam-paigns than upon their policy role; some political scientists even query whether parties have such a role. Yet there is little prima facie reason to believe that communist, socialist, Catholic and conservative regimes all carry out the same public policies — and much evidence that they differ.

4) *Reviewing resources and constraints:* The formulation of alternative policies or combinations of policies goes forward on the basis of resources available, and constraints upon choice. To note this is not to suggest that there will be a consensus about available means; judgments about the limits of choice invariably differ according to aspirations. Partisan ideologues will likely be more optimistic about the resources of government for changing society and bureaucrats are likely to think

first of constraints. In other words, judgments of what is 'practical' depend not only upon objective features of the environment, but also upon subjective perceptions.

5) *Shifting from no-decision to decision:* A debate about policy can go on for a very long time. For example, the British government deliberated about the introduction of decimal coinage in 1816; the decision to go decimal was taken 150 years later. Deliberations about a tunnel or bridge across the English Channel have been going on since 1802; the policy is still at a state of indecision. A government takes a decision because there is a routine, e.g., an annual budget cycle; there is a crisis with a known deadline, or in which delay is daily very costly, e.g., a military ultimatum or a currency crisis. Other pressures to act are thus non-routine and non-crisis.

6) *The content of choice:* The literature of decision-making and political power has concentrated upon the determinants of choice. It is equally important to consider the *content* of choice, that is, the particular program of actions to which a government commits itself. A program may take the form of a law telling people what they may or may not do, or it may authorize money and services as incentives to individuals or organizations to act as the government wishes its citizens to do. A program may provide no more than a symbolic response, e.g., a ministerial speech appealing to public opinion.

7) *Implementing policies:* A study that stops at the moment of decision is literally a study of no consequence. A government's choice of a program only has meaning through the implementation of its intentions. Implementation often occurs through the delegation and decentralization of action from the highest levels of government to local officials who may (or may not) do what the sponsors of a policy expect and wish. Pressman and Wildavsky (1973) subtitle their book on implementation *How Great Expectations in Washington are Dashed in Oakland or, Why It's Amazing that Federal Programs Work at All.* The problem of carrying out measures consistent with policy intentions is not unique to America. It faces every European government that seeks to make its economy work in accord with the government's national economic plan.

8) *The production of outputs:* The outputs of government are the goods and services produced in the course of implementing a policy.

The outputs can often be identified by standard bureaucratic documents: expenditure figures, personnel employed, and routine records of services rendered or undertaken. The records are often not comprehensive; they are likely to be more accurate in education than in police administration. The outputs of government are but one among many inputs to the social system.

9) *Impact upon society:* The impact of a given program can be consistent with the expectations of governors, exceed their expectations or contradict them by being nil, or even negative. As politicians do not like to admit failure and as it is often difficult to agree upon objectives, policies are often decided upon without a clearly specified statement of the changes they are intended to produce. After the event, governors, citizens and social scientists can each evaluate their consequences. American efforts at program evaluation (Weiss, 1972) have emphasized the difficulty of measuring the impact of programs, especially in the absence of clearly specified criteria of achievement. In such circumstances, a researcher may choose to examine what he thinks the government ought to have achieved. Alternatively, he may adopt a null hypothesis: policy X had no measurable effect on any condition in society.

10) *The routinization of feedback:* If a political objective is conceived in terms of outputs such as more schools, rather than impact, such as more learning, it is relatively straightforward to routinize the administration of a policy. There is sufficient audit-type information about the activities of education departments to guarantee that the policy is being implemented, and there is nothing to cast doubt upon the impact of the policy; this is inferred from the outputs. To monitor social conditions as well as policy outputs introduces the prospect of learning that routine measures are not successful, as routine expectations assume. What is viewed as the routinization of a policy can also be considered stage 1, the initial state, by someone concerned with the next cycle of policy-making.

11) *Deroutinizing a stable state:* The deroutinization of a stable state is the second step in another cycle of the policy process, once again placing a condition on the agenda of political controversy. Changing a more-or-less routinized program involves different political forces from starting a new policy. Administrators and their clients are interested parties. Since no policy, whatever its costs, is devoid of benefits, even

seemingly unsuccessful policies will have some entrenched support. Reciprocally, any policy, however seemingly popular, is likely to impose costs on someone or some group. The distribution of costs and benefits and the consequences of different burdens is important in determining the maintenance or the disruption of policy routines.

The foregoing is intended to call attention to the variety of stages involved in the policy process. In specific political situations, a welter of details are likely to obscure persisting patterns of events. Several stages of the policy process may be activated by different groups at the same time, e.g., demands are voiced, alternatives reviewed, and established policies implemented concurrently. The outline abstracts common properties of the policy process. These basic elements are presented as a process, rather than a theory, because this best reflects the state of knowledge of the social sciences today. As Donald Schon (1971) has argued in *Beyond the Stable State,* 'In the absence of a coherent and encompassing theory, process models provide ways of organizing the case histories of experience and relating them to characteristics of new situations'.

Ultimately, what a policy achieves is more important than the means by which it is formulated. The basic question that both politicians and citizens ask is both simple and concrete: Is this policy getting anywhere?

II ALTERNATIVE MODELS OF CHANGE

The study of public policy can emphasize either of two different, albeit complementary, concerns. One approach concentrates attention upon the activities within the control of government, ranging from the recognition of demands for action to the production of outputs. The other approach emphasizes the impact of these outputs, ranging from the elimination of the need that stimulated action, to no impact whatsoever. The first approach is central to the study of political science; the second is of concern to many kinds of social scientists, including economists, sociologists, social workers, lawyers, and urban planners. In evaluating the impact of government programs upon society, political scientists must broaden their outlook to take into account many conditions outside the control of government, ranging from the actions of other states to the influence of the weather upon agricultural production.

Politicians may wish to change or maintain government programs and/or change or maintain social conditions. A politician whose desire for change is divorced from a consideration of alternative government programs will have little to say when crucial decisions are made in the policy process. A politician concentrating upon maximizing his influence within government when the 'big' decisions are taken may be too busy to think about whatever happened as the result of what was decided. Because politicians can have either (or both) kind of objectives, models of change must be applicable both to the things that governments do (its policies) and things that happen to society in consequence (its impact). The four models of policy dynamics identified here can be applied to each set of concerns.

The similarities and differences between the four dynamic models can be summarized in graphic form. (Figure 1). In each instance, movement across the horizontal axis of the graph indicates the irreversible and inexorable progress of time. The vertical axis plots progress in terms of a policy objective. In the static model, the line is flat; government policy is to maintain the status quo. It is a line that would approximately reflect such public safety services as fire prevention. The second figure illustrates a cyclical movement in policy. The vertical axis might be measuring annual unemployment rates in a society. The third figure shows linear progress. While the line is not absolutely straight, it is moving upwards, and the rate of progress is more or less steady, it depicts a pattern of achievement that would certainly satisfy those concerned with promoting the economic growth of a country. The introduction of a second vertical axis midway through the time period of Figure 1 (d) indicates discontinuity, a different goal from that previously concerning a government. The erratic course of the new policy emphasizes the uncertainties in the first few years of a new policy. A discontinuity arises, for example, when a military dictatorship concerned with maximizing control of its citizens falls and is replaced by a regime wishing to encourage liberty.

1) *The static model:* If government policy shows no discernible change, it is static through time. A political party of conservative bent would regard static policies as actively desirable; reformist or socialist parties tend to favour policies of change. There is nothing intrinsically good or bad in maintaining the status quo. Ecologists, in their demands for the conservation of human resources, are as much against change in one sphere of life as they may be for it in another, e.g., re-organizing the

economy. Similarly, conservatives opposed to the introduction of new welfare measures may favour the introduction of new tax policies reducing their payments to government.

A government may do nothing, and within society there may be no tendencies causing change. On the other hand, the impact of a policy may be nil change, because there is a *static equilibrium* with a variety of political, social and economic pressures so evenly balanced that the net result of much activity is no net change in social conditions. Government inaction does not ensure a static society, for if a government does nothing in a changing environment, then the conditions it is concerned with may deteriorate. For example, in many countries a laissez faire transportation policy has gradually led to the deterioration of public transport systems and congestion in a transport system based on the automobile.

2) *The cyclical model:* A policy is cyclical if government alternates between one. option and then another. For example, the credit policies of Western governments lead central banks and ministers of finance to raise interest rates for money when they fear inflation, and to lower interest rates when unemployment is their principal worry. In this example from classical economics, the government reacts in opposition to market forces in an attempt to maintain a balance between two inter-related goals. In the course of a decade, a government may regard its policy as a success even if half the time unemployment is above average, and half the time below it; alternating policies are adopted with alternative consequences in order that the net effect will be no long-term rise in unemployment or in inflation.

Cyclical policies are most appropriate when governors have a good understanding of the social and economic processes that create pressures for change, and the technical knowledge and organizational capability to adopt and enforce counter-cyclical policies. Cyclical policies are easier to monitor and maintain if the policy concerns changes in degree, e.g., percent unemployed or pension payments as a percentage of industrial workers' wages, rather than changes in kind, as in an international relations cycle of peace and war. For two decades following the end of the Second World War, Keynesian economic theory was thought to provide such understanding to governments wishing to manage their economy. The problems of the international economy in the 1970s illustrate that even the most highly regarded cyclical policies may sooner or later fail to be effective.

Cyclical policies sometimes permit politicians to resolve dilemmas of

Figure 1

Four Models of Public Policy

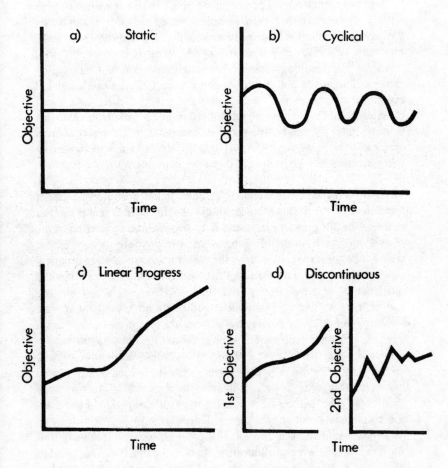

choice by making different choices at different points in time. It is in the nature of a dilemma that there is something to be said for each alternative, e.g., full employment or stable prices. Instead of keeping prices steady through continuously high unemployment, or encouraging a steady inflationary price spiral, a government can adopt alternative objectives through time; it trades off price stability against unemployment according to the political climate of the moment, sometimes favouring one phase of the cycle and sometimes the other.

A government will adopt a cyclical policy when it wishes to cope with a problem, rather than eliminate its causes. For example, no Western government would today assume that it could eliminate unemployment or inflationary pressures upon prices. It is concerned with managing the resulting tensions between these two contrasting preferences. Similarly, a police force does not expect to eliminate crime but rather to control crime. It may alter policies in a cycle as a liberal climate of opinion makes the rehabilitation of convicted criminals first priority, then a conservative reaction leads to a police crackdown on criminals at another time. Cyclical policies are not so much intended to make progress as to prevent conditions deteriorating.

3) *Linear Progress:* Many actions of government are intended to get somewhere by providing more and more benefits as time moves on. For example, health policies are intended to increase the proportion of the population free from disabling diseases and to promote a longer life for citizens. Progress may arise from the expansion of an existing program, e.g., extending the range and level of pension benefits, or from the introduction of a new policy, e.g., an innovative program of geriatric medical care. Unlike cyclical policies, which do not alter the long-term conditions of society, progressive policies are meant to create a trend upward. Proponents of public health measures do not want to see life expectancy rise for a decade, then fall, as would occur in a cyclical model. Any policy gains greatly in impact if its rate of change can be sustained from year to year. For example, a growth in gross national product of five per cent per annum, through compound interest increases national wealth by 28 per cent in five years.

The one thing constant in a model of linear progress is the criterion for measuring progress. In education, an increase in the average number of years of schooling of each young adult is assumed to be a good in itself. The changes resulting from linear progress may not, however, be regarded as blessings in all parts of society. An increase in the gross national product, while valued for the resulting wealth it brings, will be viewed negatively by those who believe that growth means an increasing depletion of natural resources. When the evaluation of change is in dispute, linear progress may imply moving upward to some, and downward to others, depending upon whether one believes that 'more means better' or 'more means worse'. In both perspectives, there is agreement that the policy is going somewhere by degrees.

4) *Discontinuity:* The biggest changes in policy, even if the least frequent, are those that involve new objectives as well as new programs. When there is such a nominal change in policy objectives, one cannot speak of a change of so many percentage points along a numerical scale, or of steps forward along an ordinal scale. The definition of a new policy objective represents discontinuity from the past. The break requires the introduction of new measures to register subsequent movement. For example, a government that shifted its economic aims from inflation and unemployment to concern with income equality would be introducing discontinuity in public policy, because it proposed a new definition of what economic policy should be about.

Discontinuous changes may be narrow or broad in their implications. A decision to shift from maintaining a 'no policy' stance to adopting a government policy may be small in its initial claims upon public resources and social consequences. At the extreme of a revolution, discontinuities affect the very structure of the regime itself, deposing one set of rulers and installing another. A discontinuity along one dimension of politics does not mean discontinuities throughout a regime. Typically, a revolution results in changing only a small proportion of the total personnel of government, albeit these are the highest-ranking officials and leaders of a regime.

Some discontinuities involve the repudiation of an established policy, and setting another in its place. For example, the United States Supreme Court decision outlawing racial segregation in schools voided the established policies of many Southern states, while simultaneously substituting the objective of racial integration. Alternatively, a new policy objective can be introduced in addition to established objectives. As Arnold Heidenheimer's chapter shows, many European governments have sought to reform secondary schools to integrate children of different social classes to provide a common comprehensive school. When added onto pre-existing commitments, the objectives of comprehensive education may result in conflicts between a multiplicity of educational goals. The accumulation of policy objectives is most evident in land use planning in urban areas. No matter how frequently or slowly urban policy-makers change their objectives concerning the built environment, the new objective can only be pursued while simultaneously taking into account the results of past building policies. Policy discontinuities differ from the piecemeal change of incremental models. For example, if the introduction of one new element into an interdependent system has spillover effects, then a discontinuity in one part makes the system as a whole different from before, e.g., if a wartime economy continues to produce many things also required in peacetime — but the whole is different because of the change of one part.

Table 1 sets out systematically the impact that different types of policy changes can have upon society. It emphasizes the contingent as against the certain nature of success. A political scientist may judge change solely in terms of government's actions. But other social scientists are likely to emphasize the impact of these programs upon society.

The models outlined here, like any social science models, are idealized simplifications of complex political processes. The appropriateness of a model often depends upon the particular point at which

TABLE 1
The Social Impact of Dynamic Policies

Government action	Impact on Society (examples)
1. STATIC	*Static* (Public health) *Variable* (Influencing voters)
2. CYCLICAL	*Cyclical* (Rise and fall in numbers of unemployed) *Non-Cyclical* (Steady rise in numbers of unemployed when government deflates and reflates)
3. LINEAR PROGRESS	*Progress* (Inter-city mileage expands with construction of motorways) *Non-progressive* (% of population in poverty unaltered by increase in funding of anti-poverty programs)
4. DISCONTINUITY	*Disruptive* (Invasion of territory by foreign army and collapse of regime) *Non-disruptive* (Condition of peasants unaltered by palace coup d'etat)

one cuts into the continuing policy process, and his time perspective. For example, the underlying trend of a cyclical policy can be viewed as static, inasmuch as the final point of the process is the same as its initial point. Similarly, linear progress may involve a cycle of ups and downs around an underlying upward trend. At one point in time, a major policy innovation can introduce discontinuity. A few years later the efforts to realize the new objective will result in a pattern resembling one of the first three categories in Figure 1 — or yet another discontinuity. The case studies that follow often invoke more than one of these models, because the authors are concerned with viewing issues in their full complexity across time.

At any given point in time, the most appropriate model of government policy will be the static model. The past commitments of government — whether measured by legislation, by public expenditure or by personnel — are so vast that no political party could hope to overturn or greatly alter the bulk of government commitments within a four or five-year grant of office by election. Any attempt to do so would either lead to organizational chaos because of the abandonment of predictable routines or else reflect fundamental disorganization in society, e.g., the massive inflation that erupted in Weimar Germany in the early 1920s. Among the actions that the government of the day does take, the most frequent are those that add on to existing commitments, as in the model of linear progress. It is far easier to amend an existing act, or to add a clause entitling additional people to welfare benefits, than it is to start a new program or a new government bureau from scratch. Cyclical policies require considerable flexibility for decision-makers, a flexibility difficult to obtain when the checks and balances of coalition government obtain, as in many European countries, or with the divided institutions of authority in America. Central banks and treasuries are atypical in the flexibility they enjoy in efforts to manage the economy — and in the degree of understanding offered them by economic theory. Governments are limited in the discontinuities they can introduce, because of the effort required to abandon one policy and introduce another. If a discontinuity reflects government intervention in an area previously unaffected directly by government, there is risk in attempting the unknown. There is, moreover, the probability (the pessimist would say, the certainty) that any small initial involvement, e.g., state aid for the arts, or food subsidies, would gradually grow far beyond the bounds of original cost estimates.

The social impact of government policy is most likely to follow a cyclical or linear model of change. It will be cyclical if the government is trying to resolve a dilemma by going back and forth between inflation and unemployment, or if it is trying to maintain a constant impact in changing conditions. For example, a government commitment to provide pensioners with a benefit that is a fixed proportion of current average earnings will require annual, semi-annual or quarterly review, in order to accommodate fluctuations in macro-economic conditions. When a new adjustment is made, pension payments will be at a peak, falling in relative value as other economic conditions inflate only to rise again with the next periodic review. The cyclical pattern thus reflects a lagged response to change. Governments seeking to improve programs often find that the path of progress is not as straight as that drawn with a ruler, but rather involves a series of changes, which cumulatively lead to progress, but not without their ups and downs. In graphic terms, the result is best represented by a straight line depicting the long-term underlying trend, and a cyclical movement around the line showing how benefits increase because the 'ups' in total are greater than the 'downs'.

It is easier for a government to create discontinuities in its own actions than to make an impact upon society that greatly alters its conditions. The institutions of free elections and competing parties presuppose that there will be alterations in government policies as party control of government changes. Moreover, politicians appear to be interested in activity for its own sake, launching new programs so that they can claim credit as the father of some scheme of betterment. But to make new programs achieve desired goals is often difficult, as President Johnson's Great Society programs unintentionally demonstrated. President Nixon's administration found out that it was also difficult to eliminate established programs. Social theorists disagree among themselves about the desirability of introducing discontinuities in society. (Olson, 1968). Some writers emphasize the presumed virtues of continuity and stability in social life, whereas others anxiously demand that governments act to change society, and change it now.

The foregoing models of change vary in their applicability according to the type of issue at hand. Linear progress or cyclical change can occur only when a policy or its impact can vary by small increments. The lines in Figure 1b, and 1c, presuppose that one can have a little more or a little less, e.g., the numbers of people covered by an income maintenance program. The choice is not either/or, as in the case of a decision to allow foreign workers to enter a country for the first time. Many of the issues of social welfare, e.g., health, education and income maintenance benefits, are amenable to changes of degree. But many of the issues of increasing importance in the 1970s, such as environmental pollution, land use, and urban redevelopment, involve choices between 'lumpy' goods. For example, the siting of an airport involves a fundamental change in land use, and not just a little more traffic noise for those living in the vicinity. Policies that involve collective goods affecting everyone (though not everyone equally) cannot easily be represented by incremental change. (See Rose, 1974). For example, either the whole of one society is at war with another, or it is not. When an issue affects everyone but affects them unequally, then achievements must be measured in at least two dimensions; for example, policies intended to promote income equality would show a rise in benefits for one group — but a fall in benefits for another.

III CONSTRAINTS UPON CHANGE AND PRESSURES TO CHANGE

Pressures to change and obstacles to change are often found in the same set of facts viewed from different angles. As Robert Jackson notes (infra, p. 213), the Chinese ideograph for 'crisis' also stands for 'opportunity'. In the relationship between government and society, change increases uncertainty if a change in one area may not correlate with a change in the other. The following paragraphs outline briefly the ways in which both social and political conditions can influence the dynamics of public policy.

Demographic change is the most certain of all forms of social or political change. But its political meaning is ambivalent. Is one to say that 'as much as' two or three per cent of the population is different each year, or that 'only' two or three per cent of the population alters? Viewed from the perspective of the government of the day, the slow turnover of a nation's population is an obstacle to change. At any given point in time, the bulk of the population of nearly every Western country has already formed its initial political outlook under a predecessor government. In the Western world of 1975, only in Spain and Sweden has a single party been in power for the lifetime of the majority of its citizens. The age profile of every society makes youth, the social group potentially most susceptible to new ideas, a minority. Any attempt to extrapolate future demands in society from the current attitudes of youth must be based upon a long-term perspective, for today's young people will not reach the age of the median adult voter until after the year 2000.

Gradually and cumulatively slow changes in the population result in much larger changes. A 2.5 per cent annual turnover in the population becomes a 12.5 per cent change in five years, and a 25 per cent change in a decade. For example, in a study of the British electorate, 1959-70, Donald Stokes calculated that approximately 22 per cent of the electorate at the beginning of the period had died or emigrated eleven years later. Of the 1970 electorate, 30 per cent had not been eligible to vote in 1959, because of their youth or because they were living outside the United Kingdom. Notwithstanding this very substantial amount of social change, the net *political* change was slight: a small increase in the proportion of electors predisposed to support the Labour Party. The change was not decisive for there was a Conservative victory at both the beginning and end of the period for analysis. (Butler and Stokes, 1975: 242).

At any given point in time, the resources of a society constrain what policy-makers can do. The government of a poor African country cannot introduce an effective national health service if the country has only one doctor for every 50,000 citizens, nor can a government nationalize oil resources if geologists have yet to discover any oil within its territory. Whatever the level of a nation's resources, a government cannot spend more than it can raise from its populace and borrow abroad. If the demands of the populace exceed the resources available, then the decision to introduce some changes will mean that governors lack the money, the manpower and the time to introduce others. Politicians must invest much time in defending the way in which they are managing the status quo, and pre-existing commitments at any given point in time pre-empt much of the margin of resources that policy-makers have to dispose. (See Davis, Dempster and Wildavsky, 1966).

Economic growth has been a policy that is immediately attractive to governors in Western and non-Western countries, because it promises a seemingly painless way to increase resources for public policy. If a nation's gross national product increases annually by a few per cent, there is a fiscal dividend to be enjoyed by society and government without raising taxes. This is true, whether a government chooses to use the growth of its gross national product to increase the state's own resources, e.g., building an army; devote its fiscal dividend to improving the living conditions of its citizens by increasing public benefits; or let citizens themselves allocate the benefits of growth by cutting taxes. The economic depression in many Western nations in the 1970s, along with continuing pressures upon governments to spend more on established policies, makes the hope of financing new policies through the 'fiscal dividend' of economic growth seem as remote in 1975 as it seemed immediately certain in 1965.

Foreign nations can influence the development of new policies in contrasting ways. Economic competition between nations may make it difficult for a country's policy-makers to finance new policies through economic growth. For example, the sharp rise in oil prices following the 1973 Middle East war reduced the resources of all Western nations. Insofar as foreign nations are perceived as military threats, they may force policy-makers to divert resources from domestic policies intended to benefit the welfare of the citizenry to defence expenditure of limited value in social terms. Yet contacts between nations can also stimulate new policies, if only through imitation. An innovation in one country may soon be copied in another, whether circumstances are appropriate to justify the lessons drawn or not. Imitation can occur among industrial nations, as when European nations introduce commercial television on the American pattern, or it can occur between advanced and relatively backward nations, as in the provision of technical assistance by Western nations to Afro-Asian countries.

Some citizens make demands upon government to act through pressure groups and political parties. But other citizens will mobilize to oppose their demands in the name of competing interests and parties. Thus, the net effect of a very large number of demands being voiced may be very small. It is misleading to label political parties as unambiguously favouring the status quo or linear progress, even when their name incorporates either term, or, like the Progressive Conservative Party in Canada, combines both labels. A labour or socialist party will resist changes intended to curb the powers of trade unions, and a conservative party may encourage industrialists to develop industry in ways that will transform or destroy natural resources, rather than conserve them. Each political party is inclined to advocate changes that benefit their own voters and client interests and to oppose changes that leave their supporters worse off.

Laws are a conservative force in every society, insofar as they represent and enforce the preferences of past governments. In a society as old as Britain, one-quarter of all the legislation currently on the statute books was passed prior to the reign of Queen Victoria, and the oldest law still extant dates from 1235. Even a government newly established by revolution will not issue a new statute book overnight. It repudiates the authority of the existing regime, while simultaneously expecting its subjects to follow the laws of its predecessors, except those that are individually and expressly repealed.

Because laws establish and regulate so much of government activity, they give policy-makers the opportunity to concentrate their attention upon the relatively few areas where the need for change is immediate. Moreover, governors can use laws as one resource to change society. Laws may provide benefits to large numbers of people (e.g., social security legislation) or compel people to do what they would not wish to do (e.g., military conscription). Decisions of the United States Supreme Court illustrate in an extreme fashion how something as seemingly inert as a written constitution may be used by judicial activists to stimulate social change.

The public bureaucracy is another force that can obstruct or impel change. The civil service socializes its recruits to accept many regulations and procedures restricting behaviour and inhibiting change. Routine and precedent offer predictable and economical ways of dispatching great volumes of detailed work within government, and are valued by bureaucrats for this reason. The importance given to seniority in promotion requires leaders of a nation's civil service to spend 20 years or more in becoming expert in established ways of governing. Not least of the reasons why civil servants are often sceptical of change is that they will have to carry out new tasks, while simultaneously getting on with existing work.

In some circumstances, professional bureaucrats can be positive forces working for change. Any increase in the activity of government means growth for an established bureaucratic agency, thus raising its status and resources, or the creation of a new agency, thus providing new jobs and promotion prospects for ambitious civil servants. (See MacDonagh, 1961). Where public servants are also professional experts, whether economists, engineers or astrophysicists, they may canvass for government to do more in ways meaningful to their profession, e.g., stimulate more economic growth, build more highways and bridges, or build more space missiles to explore outer space.

Institutions of government are obstacles to change insofar as new policies cannot be adopted without the concurrence of parts of government institutionally independent of each other. A federal system such as Germany is likely to change policies more slowly than a highly centralized government, such as Sweden, because of the need to co-ordinate policies at two levels. A government formed by a coalition of parties is likely to be slow to alter policies, for any major policy initiative is likely to create strains within its coalition, thus inhibiting action. The government of the United States — a federal system separating powers between Congress and the President, with two political parties formed by coalitions of heterogeneous groups — faces the greatest difficulties in responding promptly to demands for change.

The conventional way to assess whether policy-makers are likely to favour or oppose change is to make some kind of 'cost-benefit' analysis, to see to what extent and under what circumstances the benefits of innovation anticipated by those promoting changes are greater than the costs of overcoming the foregoing obstacles. Such a calculation assumes that politicians place 'profit-making' first. Yet the difficulties of making policy and the slowness with which governments respond suggest that the assumption is too simple.

The resistance of politicians to new policies can be better understood if one regards a politician as a man who wishes to minimize costs. Following this assumption, a politician would be hesitant to recommend a change in policy as long as it imposed visible costs upon any group capable of articulating political opposition to the policy. A good policy is not defined as one in which the benefits are greater than the costs, but rather one in which there are *no* visible or controversial costs, whatever the benefits may be. For example, increased welfare benefits can be financed by government through increased taxation *as long as* the benefits are not directly linked to changes in taxation rates. Actions can also be taken, even when costs are visible, e.g., a block of houses can be razed to build a new road as long as the affected residents are of such low social and political status that they cannot mobilize themselves to articulate protest. If costs fall visibly upon a group capable of articulating objections, no matter how small its size, its members will seek to obstruct change by claiming the political rights of members of the 17th century Polish *Sejm,* in which every member had a *liberum veto,* that is, a single dissenting voice could prevent the enactment of a specific measure and even nullify the whole work of a session of the Parliament. (See Groth, 1972: 4).

If one assumes that politicians wish to avoid costs, then it follows that the way to stimulate action from government is to organize actions, whether through interest groups, elections or street riots, making the present situation 'intolerable'. While politicians hesitate to act as long as the costs of action appear significant, in a crisis they are anxious to act (or give the appearance of changing policies) because the costs of inaction appear infinite. (Rose, 1972: 141).

IV THE PLAN OF THE BOOK

Within the compass of a single volume, one can explore most of the problems posed above. The juxtaposition of a number of case studies enables every reader to confront the following questions: To what extent does the character of change differ from country to country? To what extent do the dynamics of policy differ from problem area to problem area within a country? And, not least in significance, to what extent are the obstacles to change the same in a range of Western countries?

The comparative approach is valuable, for it bases the conclusions of the book upon a far wider range of experience than could be derived from the study of a single nation, however large or small. Comparative analysis enables one to see to what extent problems that face one Western government are the same as those that face its neighbours. When a government's program stipulates nationwide uniformity, it is only by cross-national comparison that the causes and consequences of differences can be examined. Policies that seem 'obvious' in one national context may be 'unthinkable' in another, because of differences in political culture and political ideology, not because there is anything intrinsically impossible or compelling about them. Comparison thus enables social scientists to identify empirically no-decision areas excluded from public controversy in one society, yet evident in another. Comparison also invites evaluation. To notice that welfare services or economic policies are undertaken differently in two countries not only stimulates an interest in the causes of variation, but also, in evaluating the consequences. Which policy is better, or does judgment depend primarily upon the values of the judges? Inasmuch as many judgments about public policy already involve comparison between past and present, between one part of a country and another or between one segment of society and another, cross-national comparison does not introduce anything new to the logic of social scientific analysis. It simply extends our awareness of the manifold ways in which governments respond to problems common to many lands.

In theory, the reform of local government should be among the easiest of policies for a European government to carry out, given that local government powers normally depend upon central government legislation rather than upon constitutional compacts, as in federal countries such as the United States. If a government cannot alter its own institutions, how can it expect to change the society around it? Jack Brand's study emphasizes the extent to which established institutions of government constitute political obstacles to change and what government nominally has the power to alter. It also specifies conditions that allowed institutional change to occur in both England and Sweden. On first impression, the Swedish reform appears to indicate linear progress reaching a much higher level of efficiency, and the English reform progress at a lower standard. However Brand questions this. He notes that the idea of changing local authority boundaries involves a discontinuity in symbolic identification with communities. He also notes that the static persistence of many problems of government — whatever the structures — can lead to a cycle of reform and disillusion.

While the biosphere is constantly in flux, Christopher Hood's study of the dynamics of fishing policy in the waters around Britain emphasizes the constraints upon a government's fishing policy. When government policies remain static, changes in impact can result from biological variations in the number of fish in the North Atlantic, in the economic value of fish or in the policies of other countries fishing in the same waters. When the British government has acted to counteract more or less cyclical trends, their efforts are made difficult by the fact that fish are, as it were, a 'free-floating' resource, swimming in and out of the marine jurisdiction of governments with differing policies. While there has tended to be long-term linear progress in the amount of fish caught, Hood's article makes clear how the ups and downs of fishing affect politicians with shorter-term perspectives.

The introduction of new forms of comprehensive secondary schools, bringing together children of different social backgrounds, involves a major discontinuity in European nations, where pupils of different academic aptitudes have traditionally been separated according to academic ability. Arnold Heidenheimer's chapter demonstrates that the decision in principle to introduce a discontinuity in policy can only be followed by slow linear progress in the implementation of a change from a selective to a non-selective secondary school system. The number of young people in comprehensive schools can gradually increase each year as the reform is implemented by local education authorities. The author's comparison of the actual dynamics of change in Sweden and Germany shows that the impact of Swedish policy has been steadily to emphasize discontinuity with the past, whereas the German government's initiatives now show a static trend. Heidenheimer explains why the same issue leads to pressures for change in one political system and constraints upon change in another.

The literature of social mobilization and political development depicts change in terms of a slow, seemingly inevitable expansion in the activities of government and its impact upon society. Theorists disagree, however, about the most important pressures resulting in linear progress. Guy Peter's analysis of the growth of social welfare programs in Sweden from 1865 to the present is a statistically elegant and precise attempt to test a variety of generalizations about the most important pressures for change. Because he covers more than a century of government activity in Sweden, Peters is able to demonstrate that the factors influencing the growth of social welfare expenditure are not the same in each period. In addition to the influence of growing national wealth, increased involvement of citizens in society through urbanization, increased involvement of citizens in politics through the expansion of the suffrage, and increased involvement of civil servants in providing services, are each at some point significant.

Viewed close up, long-term, seemingly inevitable pressures for change appear far from clear in their implications. The nature of politics forces government to view each step in the policy process as a question of choice – even though it may recommend its choices to the electorate as the 'only' thing that could be done. The boom in the European economy in the 1960s created a demand for more workers, met in almost every European society by the importation of foreign workers from outside industrial Europe. Ernst Gehmacher's study, commissioned by the City of Vienna and the *Arbeiterkammer*, Salzburg, describes the role that such workers have come to play in the Austrian economy, and calls attention to the policy options of the Austrian government. The study concerns present choices and probable future consequences. It points out that a static 'do nothing' government policy would itself result in significant changes in Austrian society in the foreseeable future.

Whereas most studies of discontinuities in policy emphasize the introduction of new policies, it is equally important to study the failure of existing policies. Thomas Bowden's study of the decline of the British-led Royal Irish Constabulary in the face of a challenge from Irish rebels is a careful and thought-provoking illustration of the way in which a downward trend in a regime's ability to enforce public order can lead to the greatest of all political discontinuities: the repudiation of its authority and the introduction of a new regime.

Crises compress a multitude of pressures for political change into a short space of time. Because crises arise from unexpected events and concern matters of importance to society, a government must take some action. Yet acting at great speed in areas of high uncertainty also involves risks. A cautious politician might hope that government actions would maintain the status quo, say, in response to a potential insurrectionary army. At the other extreme, a crisis may lead to discontinuity. Robert Jackson's comparative study of government activities in times of crisis in Canada, Britain, America and France emphasizes the unique properties of crisis management.

The concluding chapter by Hugh Heclo provides a framework for analyzing the elements that create different types of policy change. The studies in this volume are located within this framework. Heclo emphasizes that the most important elements in policy change are contingent, and therefore outside the bounds of mechanical certainty, or else derived from changes in the subjective manner in which both governors and governed perceive and evaluate the world about them.

The range of countries and problems represented here cuts across conventional categories of political science analysis. Some of the case studies concern government efforts to help people through welfare policies, e.g., the analysis of health and education in Sweden, and education in Germany. Christopher Hood's study concentrates attention upon the intention of fishermen to help people by hurting (that is, catching) fish. Ernst Gehmacher's Austrian study raises questions about who should be helped by employment policy: Austrians or their foreign 'guest workers'? The crises that Robert Jackson reviews are crises because it is not clear what government can do to help people, or to help itself. Two chapters remind readers that government is also concerned with helping itself, by maintaining or reforming its own institutions. The case of local government reform is a benign illustration; the repudiation of British authority in Ireland in 1921 is a bloody example. This mixture of problems accurately reflects the variety of concerns that face government: students of public policy limit the relevance of their research if they concentrate upon the actions and impact of government in only one policy area.

Because national differences can be important, whether reflected in institutions, cultural values or past actions, it is important to consider the dynamics of public policy in a variety of countries. Within a single volume, one cannot represent all the nations of the earth, or even, all Western nations. The countries studied here reflect significant and differing national experiences. Among larger European nations, Britain and Germany are examined in detail. The French 'events' of May 1968 are included in Jackson's study of crisis management; that chapter, along with Bowden's also has relevance to Italian politics. Sweden, the prototypically prosperous and politically successful Scandinavian country, can be contrasted with Ireland and Austria, two smaller European countries with less prosperity and less fortunate political histories – as well as values that originate in cultural milieux very different from that of Scandinavia. Consideration of crisis management in Canada illustrates not only North America concerns, but also problems of federal countries. American experience is intermittently referred to by many authors. The American literature of public policy is familiar, because of the vast amount of writings already available on the subject. To have included copious American examples, or to have doubled or trebled the number of policy areas considered, would have greatly increased the length of this volume, without a proportionate increase in clarity.

These models of change are analytic, rather than predictive. In an era of uncertainty, it would be pointless for political scientists to claim that they had discovered the philosopher's stone revealing secrets of the future, as well as the past. What they might hope to do is to provide models to chart where we have been and where we are heading. Consumers of public policy, as well as students and practitioners of public policy, want to know whether the actions of government are getting anywhere, and if so, whether their progress is cyclical or progressive, or can result in big discontinuities between the present and the future.

REFERENCES

ARMSTRONG, Sir William (1974) 'Sir William Armstrong talking with Desmond Wilcox', *The Listener,* No. 2348 (28 March).

BUTLER, D. E. and STOKES, D. (1975) Political Change in Britain. London: Macmillan, 2nd edition.

DAVIS, Otto, DEMPSTER, M. A. H., and WILDAVSKY, Aaron (1966) 'A Theory of the Budgetary Process', *American Political Science Review,* LX: 3 (September).

GINZBERG, Eli and SOLOW, R. M. (1974) The Great Society. New York: Basic Books.

GROTH, Alexander, J. (1972) People's Poland. San Francisco: Chandler.

HECLO, Hugh (1974) Modern Social Politics in Britain and Sweden. New Haven: Yale University Press.

MACDONAGH, Oliver (1961) A Pattern of Government Growth. London: MacGibbon & Kee.

OLSON, Mancur, (1968) 'Economics, Sociology and the Best of all Possible Worlds', *Public Interest* II.

PRESSMAN, Jeffrey, L. and WILDAVSKY, Aaron (1973) Implementation. Berkeley: University of California Press.

ROSE, Richard (1972) 'The Market for Policy Indicators', in Andrew Shonfield and Stella Shaw (eds.), Social Indicators and Social Policy. London: Heinemann.

– – –, (1973) 'Comparing Public Policy', *European Journal of Political Research,* I. 1.

– – –, (1974) 'Coping with Urban Change', in Richard Rose, (ed.), The Management of Urban Change in Britain and Germany. London & Beverly Hills: Sage.

SCHON, Donald (1971) Beyond the Stable State. London: Temple Smith.

WEISS, Carol H. (1972) Evaluating Action Programs. Boston: Allyn & Bacon.

Part One

CONSTRAINTS UPON CHANGE

Chapter II

REFORMING LOCAL GOVERNMENT: SWEDEN AND ENGLAND COMPARED

Jack Brand

Strathclyde Area Survey
University of Strathclyde
Glasgow

Structural reform is an important if infrequent aspect of all political systems, occurring when the structures of political institutions set up to meet the needs of one particular time are deemed to require change to meet changing circumstances. Structural reform in general and local government reform in particular can be regarded as a cyclical process. The institutions established because they are appropriate at one time gradually are perceived as inappropriate; they are replaced by another set of institutions which, in their turn, will have to be replaced when new conditions demand this. There is a cycle of adequacy and in-adequacy, or at least of perceptions of these two conditions. The period before the reform is marked by high hopes. Immediately after the new institutions are established there is a feeling of disillusionment caused by the administrative upheavals. Public evaluation reflects satisfaction with the new routine; sooner or later there is a slow rise in dissatis-faction, when it becomes clear that more changes are needed. I shall try to explore these cycles and the aspects of structural change as they are illustrated by local government reform in two Western European countries: England and Sweden.[1]

Since the mid-1960s major changes in local government have either happened or have been attempted in one country after another. In

Sweden and England reforms have been implemented, and have been thorough going. In 1952 there were over 2000 Swedish communes; by 1974 they had been reduced to 282. In England one form of local government, the county borough (a large independent town) disappeared altogether. The number of counties was reduced from 62 to 44 and the total of urban and rural districts and boroughs was reduced from 1356 to 333. Along with local government reform, there have also been attempts to change educational systems, parties, legislatures and many other major public institutions. To understand what has happened in local government may, therefore, give us the clue about what is happening in these other situations.

First of all it is necessary to describe the nature of the changes that took place and why they took place. I shall then present a model of the way in which the political processes of England and Sweden worked. While this is a dynamic model, a great deal of the statement of it will be an explanation of why the dynamic process did *not* take place. Finally, I shall take the differences between the two systems and use them to explain why the process took a different form in each country.

I THE CHANGES TO BE EXPLAINED

1. England

In 1972, after a great many false starts, Parliament enacted a law to reform the system of local government in England. This was the first major reorganization since 1888, although there had been several attempts between the two dates. The majority of academics and other interested independent observers would have agreed at many times during the 80 years period that a different system was necessary. When change came it was not as radical as had once been expected.

The 1888 Act set up a system of county government in England. Up to this time powers had been given to town councils and to a range of ad hoc bodies such as school boards and commissioners of police. Two levels of multi-purpose government were established: the county itself and the county district. In the late 19th century and the beginning of this century the single purpose authorities were abolished and powers were concentrated in the hands of the counties or districts. In 1902, for example, the County Councils took over the powers related to secondary education. Generally the more important services went to the county: education, major roads, police; while lesser functions such as minor roads, certain sanitary services and the provision of some local amenities went to the district. These district councils were not uniform, however, but ranked according to their powers. A Municipal Borough, often an historic and fairly large town, could run more local government services than could another type of second tier authority, the Urban District, while in Rural Districts, where there was no urban centre, the county government looked after virtually all the local government functions. The situation in rural districts was complicated further by the existence of Parish Councils which ran parish property and had the right to complain to the District or County Council if certain services were badly provided in its area. This two- or three-tier pattern was the norm for most of England but the major urban areas worked under quite a different system. A town the size of Carlisle or Leeds might be entirely within the counties of Cumberland or Yorkshire respectively; yet, because of its size or importance, it was given the right to contract completely out of the control of the county. It was not a county district but a County Borough, running not only its county services but also district services. County Boroughs were all-purpose authorities as opposed to the situation elsewhere — where local government powers were split between two and sometimes three tiers.

Over this system there stood central government. It was Parliament which brought the whole system into being in 1888 and which replaced it in 1974. Then, as now, the Whitehall departments exercised close scrutiny over the operations of the local authorities at all levels. Although larger counties and county boroughs might be able to apply some political pressure in order to secure resources or modify an instruction, the local authorities in England are creatures of Parliament and can be created or abolished at will. Nineteenth century ideas of the state representing the central elite as a check against local corruption and profligacy are an essential background for understanding contemporary arrangements.

It was central government, then, which decided to reform the system. The argument which was most important for them was that the existing areas were too small for the new demands which were being made. The whole apparatus of the welfare state had been set up since 1888 and, though it largely depended on local government for administration no changes had been made in the structure of local government to cope with it. More than this, it was pointed out that the 1888 boundaries had only been modified here and there, but virtually every large town had spilled over its boundaries, making boundaries purely administrative divisions bearing no relation to settlement patterns. Efficient administration was hampered by the unnatural divisions which

had to be made there. Finally, and most important, the needs of
physical planning were a potent argument for looking at areas as a
whole: the urban region serviced by a large town, for example. For this
a new type of local authority was required (Brand, 1974).

During the 1966-70 Labour administration a Royal Commission was
set up under the chairmanship of Lord Redcliffe-Maud (Maud, 1969).
After various attempts by the Local Government Boundary Commission in the late 1940s and the Local Government Commission in the
early 1960s to rearrange boundaries authority by authority, without
any change to the basic structure (Local Government Boundary Commission, 1947; Jones, 1963), Maud recommended that a radically new
system should be set up. A one-tier system of regions should replace the
two-tier system and the county boroughs. There was to be a massive
reduction in the number of authorities. When Labour fell in 1970, their
Conservative successors, under great political pressure from the county
interest, greatly modified the proposals.

Out of this political debate the reorganized system was established in
1974. The first striking feature is that the old county boroughs disappeared. Whereas before the reform the most important towns could
exlude themselves from the county-district system and run all the local
government services themselves, the new legislation provided that all
these previously independent units should come under the control of a
county for some of the most important services. This, in itself, was a
major political change. In the case of the six very largest conurbations,
special metropolitan areas were set up: in Merseyside, the West
Midlands and Leeds, for example. In these also, there was a two-tier
system, but the balance of power was somewhat different from that
between counties and districts. The government argued that there
would be sufficiently large populations in the Metropolitan districts to
justify giving them more services than in the case of the other districts.
In this way they were, for example, given education which is a county
function elsewhere. In general, it would be true to say that the county
councils, although reduced in number, came out of the reform with a
greatly enhanced position.

In all this there was a vigorous debate in which it became clear that
the County Councils Association had had a strong influence on the
Conservative government which took the decision to reform and which
carried it out against vigorous opposition from many sides.

2. Sweden

One critical difference between Sweden and England must be noted at once. In the years before the major nineteenth century reform, the Swedish state had gone much further in formal centralization than had been the case in England. Perhaps the most striking and important examples of this lay in the system of *'landshövdningar'* or county governors. These were royal officials leading a team of civil servants — the *länstyrelse* — who administered and still administer the counties or provinces of Sweden for the King in Council. Although there is very clear and extensive central control of local government in England there is nothing equivalent to this Scandinavian system which inevitably provides social and political as well as administrative leadership.

With this in mind it is not surprising that the nature of the debate on the 1862 reform of Swedish local government was different from that in England. Although in England a great deal was said about local freedoms and self-government, the proposal in 1862 to introduce a system of communes was, much more than in England, an attempt to provide real self-government as opposed to central administration. The legislation was in the tradition of the liberalization of society in Europe, whereas the English reform had more of the character of an administrative device.

In 1862, legislation provided for the introduction of a commune into every rural parish and into every town. In the country districts it replaced the parish meetings chaired by the local clergyman; in the towns, the magistrates. Whereas before, these bodies could carry out only functions for which they had a specific legal mandate, the new legislation provided that they should be able to undertake anything which was for the benefit of the people of their commune. Thus they could run local government services like the English local authorities — in many cases they would be required to do so by law but this was not the end of their jurisdiction. There were no differences in powers between communes of all sizes and in all parts of the country. Towns (*stader*) and country communes (*landskommuner*) were equal in that they were all responsible for administrating all the local government services and had the general power to do anything within the law which would benefit the inhabitants.

It is important to realize that, as in other continental countries, the communes were much smaller than equivalent units in England. This comes out sharply if one realizes that, even when the first move was made to reorganize the system in 1952, the government spoke in terms of a minimum population of 3000 for the proposed new communes. At this time it was widely asserted that 10,000 should be the absolute minimum for an English rural district, which was not the all-purpose authority (which the commune was and is) but was responsible for only the less important services.

It appears from this description that the new communes of 1862 must have been small but self-contained units. In a sense they were but in their conduct of their affairs they were and still are supervised by the *länstyrelse*. Thus, a committee of civil servants representing the various administrative bureaux in central government which were concerned with such local government services as education and housing and the care of the poor, exercised a detailed control over what was done. Furthermore, this was done at a much closer range than was the case in English local government and was, arguably, more all embracing.

In an attempt to democratize the system at the level of the province or *land*, a provincial assembly was set up: the *landsting*. In recent years this has become a more important body. In the 1960s for example, it was suggested that the landsting should take over the duties of the *länstyrelse* and this was associated with a suggestion that there should be a general upward move of powers from the communes to the land level (Elder, 1973). This proposal has not been acted upon. In 1862 and until after the Second World War, the landsting remained as a largely advisory body working under the shadow of the landshövdning and the länstyrelse. One further point about the 1862 structure is that there was a provision that towns over a certain size (25,000 in 1862) should not be controlled by the länstyrelse but should be 'provinces' on their own. Only two Swedish cities are in this position: Gothenburg and Stockholm. Central government supervision is carried out by a special bureau of the central government rather than by the usual sort of länstyrelse.

It was this system which operated in Sweden from 1862 until the 1950s. By that time, however, many people in Swedish public life had begun to feel that the system should be reformed. The basic problem was that the communes were being asked to take on more and more services. It was felt that communes of the smallest size, those around 3,000 for example, simply could not handle these new demands. As in England, it was felt that larger authorities would be more capable of providing these services. Added to the difficulties of running the small communes in general was the fact that Sweden was experiencing an enormous movement of population away from the country areas into the towns. The rural communes generally started with smaller populations than the towns but these demographic changes made the whole question of the viability of the rural communes much more acute. In the year before the Second World War there were annexations of neighbouring parts of rural communes into the towns, but this piece-meal approach clearly did not meet the needs of the entirely new population distribution. It was further felt that the loss of population in the rural and especially the northern communes led, through the weakening of local services, to an inequality between Swedish citizens. All should be provided for equally.

As a first move towards the modern system, the government suggested that rural communes should consult together under the guidance of the länstyrelse so as to form a series of large communes (*Storkommun*). In other words, it was envisaged that several small, weak, rural communes should come together to form one large commune by voluntary agreement so that the resulting entity would have enough resources to run all the local services at an adequate level.

In the event, the '*storkommunereform*' was not successful. There were 2281 rural communes before the reform and afterwards the number was reduced to 816 but a quarter of them were still smaller than 3000. One of the major reasons for the failure was the assumption that the communes would coalesce voluntarily. It is also arguable that there was not a great deal of central leadership since it was felt that the communes should take a leading role in putting their own house in order. In any case the central government was rather preoccupied with the difficult social and economic problems of the 1940s and 1950s.

When it became clear that the targets had not been reached in terms of numbers alone it also became clear that the 'flight from the country-side' was such that one could not exclude the towns from reform because of tradition or any other reason. The 1962 reform introduced a new element and one significantly like the new British system (SOU, 1961). Communes were to be clustered around some town or other populous place which could act as a centre. In other words, the idea of an urban region was introduced. This time the minimum population was to be 8000 − significantly larger than before but significantly smaller than the equivalent British units. This reform, which introduced the current system, was much more strictly applied. By the beginning of 1970 the number of communes was reduced to 464 and by the end of 1974 it is estimated that the number was 274. Clearly this is a radical change in terms of the sort of body that the commune is. It is no longer the small intimate body in terms of numbers of inhabitants that it was up to 1939. On the other hand the commune is basically the same body as before in terms of its powers and its competence. As before, the communes are supervised by the länstyrelse consisting of officials under the centrally appointed provincial governor: the landshövdning. It is fair to say, however, that what might be described as the provincial commune, the landsting, is rather more influential than it was and now runs such functions as hospitals. There is no doubt, however, that the bulk of the local government services are still run by the new enlarged communes. (Brantgärde, 1974).

II A MODEL FOR THE EXPLANATION OF STRUCTURAL CHANGE

Both of the reforms just described took decades to effect. They met with sturdy opposition which appeared to be invincible at one time. Why are such reforms difficult and when do they become possible? It is these two questions which I shall start to answer in this section.

Braybrooke and Lindblom (1963) drew our attention to the way in which most public agencies work. According to these two writers they use the strategy of 'disjointed incrementalism'. People making public policies operate in terms of problem situations, and they usually act in order to alleviate the condition rather than by taking measures which are thought to eliminate the problem by getting at its cause. They will try solutions which are only incrementally different from the existing solution rather than looking for a totally new way of dealing with the situation. There is a justifiable fear that taking a completely new line might lead to quite unforeseeable results. Moreover a functionary who is trained in or habituated to a certain way of doing things is unlikely to welcome changes which will simply cause more work.

The reform of local government is very much an illustration of this point. Any thorough-going reform of local government is more than an incremental change. Moreover, both bureaucracies and their political masters normally display caution over major changes. Thus, such a reform would not be easy to achieve.

If we look at the years before the reform actually took place in both countries we can see attempts to solve the problems incrementally. In Britain this took the form of installing control over the operations of the authorities by financial or other methods; for example, the operations of local authorities were necessarily superceded with a mass of administrative regulations during the war. After the war these were not removed. In fact they grew. Material shortages for housing or schools meant that central departments had the power of rationing supplies to local authorities and this was used to secure compliance with detailed regulations. In some cases functions were completely or partly taken over by central government, leaving the local government structure as it was. The removal of the local authority hospitals in 1948 from the local authorities to the National Health Service is a case in point. In other services arrangements were made for ministry inspection and advice and in some services like physical planning, teams led by ministry personnel in effect did the job of local government.

In Sweden there was some centralization of powers: in 1965, for example, the police service was nationalized. A more obvious incremental approach was the attempt of communes to work together (*samarbete*). There were many arrangements of this kind with regard to various functions: education for example and medical services especially for communes in the north. There was also some voluntary amalgamation between communes but this was not common. It did not go much of the way to solve the major problem of making communes efficient administrative units.

In order to explain why large structural changes are difficult to achieve it is necessary to move to a further level of analysis. What is it specifically about a change in the structure of institutions which makes it especially non-incremental?

It is important to see, first of all, that the reforms which finally took place in Sweden and England were large-scale changes. To have boundary commissions adjusting boundaries in an ad hoc way might cause some local discontent but a country-wide change becomes a national public issue with different ramifications. At the very least it concentrates the discussion on the reorganization at one point, where before the whole issue dragged on in a way which avoided public notice. The boundary changes, especially since they meant that much larger units were created, changed the whole system of representation in both countries in terms of the relationship between councillors and their electors. Furthermore, they altered, or were perceived to have altered, the relation between centre and locality. The relationship between local councillors and officials and central officials can change. In some cases the change takes the form of greater power to the larger local units; in others, the larger units make for easier administration by the centre. In all, then, what looks like a simple change in boundaries has much wider implications.

What makes this type of non-incremental change particularly difficult? The most important point here is that change in the structure of a society involves an alteration of the symbols of the society. The symbols stand for the ways in which, it is believed, the society lives. In the case of local government one might consider the extent to which the symbols of a town or village, in the sense of the name or the coat of arms, are used by voluntary organizations. They share the concept that this is how society is organized. The geographical area of influence of these bodies is perceived as being defined by the town or commune. The symbol of the local government unit is a symbol of community: a social concept that embraces much more than political or administrative units. Thus, structural change is threatening because it suggests that the basic values of the society (or at least of the political system) are being uprooted. At a very simple level, therefore, a proposal to reorganize local government can very easily be represented as a threat to the independent rights of the communities. This latter is considered a value in Sweden and England, for communes and towns are seen as a counterweight against the central government. An attack on local government can be interpreted as a general attack on democracy. In theory at any rate, participation in local decision-making through the elections is one of the foundations of citizen's rights. Anything which can be interpreted as diminishing or diluting these rights will be assured some opposition.

An appeal to such a value is a reliable ingredient for a rousing political speech. It is especially useful for the commentator who wants to preserve the existing situation, but its weakness is that it can be used by both sides. That is to say, it is easy to use the symbol of local independence while, in reality, advocating policies which will create more and more central control. Thus there seems to be an expectation that the rights of local communities will be deferred to in form; but simultaneously, the practice in Sweden, England and many other countries, has been to view local government as more and more an organ of central administration. One does not have to believe in the symbol to make effective use of it.

Proposals to reduce the number of countries and towns or communes in England and Sweden were criticized in identical ways. It was argued that this would increase the distance between the citizen and the level at which the decisions were being taken. In both countries the county areas were most opposed to change because this would mean amalgamation with the towns. The towns were represented as grasping, hungry for territory to build houses and eager to destroy the pure amenities of the countryside. The various local authorities not only expressed these values in the course of the arguments for reform, they themselves in a sense *were* the values. Edelman (1964) explains the situation very succinctly:

Factual premises alone are certainly not sufficient to explain administrative decision choices but factual premises in conjunction with observable role-taking are: for the role both specifies the value premises operative in a particular instance and establishes a probability that these same value premises will be operative in future decision making in the same policy area.

The institutions are the embodiment of certain roles within government. Though role-taking is often characterized as being peculiar to individuals it is also possible to think of institutions as taking a role. Moreover, the role of the institution can change: nearly every European monarchy is a clear example of this. Just as individual actors can be seen with different roles which constitute a group, so governments can be portrayed as made up of institutions which have their own roles, values and interests. It is then easy to see that these institutions 'institutionalize' the expectation that they have a right to continue to exist. When a proposal is made to change them it also means that the roles and thus the values are to be altered. This may be all right if everyone is agreed that the values embodied by the institutions need to be altered. Tactically, the defenders of the institutions which are threatened will be able to appeal to some values implied by the role system of the institution which is by no means rejected by the society. Thus the idea of the commune as a counterweight to the power of the state was heavily exploited by the Swedish communes and the demand that local government should be kept 'local' was a theme taken up by those who wanted the status quo in English local government.

Ironically, the appeal to democratic values, like the whole argument over local government reform, took place in the context of a restricted and interested public and political elite. Both in Sweden and England there was no mass participation in the debate. But it was to this restricted public that the appeals were powerful, since talk of democracy and the rights of the localities against the centre would probably carry little weight among a mass public. The interested public or elite can be socialized into caring (or thinking that it cares) about such things.

The values which were embodied by institutions such as local government were embodied in very tangible forms: in the case of local government there were the officers and councillors, the public buildings, road signs and boundary markers. The change of structure threatens precisely those individuals who clearly symbolize, by holding local office, the values in question. In exactly the same way the end of colonial rule threatens the values embodied in the Governors and Residents and District Commissioners. The end of their jobs is the visible sign that the old values are gone. A threat to reform the structures is not just a peripheral threat but one aimed at the very heart of their existence. For the officers it may be that a livelihood or at any rate a high salary are at stake. It is interesting that provision has been made to 'buy off' redundant officers with enormous 'golden handshakes' and to substantially increase the salaries of others. For the councillors the political ambitions of a lifetime may be threatened. Yet in the case of reforming political institutions these are precisely the people who have developed political skills in running the institutions. Their considerable skills will now be aimed at protecting their own positions.

In England the local government interest was expressed through the local government associations such as the Association of Municipal Corporations and the County Councils Association. Not only did the central government depend on local government for running such important services as housing and land-use planning, education and social work, but it was precisely these local government associations which were consulted by the appropriate ministries in framing any new legislation or regulations. The administrative decision creating networks between central and local government were so closely linked that they were a great barrier to reform if the local government associations were against reform.

In Sweden the local government associations certainly did not approach their English counterparts in terms of power vis-a-vis central government. On the other hand, the communes did and do implement a great deal of social policy as in England. The associations are even more important in advising the communes on the technical aspects of their responsibilities. Secondly, some 70 per cent of members of the Riksdag hold local office. This link could transmit influence two ways because there were a great many powerful local politicians who operated at the highest level of Swedish politics. It is interesting that parliamentary opposition to the reform was led by the Agrarian (*Bondeförbundet,* now the Centre) Party. It represented the rural interests which seemed to be attacked by the move to a larger scale. All other parties, although they had rural supporters, were mostly based in the town. It is not surprising that the Agrarian Party *Riksdagsmän* alone should work for the old system. Other parties were town and even Stockholm oriented.

Reform then, was obstructed in these two countries because the local political system was part of an overall political system with which it shared values and personnel. For councillors and MPs alike it was common to refer to the importance of local democracy. Again, up to the late 1950s it was not common to believe that one's own institutions were other than the best in the world. A change at one level could be presented as a more general change. Thus the very parliamentary and civil servants who could have undertaken the change felt that the change in some way threatened them. It threatened their networks of communication and it threatened their picture of how the world was. Under these circumstances a change was too unsettling.

III THE CONDITIONS OF CHANGE

Although incremental change is the habit of many political organizations, there are occasions when such an approach will be perceived as inadequate. Many of those involved may regard large changes as 'leaps in the dark' but also feel that the risk is worthwhile. Such a situation requires the development of a powerful group which regards such a large, non-incremental change as necessary; which would no longer be satisfied with adjustments of the existing situation, such as the manipulation of boundaries around the developing town.

In Britain this crucial role was taken by the planning profession, which became a dominant part of the local government machine in the 1960s. They had existed before, but by the 1960s they had attained full professional status through the building up of professional schools. Unlike other local government personnel who were trained more or less to look at their services within given administrative boundaries, planners were, by the nature of their profession, inclined to look beyond these boundaries. More important than the attitudes of the planners on the local authorities was the advocacy of regional planning by the Ministry of Town and Country Planning. It became clear to certain personnel within this Ministry and others that the problems of overspill housing, transportation, the regional planning of industry and so forth had to be directed over larger regions. Thus, outside the groups with an interest in the maintenance of the status quo, there arose a group which believed in the need for structural change and, more important, which had the political position to force through this change. In terms of the earlier discussion about incrementalism it is significant that planners are *not* incrementalists — their profession requires a broad view of the processes of change. It is also worth bearing in mind that physical planners were at this time working with economic planners, who were emphasizing industrial amalgamation and economies of scale. Local government amalgamations were only a small step away from this line of thought.

In Sweden, the model was the same but those who pushed for reform were different. Planning took a much less important role for the Swedish communes than for the British county or borough council. It was, therefore, less likely that planning would be cited as a reason for enlarging the sizes of the communes. The recognition of the place of the communes in planning came much later. In the context of further discussions on the reform of the 'länstyrelse' and 'landsting' organizations, the link between national, regional and local planning was clearly seen. Brantgärde (1974: 186-7) quite rightly suggests that it was planning of all services that created the need for the reform into 'blocks'. In Sweden, local government reform was introduced into the public debate principally by the Social Democratic Party itself. The major reason for their early involvement as champions of the reform lay in the belief that social benefits should be applied equally throughout the country; that the size of the commune and the consequent tax base should determine neither their level of enjoyment of these benefits nor the feasibility of providing sufficiently sophisticated services. This was an ideological aim which was well within the corpus of the social democratic canon. It came to the fore in the later 1940s and resulted first of all in the 1952 reform. This was the time when the social welfare state, organized by the party since the 1930s, and especially in the 1940s, could now be perfected by being made uniform throughout the country. It had been the Social Democrats who chose the communes as the instruments of this welfare state and it was they who wanted to be certain that their instrument was doing the job. In Britain, by contrast, much of the work of the welfare state was done by non-local government bodies: the health service and income maintenance programmes are examples. It was not so important for 'socialist' reasons that the reform should take place. Where there was inequality of service provision through unequal resources that matter could be solved by tax equalization grants.

Thus, the body which had the direct political interest in putting through the reforms, the Social Democratic government, was the one which, in Sweden, initiated it. This partly explains why the reform should be so much earlier than in England. It is also true that the department and bureau chiefs reported in favour of the reforms. Many of them were Social Democrats and had been appointed with their political sympathies in mind in the closely interlinked political and administrative state structure of Sweden.

Groups existed both in England and Sweden which had an interest in a change in the performance of the structure in question. The actual change of the structure itself required another development. To explain the difficulty of structural reform it was suggested that those institutions were protected by their close involvement with the values of the political system. One would expect that, when the values of the society changed, the existing institutions would be in danger. This was in fact what happened in both countries, but it happened in significantly different ways.

The reforms in both countries took place at times when other reforms were also being discussed or implemented. The reforms of the structure of local government came about (and had to come about) at a time when certain general ideas were prevalent. It was these ideas which embodied values and used symbols which were antithetical to the existing institutions and which made it possible to change them. In Britain, in the 1960s, there was a great deal of discussion about 'what's wrong with Britain'. This made reform topical in many areas, e.g., Parliament. The system of secondary education and the universities were subject to wide structural alterations. The reorganization of the health service structure was discussed and, in 1973, actually implemented. In Sweden the Riskdag became unicameral. The Land came under close scrutiny. The structure of the educational system was changed. The ideas of rationalization and a move to larger-scale units characterized changes in both societies. Thus the conditions existed for representing local government not as a counter-weight to the power of the state or as a way in which people could run their own affairs, but as outmoded, lilliputian, ridiculous and self-important. Some of these new values emphasized efficiency. Others concerned equality: of opportunity, of service, of treatment for all citizens. As opposed to this the existing local government system emphasized the importance of freedom in the sense of autonomy.

It is interesting to speculate that, if the interests which were against reform had been able to hold it off for a few years, they might have been successful. The current emphasis on the values of participation and community involvement certainly do not seem to be well served in the reform. The idea of the large authorities which have not been established would have met hostility in the name of participation which is not confined to the world of local government. Yet for Maud and for the subsequent legislation there is a quest for bigness as the necessary means to a better system. 'The movement of opinion in favour of large authorities is impressive.' (Maud, 1960: para. 110).

The development of a group with an interest in reform would not, on its own, have been sufficient to achieve the change. Such groups existed in both countries before the major reforms actually took place. Change in the value system was also necessary. The 1952 Swedish reforms were more successful than the early ones in Britain but they did not go nearly as far as the government had intended. This is not to say that the groups interested in change did not alter the situation. In England many of the functions of the local government became subject to tighter and tighter controls, and the work of the planning departments, for example, was very nearly taken over by central departments for some aspects of planning in certain important areas. In Sweden the same sort of thing happened and communes were encouraged to develop ad hoc cooperation. The point is, however, that they would not make the transition from these purely functional rearrangements to a real structural change without an open acknowledgement that the value system was different, e.g. by surrendering symbols of power and local autonomy. To do this there had to be acceptance of the new values.

IV THE EFFECT OF POLITICAL STRUCTURE

Up to now the emphasis of the article has been on the similarities of the Swedish and English developments. They were not identical, however, and it is important to explain this too.

In writing about Sweden many people have discussed the apparent rationality of the society and the extra-ordinary way in which this affects the political system. The approach is evident in Elder (1970: 186-187):

> The spirit of *saklighet* rates highly a cool, objective and dispassionate approach to questions of public policy. It antedates the era of modern parliamentary government . . . two strands may be detected. First, an essentially conservative belief that the national interest is best served by cooperation across factional barriers; and secondly, an essentially liberal faith in the capacity of un-emotional reasoned arguments to winnow out the best possible solution to any given problem and so to bring about a steady continuous progress in human affairs.[2]

While I do not want to deny a role for political culture, it is a concept which is rather difficult to be precise about even with the help of survey research. I should like to suggest that there are certain institutional features of Swedish politics and society different from the situation in England which explain the different outcomes of the reform. Such features are more visible than others which are discussed in the context of the political culture. Thus, for example, Anton (1969: 94) has said:

Let me emphasise that the systems of 'expert' or specialist roles operating in a
deliberative, rational, open and consensual fashion represents the 'normal' in
Swedish decision making. Systems operating in this fashion are found at every
level and for every issue . . . This pattern, in short, represents a national style
which is itself a reflection of Swedish political culture.

Perhaps the most obvious difference between the English and the
Swedish reforms was that the Swedish one came earlier and, in general,
seemed to be easier to execute. Part of the explanation for this has
already been given. The Social Democratic government was a prime
mover in the changes whereas the Labour government only accepted
change after a great deal of hesitation. Some of this hesitation related
to a fear that the Labour city strongholds would be swamped with
Conservative suburban voters if boundaries were reorganized. The
Swedish Social Democratic vote was not so dependent on the inner city
vote. Swedish manual workers are more widely dispersed since the
Swedish policy of abolishing the old slums had long been implemented.

There are further structural differences, which lie behind this difference between the two countries. The local authorities were much
smaller in Sweden than in England and thus, for a government which
wanted to use the communes in any way for administration, a change
was that much more necessary. The smaller scale of the communes also
implied that there were not, as in England, a fair number of large towns
or counties which were themselves political bases and which could be
used to inhibit the attack of the reformers. The Swedish local government associations were unlike the County Councils Association and the
Association of Municipal Corporations, being more oriented towards
technical advice for their members (for which they maintained staffs
much larger than their English counterparts) and less oriented towards
political maneuvering vis-a-vis the government. The small size of their
membership made this technical emphasis necessary and also made their
political force rather weak. In England, the Rural District Councils
Association and the Urban District Councils Association were also weak
politically as compared with the associations of the larger local
authorities: the counties and the county boroughs or even the
boroughs.

A point often made about Swedish administration is its decentral-
ized nature and the independence of the local authorities. (Marshall,
1967: 3). Both these properties have to be explained and earlier
comments have to be somewhat modified. Swedish central government
is unique in having its operations divided into ministries which are
policy making bodies with virtually no administrative responsibilities

and agencies for administering programmes and which take a great deal of their instructions from the ministries but are separate from them. It is arguable that one reason why local government reform came to Sweden earlier than in Britain was that such a body did exist: the Ministry of Local Government and Development. It had a policy-making role and was not intertwined with the existing local government structure in the job of administration. The Swedish ministry has a specific duty to plan for the future whereas in England this sort of forward planning is relatively new. When local government reform was first being considered in England there was no organization in the government whose role it was to detatch itself from the day-to-day running of the machine. It was to be expected that the nature of the English structure would lead to more of an emphasis on incrementalism.

The argument about the decentralization of the Swedish system is often extended to saying that there is more local autonomy than in other countries. This point is rather controversial. Sweden is divided into 24 *län* or provinces but the länstyrelse, presided over by the landshövdning, which is responsible for the direction of local government functions, is made up of regionally based civil servants as we have seen. They represent the central government albeit at local level. The landsting is rather a weak council appointed by the communes in the län. One cannot say that, by the nature of the län administration the local authorities have more independence. On the contrary, the länstyrelse makes it easier for the central government to exercise surveillance over the work of the communes. It is significant that, when the 1962 reform was being planned as a result of the partial failure of the 1952 reforms, it was suggested that the län administration could take over many local government functions. This was an extremely powerful argument in making the local authorities agree to reform. In England there was no equivalent arm of the central government; when the Regional Economic Councils were set up by the Labour Government in 1966, local authority associations feared and objected to the creation of bodies which could threaten their powers. The Regional Economic Councils were, as it turned out, merely advisory and largely impotent bodies.

Integration of local and central government not only exists at the bureaucratic level but also among politicians. Anton calculated that 70 per cent of the Swedish Riskdagsmen held local office. Since they were generally among the most important of the local politicians it is not surprising that once the importance of reform had been accepted in the parliamentary circles, it would also be acceptable in the communes. Such an overlap does not exist at Westminster. The time demands of the British Parliament make it extremely difficult for an MP to hold local office and it is very easy for tension to arise between the London and national party oriented member and his local council party colleagues.

There is a further point about the operation of the Swedish system which is relevant to the argument. Anton has already been quoted when he speaks about the tradition of 'saklighet'. (1969: 94), or rationality of public decisions and this is underpinned by the nature of the commissions of enquiry and the parliamentary commissions which tend to have a much heavier representation of experts and less of politicians than in Britain. It was not simply that the Swedish political style emphasises rationality, but that it acknowledges the role of the expert to legitimize this unbiased and informed approach. Elder speaks about the tradition of the 'amateur' in British Royal Commissions and other methods of enquiry. (Elder, 1970). It may be that this tradition played its part in getting an orderly and early settlement of the question but there is no doubt that the British 'amateur' tradition also involved the introduction of 'political' considerations. Here policy is to be understood as what was conventionally considered to be possible. The Swedish use of experts seemed to put more emphasis on the search for new options. There was less emphasis on incremental solutions.

V CONCLUSION

Is it possible to generalize beyond these reorganizations in Sweden and England? First, I have suggested that structural change depends on the development of a powerful group which is marginal to the structure to be reformed, but which has an interest in its performance. Secondly, I have argued that such a group will be able to change the structure itself only when there is a change in the publicly accepted general value system, making non-incremental reform acceptable. These points are, I think, relevent to any situation which requires structural change. The last section of the chapter notes other features of the system itself which make structural change more or less easy.

One such feature is the position in the political system of the structure to be reformed. It was important that the Swedish communes were smaller than their English local equivalents. The lack of power was not a question of geographical or population size so much as the fact that they were called on to perform functions for which they were inadequate. The French communes are in many instances smaller than those in Sweden but there has been no reform there perhaps because of the political function which they perform and the powerful interest of many large towns.

A further important structural feature is the existence or absence of a body with political influence whose particular job it is to consider long-term planning and not simply the exigencies of the existing situation. In Sweden, the Ministry played this role but the Ministry of Housing and Local Government in England had not developed this function to the same degree.

In the beginning of this essay I drew attention to the cyclical nature of change in structural reform. I have proposed a model of the process of change, of the dynamics of change, in addition to my original reference to the cycle of adequacy and inadequacy. I have argued that the dynamics of change have to be seen in terms of demands and changes in the perceptions of certain groups. In England it was the planners and in Sweden the Social Democratic Party who had an interest in the change. In each case the crucial consideration is: who makes the evaluation, in terms of what values and symbols, and with what power to implement these values? This itself is part of the cycle since these groups have themselves become committed to the new institutions and, presumably, will be challenged when other groups arise. The rise to public influence of such new groups has to do with the public acceptability of certain symbols. I would suggest that there is a further cyclical element here in the context of public institutions. They appear to move between periods of emphasizing the symbols of administrative efficiency and those of democracy and public participation. An over-emphasis in one seems to lead to a balancing emphasis in the other. In modern times, however, the reality as opposed to the rhetoric is more likely to be an emphasis on central administration. In this there seems to be a linear as opposed to a cyclical movement in the direction of growth for central administration. However, there is also a both real and symbolic cyclical process of change.

NOTES

1. This paper is devoted to the reform in England. The local government systems in Scotland, Wales and Northern Ireland were all different from that in England before the reform and they were all reformed within a year or two of the English reforms. The resulting systems were again different from the new English system. One important reason for the differences in the patterns between Scotland and Wales on the one hand and England on the other was the larger rural element in the former two countries as compared to the latter.

2. It is interesting here to compare an account of 'Sachlichkeit' in Austrian culture. See Steiner, 1972: 188, 281, 425.

REFERENCES

ANTON, T. (1969) 'Policy Making and Political Culture in Sweden', *Scandinavian Political Studies* 4, Stockholm.

BRAND, J. (1974) The Reform of Local Government. London: Croom Helm.

BRANTGÄRDE, L. (1974) 'Kommunerna och Kommunblocks Bildningen' Lund, CWK Gleerup.

BRAYBROOKE, D. & C. E. LINDBLOM (1963) 'A Strategy of Decision'. New York: Free Press.

EDELMAN, M. (1964) The Symbolic Uses of Politics. Urbana: University of Illinois Press.

ELDER, Neil (1970) Government in Sweden. London: Pergamon Press.

――― (1973) 'Regionalism and the Publicity Principle in Sweden', Research Paper 3. *Commission on the Constitution,* London: HMSO.

JONES, G. (1963) 'The Local Government Commission & County Borough Extensions', *Public Administration* 41.

LARSSON, Åke & N. HEDFORS (1961) Kommunindelning och Självstyrelse. Stockholm: Tidens Förlag.

LOCAL GOVERNMENT BOUNDARY COMMISSION (1947) Report, House of Commons Paper, No. 150.

MARSHALL, A. H. (1967) Management in Local Government, 4, Committee on Management in Local Government, Ministry of Housing and Local Government. London: HMSO.

MAUD, Lord Redcliffe- (1969) The Local Government System in England. Cmnd. 4040. London: HMSO.

RING, Hans (1971) Kommunal Självstyrelse och Kommunala Reformer. Gothenburg: Kommunalförskning gruppen.

STATENS OFFENTLIGE UTREDNINGAR (SOU) (1961: 9) Principer för en ny kommunindelning. Stockholm.

STEINER, Kurt (1972) Politics in Austria. Boston: Little, Brown.

Chapter III

THE POLITICS OF THE BIOSPHERE:
THE DYNAMICS OF FISHING POLICY

Christopher C. Hood

University of Glasgow

Cyclicality is a feature of many policy fields and many types of policy are concerned with counteracting cycles or adapting to them. Agriculture and fishing are clear examples of this. Pre-industrial societies were geared very closely to the rhythms and fluctuations of nature, and even in the supposedly post-industrial world, the business of feeding people is still a highly uncertain affair, with alternating gluts and shortages of key commodities. For example, the five-year planning cycle was adopted in the USSR as the shortest period within which the effects of good and bad harvests could be expected to cancel out.

The 'feast-and-famine' cycle does not result simply from unanticipatable variations in nature's bounty in the biosphere. For example, in semi-planned economies of the Western type, the 'law of anticipated reactions' results in actual production veering wildly in response to regulatory and market changes, with producers helping to create a glut by reactions to shortages, and vice versa. Without attempting an exhaustive classification, we should at least distinguish between cycles in policy outputs and cycles in policy inputs.

So far as cycles in policy inputs are concerned, three main types are easily distinguishable. First, there are economic cycles such as the trade cycle. This perhaps should be subdivided into long-term and short-term components; for example a temporary decrease in supplies of fish may result in an increase in revenue as fish are in short supply. In the long term the reverse may be the case owing to alterations in patterns of consumption and processing. Second, there are biological cycles such as harvest cycles or weather cycles; and third, there are electoral cycles impinging on the policy process, varying in predictability according to whether or not the government has a fixed-term of office. Cycles in policy outputs cover programme implementation, agency reorganization cycles, regulation-response cycles, or changing policy outputs through sequential adoption of incompatible alternatives — the dilemma situation outlined by Richard Rose in the introduction. If one looks hard enough, all sorts of more esoteric cycles can be discerned; for example, the biological rhythms of individual policy-makers may be relevant for policy outcomes in some circumstances, particularly where very rapid decisions are involved.

What we are interested in is how cycles in inputs relate to cycles in outputs. There are three broad possibilities here. One is the case of a change in outputs in relation to a change in inputs; the second is a change of outputs in relation to no change in inputs, and the third is no change in outputs in relation to a change in inputs, such as no policy change after a change in government.

One can go on to ask questions about the effectiveness of government adaptations to changing inputs. Policy fields with cyclical inputs such as fishing present a peculiar danger of counter-productive policy outcomes, because policy outputs can vary as a lagged function of inputs. Some examples of this problem will be given shortly. On the other hand, where inputs are of a linear type, mis-timing of policy outputs is likely to be ineffective rather than counter-productive (Hood, 1974).

CYCLES AND FISHING POLICY

Fishing is a cyclical policy field par excellence; more so, in fact, than agriculture, because it is still a hunting industry to a large extent and therefore control over production is at best tenuous. Even the electoral cycle is not important as a dynamic input because British fishing policy, like agriculture, has been non-partisan for the past 30 years or so with negligible exceptions. (In Iceland, on the other hand, electoral changes have been much more important, and this has affected British-Icelandic fisheries negotiations on several occasions.) An absence of party political controversy might be expected to lead to a long-range planning style of policy-making, but this is difficult to achieve, owing to the effects of biological and economic cycles which have traditionally been the chief factors responsible for policy change.

The biological cycles involved are of several types. First, there are day-to-day fluctuations in fish catches owing to weather conditions and the like. Then there are seasonal cycles, such as migration cycles and spawning cycles. Most fish come near coastlines to spawn, where they are vulnerable to capture. This is especially the case for anadromous fish, which go up rivers to spawn; measures for the protection of spawning salmon go back to the Middle Ages in Britain. Migration cycles clearly present particular problems in the determination of national *(sic)* jurisdictions, for example the deep-sea catching of Scottish-spawned salmon off Greenland by Danish vessels which began in 1965.[1] They also affect administrative structures; for example, the herring seasons follow one another in a roughly clockwise pattern round the British Isles, necessitating a mobile force of port inspection staff and the like.

Finally, there are fish population fluctuations, both of long swings, for example, herring[2] and year-to-year fluctuations in the abundance of stocks, often coupled with longer-term trends. Figures I and II illustrate the year-to-year fluctuations in the North Sea haddock and cod stocks by giving data of catches from English East Coast ports.[3] These population movements give wide scope for disagreement: what one man asserts to be a cycle another asserts to be a trend. It is to settle these kinds of disagreements that governments have established fisheries laboratories over the past century. But forecasting changes in fish populations is almost as hazardous a task as is forecasting human populations.

Economic cycles add another dynamic input to government policy. They present challenges such as how to devise schemes of subsidization which cater for cyclical changes without propping up inefficient operators at the expense of more efficient operators. This is a persistent bugbear of subsidy schemes. A recent British effort to cope with this problem in the deep sea fleet was to base operating subsidies on a negative value-added tax. A global subsidy for the whole fleet was first determined using a formula which related the total sum inversely to the total profits made by the fishing fleet. Then each vessel's share of the total sum was determined in proportion to its share of the total profits.[4]

Many of the cyclical processes which have been described in relation to fishing are not shared by other undersea resources, such as oil and minerals. Such processes can easily frustrate long-term policies of support for fishing and even result in counter-productive responses at several levels. This can be seen in long-term processes of change. Fishing has moved through three broad phases during this century. In the early

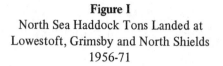

Figure I
North Sea Haddock Tons Landed at
Lowestoft, Grimsby and North Shields
1956-71

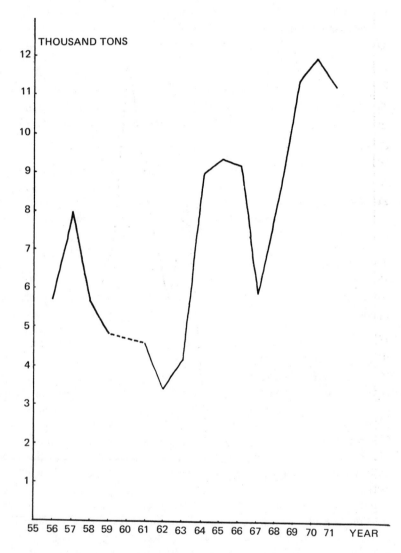

Sources: Ministry of Agriculture, Fisheries and Food (Fisheries Laboratory, Lowestoft) *Fishing Prospects* 1956-73.

Figure II
North Sea Cod Tons Landed at
Grimsby and North Shields 1956-71

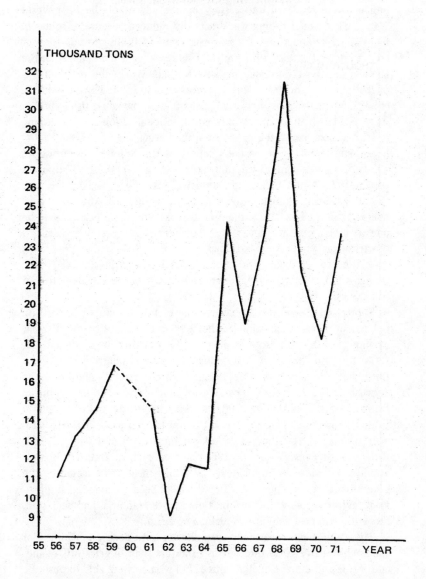

Sources: Ministry of Agriculture, Fisheries and Food (Fisheries Laboratory, Lowestoft) *Fishing Prospects* 1956-73.

twentieth century there were fears of shortage and over-fishing in the North Sea[5] and the North-East Atlantic; this led to moves for scientific regulation of the stocks and attempts to find new fisheries. But these policies were rendered unnecessary by the advent of the First World War, during which fishing was drastically reduced because of mines in the fishing grounds and the requisitioning of fishing vessels for war service. After the war, with prolific fish stocks and the collapse of the Russian and East European markets for salted fish, the problem was one of glut not shortage. This was more evident in the herring industry (traditionally, the most important fish) than in the white fish industry. As a result of this distress, moves for rationalization and marketing restriction (similar to the agricultural marketing schemes of the 1930s) began in the inter-war period (Report of the Sea Fish Commission, 1934); a 10 per cent ad valorem tariff was also imposed on imported fish in 1933. But the Second World War intervened, and by the time that the Herring Industry Board and the White Fish Authority were operating in the late 1940s, the problem was once more beginning to be one of shortage rather than glut. In the immediate post-war years this shortage was a relatively 'artificial' one owing to the fact that fleets took time to build up again after requisitioning during the war years, though stocks were good. Later shortages were created by depletion of fish stocks.

Shorter-term changes can have similar counter-productive effects on policy outcomes. For example, the Herring Industry Board built four herring meal and oil factories in the 1950s at Stornoway, Peterhead, Lowestoft and the Isle of Man to dispose of surplus herring. But by the time that the factories were finished, catches were falling and the Scottish Office had altered its subsidy policy. Morover, the Peruvian fishmeal boom, starting in 1960, knocked the bottom out of the world fishmeal market. When the Fleck Committee reported in 1961, Peruvian fishmeal was selling at 12/6d per unit, compared with 21/- for British herring meal (Report, 1961) and the Herring Industry Board's attempt to secure an import levy on herring meal was rejected by the government. Accordingly, the Board was obliged to abandon the fishmeal factories policy. But by the time that the factories had been sold, the world fishmeal market was picking up again.

The same dilemma attends even shorter-term decision-making. For example, in early 1968 three British trawlers sank in gales off Iceland, and in the subsequent hysteria three Hull women were able to push the Labour government into taking panic safety measures without (so it is said) consulting the responsible civil service officials on the spot. The result was that the British trawler fleet was compulsorily withdrawn from Icelandic waters after the gales had died down and the fishing was perfect.

The pattern of subsidization is also affected by the cyclical character of the industry. Here it is the economic cycle of fish prices (which is related to some extent to abundance – see Fig. IV) which seems to be the key factor. Fig. III illustrates this point.[6] Quite simply, the market is not allowed to work in a pure fashion to regulate fishing activity. Instead, the government steps in with extra subsidies at every major point of depression in order to keep the fleets going. Surplus fish can be frozen and put into cold storage.[7] The same sort of thing has applied in the past with tariff and quota increases: for example, in 1966 the British government removed the tariff on frozen fillets imported from the EFTA (European Free Trade Association) countries, and replaced the tariff by import quotas. In 1968, the tariff was reimposed (this was particularly damaging to Icelandic fish exports); in 1970 it was removed again, to be replaced by minimum import prices.

Because the timing of subsidy initiatives is coincident with price fluctuations, the law of diminishing returns (which would otherwise operate to conserve fish stocks) does not operate. Note also that the cyclical character of these fluctuations makes it very difficult to determine the effectiveness of the policy changes (the same is true of the the extensions of national fishery limits). Do subsidy increases worsen the cycles, make them smoother than they would otherwise be, or make no difference? The data given here would support all of these contradictory assertions.

EXTERNALITIES

While natural cycles interacting with government programmes were important as the older dynamic in fishing policy, externalities – the impact of one fishing vessel or fleet on another – are more important now. Indeed, over-fishing is a classic textbook example of 'external diseconomies'. In principle, it is in everybody's interest to stop fishing at the point of maximum sustainable yield (that is, the point at which the available food supply is used for maximum growth rather than for the maintenance of full-grown fish – a familiar concept in farming). But voluntary collective action would be needed to prevent fishing beyond sustainable yield, and fishing does not meet any of the conditions which Olson (1971) considers to facilitate such voluntary action..

Figure III. Catch Prices and Subsidy Measures 1945-70

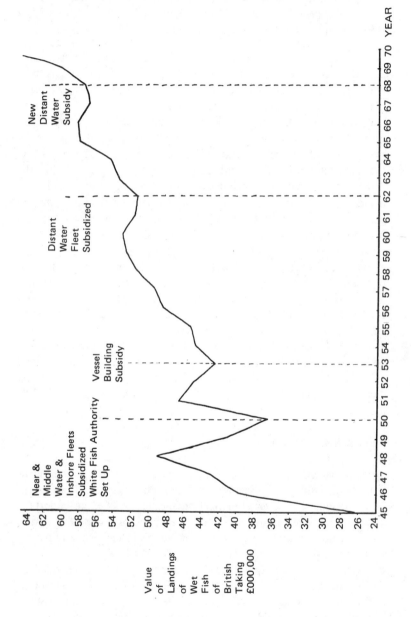

The result is that fishing fleets land larger catches than can be sustained in the long-term, causing a depletion or even exhaustion of stocks. In the 1880s T. H. Huxley was saying that the resources of the sea were inexhaustible, and as recently as 1944, the Elliott Committee on the Herring Industry could remark, 'It is said that man is one of the least important of living creatures in his inroads upon the herring shoals' (p. 5, para. 8). This is not the case today. In 1972 the British official report on *Fishing Prospects* remarked, '. . . We are now faced with a situation in which non-biological factors are having as much, or more, effect in determining potential catches than the biological processes . . . .' Indeed, the present world fish catch (about 60m. tons) could be obtained (and possibly increased) by a much smaller fleet of fishing vessels. It has been estimated, for example, that the present haul of cod from the North-East Atlantic could technically be taken at half the present cost (FAO, 1968).

Where there are economic externalities, there are arenas of political conflict; and probably it is because there are so many externalities involved that fishing has always been such a highly 'political' industry. There are two main arenas involved, namely those of *inter*national and of *intra*-national conflict. The microcosmic politics of 'deep-sea' fishing, the national politics of 'inshore' versus 'deep-sea' fishing, and the macrocosmic politics of world deep-sea fishing interact in a dynamic process.

The two main conflicts within a nation or state involve: (i) longshore fishermen versus 'nomad' fishermen ('nomads' are usually otter- or beam-trawlermen, but in some cases seine-netters come into the same category); (ii) 'Inshore' fishermen versus 'deep-sea' fishermen. The history of conflicts between longshore fishermen and 'nomad' fishermen is rich in the United Kingdom, particularly in Scotland, which has a three-mile limit within which trawling and seining is largely prohibited (though this prohibition is not effectively enforced). The closure of many overseas fishing grounds through the extension of national fishery limits, combined with the effect of rising fuel costs, will probably induce more big British trawlers to fish inshore in the future, and thus exacerbate the conflicts between nomads and locally-based fishermen. Similar prohibitions on large trawlers fishing inshore apply in Norway, and in some cases, such as Japan and Alaska, coastal fishing was restricted to sailing vessels until comparatively recently (Tussing, Morehouse and Babb, 1972). Iceland exhibits a similar pattern; indeed in Iceland, longshoremen are of much greater importance than elsewhere, since up to 10 per cent of the country's total cod catch is taken by hand line (Government of Iceland, 1972: 20). The increasing economic importance of shellfishing has led to conflict between shellfishermen and trawlermen. In the United States, shellfishermen have dumped old cars in the sea to form artificial reefs and therefore to keep trawlermen away, and there are proposals to do the same thing off the West coast of Scotland.[8] But even shellfishermen are by no means a united group: there are fierce conflicts between traditional pot fishermen and often part-time sub-aqua fishermen.

Conflicts are very often activated by conservation measures, whether international or domestic (and there are some odd cases which fall between these two categories, such as Isle of Man fisheries). Conservation measures usually seek to reduce the efficiency of the fishing effort, by means such as the enlargement of net mesh sizes to remove smaller fish from the catch rather than by the establishment of property rights by limiting entry to the fishing grounds. In practice, such measures often strike at the more efficient fishing vessels (for example, by permitting only sailing vessels in some areas) and also characteristically contain exemptions for local longshore fishing boats. For example, international close seasons on herring fishing in the North Sea and Skaggerak were established by the NEAFC (North East Atlantic Fisheries Commission) in 1971. But local longshore boats were exempt from the ban, and for some years before the NEAFC action there had been conflict between English longshoremen and Scottish nomad fishermen over the issue of a possible United Kingdom ban on herring fishing on the English East coast by large trawlers.

The Moray Firth in Scotland is an area particularly rich in disputes between fishermen, and the result has been an extraordinarily complicated maze of regulations and close seasons for different types of fishing gear (Report 1970: Appendix 5, 188). This has also produced the curious anomaly that British government regulation over fishing methods by British trawlers has extended into a sea area outside the international fishery limit lines. The result is that British trawlers have in the past been banned from the Firth for much of the year by United Kingdom regulations (Bylaw No. 10 of the Herring Fishery (Scotland) Act 1889), while foreign and EEC trawlers could fish within 12 or 16 miles of the beaches. The Moray Firth is perhaps an extreme example of intra-national disputes between groups of fishermen, but the broad pattern of conflict is by no means unusual in inlets of this type. Armed conflict in such disputes is relatively rare, but it can happen, as with the case of the Chesapeake Bay oyster fisheries in the United States (Rothschild, 1972).

One might expect to find a connection between local regulative control of fishermen and measures to protect local fishermen, but this does not seem to be invariably the case. For example, measures to protect local fishermen are a feature of American and Norwegian fishing regulation, where fishing is in large part under the control of local authorities (and state governments in the case of the United States). But similar measures may be found in countries where fishing regulation is centrally controlled, and cases may also be found where local control of fisheries is not associated with measures to protect local fishermen. The United Kingdom can provide examples of both cases, because there is no single central fisheries ministry. Instead, fisheries control is divided between the Scottish Department of Agriculture and Fisheries and the Ministry of Agriculture for England and Wales. The Scottish system of regulation is centralized in the Scottish Office (except for the 45 Salmon Fishery District Boards, which are relatively insignificant), but measures to protect local fishermen are a marked feature of the system. On the other hand, there is a large element of regional control in the English and Welsh systems, with 11 Sea Fisheries Committees; but local fishermen enjoy much less protection than in Scotland.

The second level of conflict at intra-national level, that of inshore fishermen versus deep-sea fishermen (in the sense of vessels fishing off the land shelf of other countries) brings out clearly the interaction of domestic and international conflict. This is perhaps easiest to show over the question of fishing limits. Inshore fishermen (an imprecise term, here used to refer to fishermen operating largely within the continental shelf adjacent to their national coastlines) characteristically press for the extension of national fishing limits. This is to protect their operations from competition from increasingly capital-intensive high seas fishing fleets (especially the Russian, Polish and Japanese fleets and, to a lesser extent, those of the traditional North Atlantic fishing nations). This is particularly noticeable in traditional fishing grounds, where catches are fairly static and prices, especially of cod, have been rising, albeit with periodic downward movements (see Fig. III). The USSR, Japan and South-West Africa have very rapidly growing fleets in waters traditionally less exploited and have not yet experienced much conflict of this kind. The same limit extension trends are discernible in Latin-American waters, where states such as Peru and Chile are major proponents of 200-mile fishing limits.

International law governing limit extensions is imprecise and in a state of flux. The general trend is for an increasing number of states to claim exclusive fishing rights in waters from 12 to 200 miles off their land shore. The traditional limit has been three miles, but large territorial fishing limits were also known in the seventeenth and eighteenth centuries. There is obviously a strong demonstration effect[9] here, in that countries tend to follow one another in staking out larger limits. There is also a more direct chain-reaction stimulus in that the extension of one country's limits will tend to put pressure on the other coastal areas in the vicinity where fishing is more open. For example, the limitation of catches in Icelandic and Faroese waters has inevitably put pressure on North Scottish waters by driving displaced fleets there. Yet any counter-reaction by the British government to extend fishery limits would reopen the Pandora's Box of EEC fishing policy (Hood, 1973).

More than 30 states have now extended their offshore exclusive fishing limits, and the number is increasing steadily. This has led to minor armed conflicts in some cases, for example between Morocco and Spain and between the United Kingdom and Iceland (Cmnd. 5341, 1973), and may well do so elsewhere if protein prices continue to spiral upwards. The potential for such conflicts may well be greatest in sea areas where under-developed countries are rapidly expanding their trawling fleets, such as the West Central or South East Pacific. By comparison, the fishing effort in the North Sea is relatively stable and catches for some time have been fluctuating without any long-term increase (Coull, 1972). This is now beginning to be true of the North-East Atlantic as well.

Logically, the process of extending limits could continue until all states have annexed their adjacent continental shelves for the exclusive use of their own fishermen. This has already happened with mineral rights, but fishing rights have not been included in the definition of resources of continental shelves for such purposes (Report, 1973: 23-4). If this happened, it would mean that there would no longer be any deep sea fishermen working off other countries' continental shelves. There is already a trend in this direction. But two factors have tended to limit this process in the past to some extent.

First, if a country is or becomes an overall exporter of fish, replacing wholly or in part other national fleets in supplying fish to their domestic markets, the gateways to such export markets will by definition be controlled by antagonistic governments or producer organizations, who are thereby in a position to make direct counter-threats in terms of tariffs, quotas and boycotts, as well as indirect threats. This has been the case, for example, in every Anglo-Icelandic fishery dispute since World War II and in the 1964 Anglo-Faroese[10] dispute (Williamson, 1970). Earlier British boycotts of Icelandic and Faroese fish were largely ineffective (if not actually counter-productive), but in the 1972-3 dispute, Britain and West Germany combined to block Iceland's trade agreement with the EEC, thus depriving Iceland of tariff concessions to a huge net importing area which accounts for two-thirds of Iceland's fish exports. The Norwegian government was in the same dilemma concerning EEC entry. The Norwegian Fishermen's Association and inshore fishermen wanted to preserve their monopoly of coastal fishing waters (closed to British trawlers in 1970 after a 10-year phase-out period) whereas processing and marketing interests wanted to reap the benefits of being inside the EEC tariff wall, a huge and under-supplied market for fish.

The other limiting factor is that every extension of fishing limits invites reciprocal action by other governments under similar domestic pressures. Thus, deep-sea fishermen stand to lose what the inshoremen gain and are likely to set up counter-pressures at some point. This emerged quite explicitly in the 1971 EEC negotiations about fishery policy, when the British deep-sea trawlermen and the inshore fishermen were pulling the British government in opposite directions over limits. The same sort of conflict has occurred with the prospect of a 200-mile limit, since the British deep-sea fishermen hope that reciprocal swapping deals could be made with other fishing states such as Norway and Iceland, whereas the inshore fishermen are opposed to the idea of such swapping. Even countries such as Iceland and Faroe have deep-sea fishing fleets which are vulnerable to counter-measures; for example, Icelandic, Faroese and Norwegian boats fish for herring off the Scottish Shetlands just outside the 12-mile limit, and much of the Faroese catch is obtained off Greenland and Iceland. As limits extend further outwards, there comes a point at which previously inshore fishermen become classified as seep sea. For example, inshore Scottish fishing interests who eagerly supported the idea of a 50-mile limit are much less keen on the idea of a 200-mile limit, which would shut out many of the larger type of Scottish seine net vessels from the Norwegian coast as well as closing the Arctic waters to the big English trawlers.

INTERNATIONAL CONFLICTS

International conflicts between governments take two main forms: subsidy competition, and conflict over fishing limits. In both cases, externalities are often worsened by cyclicality, with rounds of international conflict triggered to some extent by biological cycles in the supply of fish.

The time-sequencing of major British subsidy measures (Fig. III) does not allow market forces to work to their fullest possible extent, in the sense of reduced fish prices lowering the level of fishing activity. There is certainly a demonstrable international tendency for upward spiralling of subsidization since 1947 (OECD, 1965, 1966, 1970). If the British pattern is typical, an international dynamic emerges in the form of rounds of subsidy increases activated by biological and economic cycles. In some ways this is a perverse dynamic in the same way as rounds of tariff increases. All governments might prefer lower levels of subsidy, but any individual government may face the prospect of bankruptcy among its fishermen if international competitors enjoy much higher levels of subsidy from their respective governments. International bodies such as the OECD try to prevent a spiral of competitive subsidization, but with comparatively little success.

A similar chain-reaction applies to the extension of fishing limits. If subsidy measures are introduced to encourage fishing when prices go down, it seems logical to expect extensions of fishing limits to protect stocks and monopolize coastal fishing rights when prices are going up. In general, this seems to be the case. Figure IV shows the time-sequencing of the major extensions of fishing limits by Northern European countries since 1951, in relation to catch weights, catch rates and the prices obtained for their catches by the British distant water fishing fleet.

It is the catch *rate* rather than the total catch weight which is the most accurate measure of the abundance of fish in the sea, since it measures the ease with which fish may be caught. But catch weights may be maintained or increased by increasing the time spent fishing, even when biological abundance is declining, and in fact fishermen do tend to compensate for falling catch rates by greater fishing activity. If catch rate is therefore taken as measuring the abundance of fish stocks in the sea, it can be seen from Figure IV that scarcity of fish in the sea tends to be reflected fairly accurately in catch values and that extensions of fishing limits almost always come when catch rates are falling sharply. Therefore, the timing of extensions of fishing limits coincides with the biological cycle as well as with the economic one.[11]

The geopolitical (or aquapolitical) power of governments varies according to the measure of significance employed. The rankings come out differently depending upon whether one takes the value or the quantity of fish as the index. For example, some countries catch a lot

Figure IV

Major North European and N.E. Atlantic Fishing Limit Extensions with
UK Distant Water Catches, Catch Values and Catch Rates (Iceland Cod)
1951-71

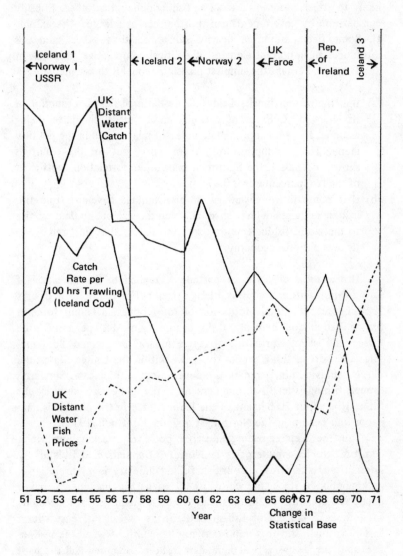

Source: White Fish Authority Annual Reports 1951-72.

of 'trash' fish for processing into meal and oil which is far less valuable than fish used directly for food. For example, the United Kingdom would be much higher in a value league than in a quantity league (Gould, 1974: 4).

Measures of fishing significance show that some governments are likely to attach more importance to fishing policy than others. Subsidy competition by governments can thus be seen as a league[12] (see Table I). Some fleets are more heavily subsidized than others, and this introduces an important element of political comparative advantage or disadvantage. Perhaps the simplest plausible model is to assume:

(a) that the proportional subsidy of any national fleet is a function of its share of GNP or of national employment, the latter being assumed to be an approximate index of relative pull in the political arena. This assumption may seem naive, but for the countries shown in Table I, the Spearman rank order correlation coefficient of the two percentages is 0.87.[13]

(b) that comparative advantage or disadvantage develops from this insofar as there are imbalances between the size of any fleet relative to the world fishing economy and the size of that fleet relative to its own national economy.

This analysis may also be partially extended to the allocation of subsidization within domestic fishing systems. For example, on Coull's 1960 figures, the total proportion of the Norwegian labour force in fishing is about four percent but this becomes almost 20 percent for the three counties of Northern Norway: Finmark, Troms and Nordland. The same sort of thing applies to Alaska within the United States; the Faroe islands within Denmark is an even more striking case. Similarly, though fishing is less than one percent of the United Kingdom labour force, it is about 10 percent of the labour force in the Shetlands, and about four percent in the North-East of Scotland (Coull, 1972).

Thus the deep-sea fishing industry is politically weak within Britain compared to its counterparts in Norway, Denmark and Ireland. By international standards, the British fishing industry is relatively large, ranking about 15th in the world fishery league with an annual catch of about 900,000 tons (UN Statistical Yearbook figures). But it accounts for only 0.25 percent of British GNP, so its overall influence within Britain is small. But it is important to distinguish between the inshore fleet and the deep-sea fleet here. The inshore fishermen and the peripheral constituencies which they affect are of some significance in

TABLE I

Fishing Subsidy League Table

	(1) Total Grants and Loans 1969 $m.	(2) Catch values 1965 $m.	(3) Catch Weights 1969 000 metric tons	(4) National Income 1969 $m. 000s	(5) (1) as % of (4) %	(6) (2) as % of (4) %
1.	Japan 156	Japan 1343	Japan 8623	Japan 136	Iceland 2.26	Iceland 72.0
2.	Norway 65	Spain 262	Norway 2481	W. Germany 124	Norway 0.86	Norway 2.12
3.	Denmark 30.6	W. Germany 237	Spain 1486	France 98.8	Denmark 0.28	Portugal 1.40
4.	W. Germany 13.6	France 237	Denmark 1275	UK 83.8	Portugal 0.13	Spain 1.08
5.	UK 13.4	Norway 152	UK 1083	Italy 66.6	Japan 0.11	Japan 0.98
6.	Spain 12.8	Italy 151	France 746	Spain 24.2	Spain 0.052	Denmark 0.87
7.	Italy 10.7	UK 125	Iceland 689	Netherlands 23.1	Netherlands 0.051	France 0.24
8.	France 6.5	Iceland 125	Germany 651	Belgium 18.2	W. Germany 0.019	Netherlands 0.23
9.	Portugal 6.0	Denmark 94	Portugal 457	Denmark 10.7	Italy 0.016	Italy 0.22
10.	Iceland 3.9	Portugal 63	Italy 353	Norway 7.5	UK 0.016	W. Germany 0.19
11.	Netherlands 1.1	Netherlands 53	Netherlands 323	Portugal* 4.3	France 0.006	UK 0.14
12.	Belgium 1.0	Belgium 15	Belgium 58	Iceland* 0.1	Belgium 0.006	Belgium 0.08
	Source: OECD	OECD	UN Statistical Yearbook 1970	UN Statistical Yearbook 1970	UN	

Rank Order correlation of Cols (5) and (6) using Spearman's formula for rank order correlation = 0.8740.

* = very approximate

British politics, especially in Scotland, which accounts for nearly half of Britain's inshore fishermen (about 9,220 out of 21,000) and for the bulk of the inshore fleet by tonnage. By comparison, the deep-sea fleet is much more concentrated in a few key ports, and thus affects fewer constituencies. For example, Hull and Grimsby have about 75 percent of all white fish landings in England, and in 1970 the average number of vessels owned by deep sea trawling companies was 11.8 ships, whereas most inshore vessels are individually owned (White Fish Authority, 1971).

Two main consequences arise. One is that the inshore fleet has tended to obtain considerably higher proportional subsidies than the deep-sea fleet. The other is that in the past, British governments have been inclined to 'sell out' their deep-sea fishermen over fishing limits (often this has been accompanied by bribes in the form of extra subsidies). This propensity to 'sell out' arises partly because the issue is relatively less important to the British government than to the other North Atlantic fishing nations, and partly because of the reciprocal advantages to inshore fishermen which accrue from higher limits all round. For example, in the EEC fishing limits negotiations in 1971, the deep-sea industry's position was weakened by the fact that the votes of about 20 Conservative (inshore) fishing constituency MPs were required for the policy of EEC entry, and it is said that this is what delayed the United Kingdom's Parliamentary vote on EEC entry from July to October 1971. (In the event, Norway did not join the EEC, so in fact the deep-sea fleet would have gained nothing from being able to exploit other EEC fishing grounds even if it had won its case with the British government in support of a 'common waters' EEC fishing policy.) But since Britain's accession to the EEC, the past strategy of 'surrenders' to Iceland, Faroe and Norway, accompanied by higher subsidies or by extensions of domestic fishing limits, has become harder to operate, at least within the rules of the EEC. EEC rules outlaw competitive subsidization and permit the fishing fleets of all EEC countries to operate within a six-mile limit of the coastline of any EEC country. This limit is extended to 12 miles of the coastline for areas which are highly dependent on coastal fishing, such as the North of Scotland. Even this six-mile limit is due to go in 1982 unless the Council of Ministers votes unanimously for its retention — and the French government has already said that it would veto such a move.

Thus the older pattern of policy change is complicated by EEC membership. Indeed, one possible development would be to establish a common EEC fishery unit (probably between 50 and 200 miles off member countries' coastlines). This would involve the abandonment of the older pattern of deep-sea fishing altogether and would turn much of the North Sea into an EEC lake in much the same way as has happened with oil (though it is not easy to see how in practice Soviet trawlers could be excluded from such waters). Distant water trawling interests in Britain are already beginning to think along these lines. It seems very likely from the above analysis that such a move would only replace international conflict with intra-national and intra-EEC conflict of probably equal intensity, and electoral arithmetic would again probably work against the capital-intensive distant water trawling companies in favour of the present inshore fishing interests.

SUMMARY AND CONCLUSION

This chapter has concentrated largely on the behavioural analysis of policy cycles. It has not, for example, explored the role of bureaucracies or any of the internal processes of government. Fishing policy has been analyzed in terms of the twin dynamics of externalities and cycles. Externalities occasion ratchet-effects, demonstration effects, reciprocal measures and the like, and cycles are the prime determinants of changes and even reversals of policy.

A third element which plays a part in policy dynamics, but which has not been mentioned up to now, is policy effectiveness. Here we have considered merely what governments do (policy outputs) without considering the effectiveness or otherwise of their actions (policy outcomes). But clearly the effectiveness of a given policy measure will have something to do with the pattern of subsequent policy-making. In fishing, there is a tendency to develop steadily more complicated modes of regulation, for two reasons. One reason is that regulation-response cycles set in, with fishermen changing their activities in such a way as to defeat policy effectiveness. For example, closed areas and seasons tend to lead to more intensive fishing in the times and places which remain open. Such regulation-response cycles are partly responsible for the adoption of increasingly complex regulations, and such regulations are very often harder to enforce than earlier measures. (Tussing, Morehouse and Babb, 1972: 283).

The other factor responsible for the tendency towards more complex regulation is simply that no single measure is wholly satisfactory. For example, in conservation, measures to prevent fishermen using very fine mesh nets which do not allow young fish to escape capture, are inherently limited, because net meshes cannot be reasonably enlarged beyond a certain point. Similarly, measures laying down minimum sizes for the fish which are landed at quays, in order to protect young fish, are also only limitedly effective, because they do not prevent young fish from being *caught,* only from being *landed.* Closed areas and close seasons have drawbacks, too. All of these measures are difficult to police as well as being inherently limited in effectiveness. The policing problem applies a fortiori where such measures are being taken by regional international fishing commissions such as the North East Atlantic Fisheries Commission, which require unanimity among their member states for their regulations to be effective.

Policing problems of this type are by no means unique to fishing. Moreover, it is often difficult to appraise policy effectiveness accurately, because in some cases governments deliberately do not enforce policies as much as they could. For example, the prohibitions on trawling and seining within three miles of the coastline in Scotland have been accepted in the past partly because they have not been very seriously enforced. The Fisheries Department has for a long time used for this purpose several 30-year-old coal-burning minesweepers, which are very slow and whose funnel smoke can be seen from a great distance (Cmnd. 4453, 1970: 141-51 and 158, para. 323). Reciprocally, the bitter pill constituted by the surrender of some of Britain's fishing limits to EEC countries in 1971 was sweetened by an assurance that the limits which remained would be more strictly enforced than in the past; the grant for the Fishery Protection Service was raised from £1m. to £1.5m. in December 1971 and the protection fleet is now being expanded and renewed.

Third, what has been described here is a historical pattern which may well be becoming obsolete. Periodic relative down-turns of fish prices are still likely to occur, but to some extent the older policy dynamic of pure cyclicality has been replaced by the dynamics of externality and the attendant problems of positive feedback, i.e. higher prices — more intensive fishing — fewer fish — higher prices, and so on. So far as extensions of fishing limits are concerned, the international chain-reaction is now likely to go faster and without a strong link to the biological cycles. Technological developments may also upset the older pattern of change. For example, various countries are developing acoustic and other devices for 'shepherding' fish instead of allowing them to roam naturally. If such devises are seriously adopted, this is likely to be a recipe for disputes both at the national and international levels, because the problem would then turn on exclusive rights to fish for given fish stocks rather than exclusive rights to fish in particular sea areas, as at present. But this sort of technological development is still futuristic, and it is doubtful if the older pattern of cyclical processes will ever entirely disappear. The basic reason for the likely persistence of an element of cyclicality is that fish is much more perishable than most other foods and cold storage facilities are expensive and only adaptable within limits.

The initial dichotomization of policy dynamics into cyclical and linear progressions begins to look over-neat. These categories are not entirely exclusive. Fishing policy dynamics looks like a case of linearity *plus* cycles – a linear trend activated by cyclical processes.

NOTES

1. Now to be phased out under a 1972 ICNAF (International Commission for North-West Atlantic Fisheries) resolution, ratified by Denmark in March 1973.

2. See for example, Einar Lea's famous studies of Norwegian herring cycles; for a brief account, see Coull, 1972.

3. Fuller data for the North Sea are given in Gould (1974: Figs. 2 and 3).

4. Note the ingenuity of this scheme. For details, see House of Commons Debates 778, c.272 (written answers).

5. In fact, for the North Sea, an official committee considered the problem of over-fishing as early as 1893 (see also Aflalo, 1904: 59 and 177-80).

6. In the period subsequent to that covered by this chapter, the pattern has continued: rising fish prices accompanied by reductions in subsidization in 1973, followed by a relative down-turn in prices in 1974-75, which has produced extra subsidies.

7. The policy dilemmas which are created by non-market processes do not necessarily prove that pure market processes would produce better results; but we are not concerned here with prescriptive arguments of that kind.

8. Other issues in this arena, which overlaps with the deep-sea versus inshore arena, are the conflicts between beam trawlermen and other types of fishermen, particularly on the South Coast of England, and the conflicts between conventional fishermen and industrial fishermen (fishermen catching fish for reduction to meal and oil rather than for consumption as fresh food) (Elliot, 1974).

9. The applicability of this concept was pointed out by Ian McSween of the White Fish Authority.

10. The Faroe islands are not in fact a sovereign state, but a very largely self-governing province of Denmark, except for foreign affairs and defence (Williamson, 1970; West, 1972). But the high political autonomy of the islands and their almost total dependence on fishing makes it convenient to distinguish them from Denmark for the purposes of this chapter.

11. On the other hand, it is worth remembering that Iceland was committed to extension of her fishing limits as early as 1949, and tried to effect such an extension whenever suitable opportunity seemed to present itself, for example in 1952 and in 1956; and the Faroese were merely following suit.

12. These figures should be treated cautiously, since, as has already been mentioned, international bodies like OECD and EEC discourage excessive subsidization and therefore governments are apt to keep accounts in such a way as to understate the extent of their bounty. But if all governments have an equal propensity to such deceit, the rankings in the league should not be affected.

13. Note that, like Pennock's study of agricultural subsidization in Britain and the USA, this suggests that different styles of government may make less difference to policy outputs than is traditionally assumed (Pennock, 1969).

REFERENCES

AFLALO, F. G. (1904) The Sea Fishing Industry of England and Wales. London: Edward Stanford.

COULL, J. R. (1972) The Fisheries of Europe. London: G. Bell and Sons.

ELLIOTT COMMITTEE REPORT ON THE HERRING INDUSTRY (1944) London: HMSO Cmd. 6503.

ELLIOT, G. H. (1974) 'The Case for Fishmeal', unpublished paper.

FAO, (1968) The State of World Fisheries. Rome: FAO.

GOULD, R. (1974) 'The Economic and Political Importance of North Sea Fish Stocks and Fishing Industries', Paper presented to RIIA North Sea Study Group, Edinburgh (May).

GOVERNMENT OF ICELAND (MINISTRY OF FOREIGN AFFAIRS) (1972) Fisheries Jurisdiction in Iceland. Reykjavik.

HOOD, C. C. (1973) 'British Fishing and the Iceland Saga', *The Political Quarterly* 44 (3).

———, (1974) 'Administrative Diseases: Some Types of Dysfunctionality in Administration', *Public Administration,* 52, 439-54.

MINISTRY OF AGRICULTURE FISHERIES AND FOOD, FISHERIES LABORATORY, LOWESTOFT (1972) Fishing Prospects 1972-3.

OLSON, M. (1971) The Logic of Collective Action. New York: Schocken Books (revised edition).

OECD (1965) Subsidies and Other Financial Support to the Fishing Industries of
OECD Member Countries. Paris: OECD.

———, (1966) Fishery Policies and Economies. Paris: OECD.

———, (1970) Financial Support to the Fishing Industry. Paris: OECD.

PENNOCK, J. R. (1969) 'Agricultural Subsidies in Britain and America', in R.
Rose (ed.), Policy-Making in Britain. London: Macmillan.

REPORT OF THE SEA FISH COMMISSION (1934) London: HMSO, Cmd.
4677.

REPORT OF THE COMMITTEE OF INQUIRY INTO THE FISHING
INDUSTRY (1961) London: HMSO, Cmnd. 1266.

REPORT OF THE HOUSE OF COMMONS ESTIMATES COMMITTEE (1966)
London: HMSO, HC 274, 1966-7.

REPORT OF THE COMMITTEE ON SCOTTISH INSHORE FISHERIES (1970)
London: HMSO, Cmnd. 4453.

REPORT ON THE FISHING DISPUTE BETWEEN THE UK AND ICELAND
(1973) London: HMSO, Cmnd. 5341.

ROTHSCHILD, D. (ed.) (1972) World Fisheries Policy. London: University of
Washington Press.

TUSSING, A. R., M. MOREHOUSE and J. D. BABB, Jr. (1972) Alaska Fisheries
Policy. Alaska: Institute of Social, Economic and Government Research,
University of Alaska.

WEST, J. F. (1972) Faroe: The Emergence of a Nation. London: C. Hurst and Co.

WHITE FISH AUTHORITY (1971) Annual Report for Year ended March 31,
1971. London: HMSO, HC 435, 1970-1.

WILLIAMSON, K. (1970) The Atlantic Islands. London: Routledge and Kegan
Paul (second edition).

Chapter IV

THE POLITICS OF EDUCATIONAL REFORM IN SWEDEN AND WEST GERMANY

Arnold J. Heidenheimer

Washington University, St. Louis

Basic reforms are attempted in education systems very infrequently, partly because they are difficult to initiate and take many years to follow-up implementation to bring to full fruition. In the 1950s and 1960s, both Sweden and West Germany sought to reorganize their secondary system of education in response to similar arguments and stimuli — including the presence in office of Social Democratic-led governments. Yet the results of their efforts have diverged sharply. In Sweden, changes initially undertaken on an experimental basis in the early 1950s have shown linear progress — and at times an accelerating rate of progress. In Germany, by contrast, the pace of reform, as characterized by a slight upward trend in the number of new-type secondary schools, does not appear to be maintaining the necessary momentum.

Few national policies in post-1945 Western Europe have exhibited such similar fundamental characteristics, and so many variations regarding substantive detail, pace, and style of reform, as the initiatives to replace the established European tri-partite systems of secondary schools dividing pupils according to their academic ability with comprehensive schools mixing pupils of all levels of ability (similar to the American high school model). The attempt to compare the reform initiatives in Sweden and West Germany is challenging because the two countries rank near the top and bottom of the European Countries in the degree to which they have implemented 'comprehensivization'. Sweden now has all of its secondary students in such schools, and

This article is reprinted in slightly amended form from *Comparative Education Review* (October 1974) with the permission of the publisher.

Britain teaches about half in this way; West Germany, however, enrolls only about three per-cent of its junior secondary pupils in Gesamt-schulen (i.e., Comprehensives). How do such factors as the reception of new research findings, the pro- and counter-reform positions of interest groups and the leadership of party politicians and bureaucrats, help to explain why Sweden led and Germany lagged? What inhibited strong German reform initiatives in the 1950s and 1960s, and what slowed an energetic attempt at 'takeoff' even after the German Social Democrats won control of the Federal government in 1969?

In the 1940s both nations' education systems were still very similar in their reliance on tripartite school structures based on early differen-tiation. Indeed the German system had earlier served as a model for the Swedes. Until the beginning of the 1950s Sweden's schools were a reflection of the traditional European dualistic pattern (Husén, 1965: 209). Then the Swedes pursued a step-by-step policy of integrating parallel school types, first at the lower secondary (1950-62), and then at the upper secondary level (1964-71). In the process they greatly increased access, particularly of working-class children, and eliminated most standard examinations and other criteria of selectivity, even to the point of abolishing the Abitur examination at the conclusion of the academic Gymnasium school. This 'revolutionary reorientation of Swedish education from a selective to an egalitarian basis' (Paulston, 1968: 116) culminated in 1971 when the three types of secondary schools then being attended by the majority of 16-19 year-olds were merged into integrated schools, thus achieving full comprehensivization. By contrast German conditions in the mid-1960s were characterized by the authors of *Two Decades of Non-Reform in West German Education* with these words:

> Important decisions about a pupil's future career are usually made when he is ten years old; not more than one out of every five pupils attempts secondary education, and the majority of these eventually fail; only five to six percent of secondary school graduates are children of workers; about two-thirds of all boys and girls have practically completed general schooling at the age of 14 or 15 (Robinsohn and Kuhlmann, 1967: 319).

I SOCIO-CULTURAL CONTROVERSIES OVER EDUCATIONAL PRIORITIES

A. Differentiation and the 'Pool of Ability': An initial barrier to reform initiatives in both countries was the conventional wisdom regarding the distribution of learning abilities sincerely upheld by prestigious academic experts on pedagogy. Thus the Swedish professors of educational psychology were unanimous in recommending an early 'creaming off' of able students to the 1940 Experts Committee which considered but failed to endorse, fundamental reorganization. One stated that in undifferentiated classes an able student 'does not meet the competition which will motivate him'; another pointed out that 'according to modern intelligence research no really weighty arguments can be stated in favor of a postponement of the selection of pupils'; another could not 'remember any psychologist who had advocated the suitability of a six or eight year common school (Husén, 1962: 11-12). Sweden was notable in that 'Education entered university faculties in Sweden earlier than either psychology or sociology' so that its faculties became 'the initial home of behavorial studies' (Scheuerl, 1968: 102). In selecting research advisers, the 1946 committee side-stepped the conservatives, who had contributed to the 1940 stalemate, and initiated a pattern of throwing support, and later ample funds, to empirical researchers. To meet objections from sceptics, the Riksdag had, in passing the 1950 Act, 'accepted the idea of the comprehensive school, but only if the experimental activities would show its suitability'. This launched a period of productive research activity.

B. Obstacles Peculiar to Germany: The relative imperviousness of German educators to demands articulated through the political structures may most importantly, and paradoxically, be explained in terms of preceding attempts to politicize the system made, although mainly during the Nazi era, also during the phase of Occupation 'reeducation' policies. Schools and universities had been key objects of Nazi takeovers, and post-1949 changes were largely in the direction of a return to the patterns of the Weimar era. Thus older pedagogical othodoxies and traditions were re-established in Germany just when they were being challenged in Sweden. Insofar as denazification removed active Nazi party members from educational and administrative positions, it eliminated much of the younger generation who had begun their careers under the Third Reich. Hence, a disproportionate number of key university and administrative posts went to older men born before 1900. Insofar as societal needs had been interpreted in widely varying ways by the Nazis and the post-war occupation authorities, these elites tended to regard a measure of non-responsiveness to political direction as a prerequisite for the restoration of a liberal pluralist society. German educators who claimed that only some five percent of the population were gifted enough to benefit from higher education, based their assertion on the opinions of 'experts' who held that 'ability is a biological category . . . unconditionally rooted in hereditary traits'. And as late as 1967 relatively liberal professors of pedagogy were offering separate theories for each category of school, while cautiously prognosticating that 'one can perceive a development which will lead the three German school forms closer to each other, and emphasize their common functions, without basically touching the tripartite pattern' (Scheuerl, 1968).

C. Social Goals and Educational Perspectives: In both countries long-established class-based attitudes toward the utilization of educational opportunities constituted a serious handicap to reform. Because the gymnasia had for so long been virtual middle-class monopolies, working-class families did not see them as natural routes of social mobility. They often discouraged their children from trying to enter them, even when barriers were lowered.

The Swedes set up administrative structures to counteract such parental influences, but found that working-class children generally did less well on tests than middle-class children of the same intelligence. This led them to the conclusion that

> There is not the slightest doubt that children from 'better' homes, especially from middle-class homes where the parents have a relatively good education and care a lot for the education of their children, are far better off in a selective and competitive system than children from working-class homes (Husén, 1962: 54).

Opponents of comprehensivization argued that social goals should not be achieved at the cost of lowering 'educational' objectives. But the reformers and their parliamentarian allies in Sweden took the position that 'certain social goals were more important than purely pedagogical ones', and that 'the differentiation of aptitudes and the possibilities of assessing them' were subsidiary to the goal of 'creating social and cultural unity'. In sharp contrast, German defenders of tripartism writing, in the secondary teachers journal, were in 1965 taking a diametrically opposed position. They held that the school system needed to 'free itself from a sociological dirigism'. The school and its educational mission must not be subordinated altogether to the requirements of necessary social change. 'The tripartite school system corresponds to the needs of the individual, and the differentiated demands of society' (Nixdorff, 1969: 146).

Support for the reform argument that comprehensivization need not, if well funded and planned, lead to a lowered learning level among bright students, emerged from an experiment during the late 1950s in which Stockholm was divided into two sectors: a northern one maintained divided schools, and a southern one allowed no separation until the ninth grade. The results showed that:

> the comprehensive system had a greater total yield by the age of fifteen than the selective one. On the whole, bright pupils performed better in the selective system at an early age, but by the age of fifteen there was no difference, whereas poorer ability pupils performed better throughout in the comprehensive system (Husén, 1965: 219; see also Beck, 1971: 155-156).

In 1965 Sweden already had 14 percent of an age group graduating from the Gymnasium, whereas in West Germany in 1967, only 8 percent were graduating (OECD, 1969: 37).

A major cause for continuing the gross under-representation of children of industrial and agricultural workers in the German intermediary and secondary schools was found to be the 'low level of aspiration of the parents themselves' (Robinsohn and Kuhlmann, 1967: 313). German parents feared that the gymnasium's reliance on parent assistance in home-work assignment would show up their own failings, that children would grow up to think they were their parents' betters, and that the far-off material rewards of white-collar jobs would not be greater than what manual work could offer. Thus in the 1960s German reformers were still demanding that 'parents should be subjected to propaganda designed to persuade them that it is their duty to give their children the longest possible education', and calling for the expansion of 'pre-school education in order to break down in particular the resistance of uneducated parents' (Edding, 1967: 108).

In Sweden such resistance was also initially present, especially since the labor movement had down-graded educational reform objectives during the 1930s. However, the working-class children born then had a generation later become reoriented in regard to the opportunities they wanted for their children. In the mid-1960s fully one-third of working-class parents born around 1930 said they wanted their children not only to finish secondary school, but also to go on to the university (Husén, 1969: 481; and Tomasson, 1970: 150). This was some six times the proportion that had attended the university in Sweden in 1940, or in Germany in the early 1960s (Husén, 1971: 81).

D. Teachers' Attitudes: The much more rapid accomplishment of the integration of parallel school types is not attributable to the more favorable attitudes of Swedish, as compared to German Gymnasium teachers. 'The theory held by most Swedish secondary teachers was that both categories of students would gain from early separation. The theoretically geared would not be hampered by their slow-learning class-mates, and the latter would be saved the feeling of inferiority that would be caused by constant confrontation with their peers' (Husén, 1965: 218). In 1948 the tentative plan for integrating Folksskola and Realskola at the junior secondary level (ages 10-15 years), was turned down by all but three of the 234 secondary school faculties to whom it was submitted. A decade later they were nevertheless selectively established on a trial basis. A survey in 1961 of secondary teachers who had taught in them, showed that: 94 percent thought the burden of work was greater; 60 percent believed that the comprehensive school's disadvantages outweighed their advantages, while only 3 percent evaluated in the reverse order; those who held that social training and social relations in class rooms had worsened outnumbered by 10 to one those who held that they had been improved (Husén and Boalt, 1968: 136-137).

Husén holds that 'since for the overwhelming majority of secondary teachers vital vested interests were at stake, another reaction could hardly be expected'. He attributes their hostility in good part to a loss of power. 'The elitist secondary school was an institution where the teachers were instrumental in deciding the fate of the students. They were in the last run the gate-keepers of the Establishment' (Husén, 1969: 482). The diminished significance of grades and entrance requirements undercut that power in the emerging comprehensive school model. In Germany many teachers and parents tended to regard the elite Gymnasium as an end in itself. Discussing the under-representation of working-class children at Gymnasia in 1966, they argued that the reasons lay not 'in the Gymnasium itself', but with 'the working class which still has not acquired the proper attitudes toward the Gymnasium, and instead still holds prejudicial attitudes which cause them not to have the children apply for admission to the Gymnasium' (Nixdorff, 1969: 145).

The lower secondary school level came to be a crucial embattled territory between the secondary school teachers with university degrees in specialized disciplines, and the more generalist primary school teachers who had been trained in teacher training schools of lower status. Because the former were fewer in number and took longer to produce, the rapid organization of a common secondary cycle between 11 or 12 to 14 or 15 years of age meant in many countries that teaching would primarily be entrusted to primary school teachers. Their control of a cycle viewed as crucial for the transmission of high culture was violently criticized by much of educated opinion. In Germany this resistance was successful in holding down expansion and impeding rapid integration of the lower secondary cycle because the possible transition conditions were judged unacceptable. Limited enrollment in the lower secondary cycle necessarily reduced recruitment to the upper secondary levels, graduation from which would entitle students to enter the university to achieve degree requirements for secondary school teaching. According to Poignant (1969: 291-294) the frustration of expansion produced in Germany 'a really vicious cycle: In order to train more teachers, more students must graduate from secondary school, but in order to enable more students to graduate from secondary school, it is essential first of all to train more teachers'. Husén in 1965 cited the Federal Republic as 'a present-day European example of a failure to plan' (Husén, 1965: 223).

II THE INTEREST GROUP AND PARTY BASIS OF REFORM AND RESISTANCE COALITIONS

By successfully achieving parliamentary acceptance of their comprehensivization reform proposals on the basis of strong interest group support, the Swedish school commissions and education ministers of the 1940s and 1950s, were able to count on strong allies among the elementary school teachers and the larger union federations. Support for comprehensive citizenship training had been traditional in the Swedish Folk Teachers Association since its founding in the 1880s, and during the debates of the 1920s its organs had been powerful vehicles for the dissemination of progressive education ideas of American origin. The political climate after 1945 gave the pedagogically pro-American elementary teacher associations an advantage over the more 'Germanophile' Gymnasium teachers, and their support of the 1948 reform proposals was strong. Their attitudes in favor of reform was re-enforced by the realization that the establishment of a common lower secondary cycle would open the way for 'a partial reduction of dualism in the two teacher levels, more favorable conditions of advancement . . and for the long-cherished goal of achieving parity of prestige and training with the elite corps of university-trained secondary school teachers' (Paulston, 1968: 119-123).

The elementary teachers were ideologically and organizationally well placed to help mobilize a powerful supportive coalition. A strong constituent union of the Central Organization of Salaried Employees (TCO), 500,000 members), they were abel to influence a numerous voting bloc of Liberals and Social Democrats. The proportion of unionized white-collar workers was more than twice as high as in Germany, i.e. two-thirds of them belonged to TCO unions which had sizable representation on both the Socialist and Liberal benches in parliament. Their links to the popular movements, as represented by the large Cooperative Society and the powerful Trade Union Federation, were built on a mutual interest in the 'battle against institutionalized privilege'. Thus the Co-ops published a book whose author argued that 'the protracted resistance of the secondary school to fundamental change could only be constructively overcome by a united effort of the whole movement' (Paulston, 1968: 120). The comments and remisser submitted to government by the large mass organizations were correspondingly supportive.

In Germany the organization which represents the largest proportion of elementary school teachers, the Education and Scientific Workers Union (GEW), long remained much more ambivalent toward comprehensive reforms. Its relatively low coverage — less than 50 percent of elementary school teachers — has been due to the fact that considerations of status, religion and class kept many teachers from joining its ranks. Catholic teachers in denominational schools have their own competing organizations, and special interests. When the GEW in 1949 affiliated to the Federation of German Trade Unions (DGB), large components of South German teachers refused to go along. Pedagogically conservative groups also constituted an internal barrier against progressive ideas. The anxiety not to offend groups of members or potential members long kept the GEW's school reform programs scarcely ahead of the conservative official commissions, and its endorsement of a comprehensive school model in the form of the differentiated Gesamtschule did not occur until the mid-1960s.

In the face of less energetic challenges, the dominant German Gymnasium teacher's association, the Philologenverband, was able to 'safeguard all the advantages which its members traditionally enjoyed over the elementary teachers' (Fuhrig, 1969: 106). Such as those covering remuneration, working conditions and social prestige. When the Education ministers sought to introduce a unified schema for teacher education in 1970, the Philologenverband attacked the program and demanded that upper secondary teachers be required to study a minimum of ten semesters compared with a six semester threshold for teachers at lower levels. Such action caused the Frankfurter Rundschau to comment 'The Philologenverband is holding fast to its structured way of thinking and to the corporative structuring of the teaching body' (Schmiederer, 1971: 111). As an affiliate of the professional and white collar Civil Servants Federation, the Philologenverband possessed influential allies throughout the higher levels of the bureaucracy, while its contacts with middle-class parents associations allowed it to form powerful resistance coalitions where Land ministers of education proposed reforms of the tripartite structure. Such an alliance was responsible for the defeat of a Social Democratic administration which tried to force the pace of comprehensivization in Hamburg during the 1950s.

The limited effect of party dominance is illustrated by a comparison between Sweden and the land of Hessen, which possess populations not dissimilar in size and social structure. Like Sweden, Hessen was continuously led by a Social Democratic government in the post-1945 period. Unlike other German Laender it did not have denominationally separated schools, is predominantly Protestant in religion and has had strong teachers union representation in the Landtag. Still, in the mid-1960s one third of Hessen's small communes had not produced a single Gymnasium graduate in the preceding decade (Van de Graaff, 1967: 77), and working class attendance in the city gymnasia had increased only marginally. Nixdorff (1969: 79) found that this was the by-product of an SPD policy under which 'the school bills of the 1950s provided for an organizational consolidation of the traditional school system, with no dramatic changes in the 1950s or early 1960s, and only small and modest changes beginning in the mid-1960s'. This slow pattern of change constituted a defensive victory for the alliance of teachers and parents' associations which the Hessen Philologenverband had organized.[1] The SPD's unwillingness to try to take the 'fortress gymnasium' by political means was attested to by the fact that the State Parents' Council, which exercised influential veto powers and contained only one SPD member on a 15-member executive board, was allowed to remain the instrument of parents of Gymnasium students (Nixdorff, 1969: 154).

Although the nature of their arguments were during the early stages of the controversy rather similar to those successfully employed in Germany, the Swedish Secondary School teacher organization (LR) was much less successful in retarding the reform movement once the rest of 'Organized Sweden' had begun to move toward a pro-reform consensus. The peak professional association to which they belonged, SACO, had only been founded in 1947 and took some time to build the aggregate membership of 100,000, which it achieved toward the end of the 1960s. During the 1950s they were rather isolated, and banked on the hope that the research findings based on the comprehensive school models would bear out their dire warnings and lead to a reversal of policy. Instead they were swamped in the plethora of research findings and pro-reform propaganda which demolished the 'limited pool of ability' argument and demonstrated that some loss of standards was compensated by numerous social, as well as intellectual, gains. After the 1962 act finalized the nine-year comprehensive school, the secondary teachers decided to collaborate more positively in planning the revision of the upper secondary cycle.

Limitations on the capacity of large political parties to act as instruments for identifying new social needs is illustrated by the fact that the Swedish Social Democrats may have, even during the crucial 1944-6 period, lagged behind other groups, including the Communists, in articulating specific reform goals (Paulston, 1968: 92-93).[2] On the other hand it is significant to note that at no time over a 20 year period until 1969 did a Swedish party take a clear-cut parliamentary stand *against* comprehensivization, while in Germany no major Federal or Land party took a clear-cut position for its full implementation. One may credit the consensual emphasis in Swedish political culture, and the ways it had operated to bring about acceptance of government initiative in the welfare and housing reforms of the 1930s, as facilitating the role of Social Democratic post-war governments in sponsoring a radical educational reform without suffering serious erosion of electoral support. This gave the government advantages in interacting with and coordinating both the elite and mass processes. After more than a decade in power, the Swedish Democrats had established viable links to large segments of the younger administrative and intellectual elite whose energies needed to be marshalled for promoting the reform effort. The efforts led to a situation where, in the 1950 Riksdag debates on the proposals of the Schools Commission, strong criticism was articulated by individual parliamentarians of the non-Socialist parties. These parties however held back from opposition on the final votes so the bill was passed almost unanimously. In 1962, draft legislation which was to finalize the structure of the nine-year comprehensive school reached inter-party committee agreement. In part this was through the mediation of the Liberal party leader Gunnar Helen, and came about in the face of secondary teacher criticism. The Conservative party leader, Gunnar Heckscher, was unable to defend the compromise against sharp criticism from teachers and others, with the result that some Conservative backbenchers voted against the bill (Hagelin, 1968: 142).

In Germany the lack of elite reorientation caused reform proposals to entail the risk of alienating just those segments of white-collar and professional strata which the SPD needed to attract in order to apprxomate the strong electoral position of the Swedish Social Democrats. Under these conditions reformers in the SPD were held back by the experience of the few innovative Land education ministers; their political careers were badly set back when the electorate or party colleagues refused to extend the necessary political or budgetary support to carry integration efforts forward. Indeed, it is highly significant that both Tage Erlander and Olof Palme could use their positions as Education ministers and their close association with comprehensive school reform as stepping stones leading to the positions of party leader and prime minister. In Germany those politicians which achieved pre-eminence in the SPD during the same period — men such as Willy Brandt, Helmut Schmidt, Herbert Wehner and Karl Schiller — all built their reputations on the basis of achivements in the areas of foreign and economic policy.

III GERMANY 1969-72: THE RISE AND DECLINE OF THE IMPETUS FOR REFORM

In Sweden, innovating social science researchers and bureaucratic reformers restructured the perception of educational realities which had previously been adhered to by the leaders of socio-cultural and political opinion. They produced the theories, research and potential arguments with which the decision makers could defend their choice to upset traditional patterns. The Swedish Study Commissions intensely exploited the research potential of experimental structures and fed findings back into the planning efforts for the next step. They thus established a model for 'rolling reform', which is distinguished from both linear progress and discontinuous change models, in that it projects long-term restructuring goals, but implements them in small and partial steps, so as to utilize both the practical and theoretical insights gained in modifying original blue-prints. The closest research equivalent which the Germans created before 1965 was the 1953 Deutscher Ausschuss, which relied much more heavily on the personal knowledge of its expert members, had little in the way of staff and funds and took six years to produce the 1959 Framework Plan, whose recommendations were only fragmentarily adopted by the Laender governments.[3]

A decade later, in February 1969, a much more influential set of recommendations for educational reform was submitted by the Bildungsrat, a prestigious commission composed of educational researchers and administrators which had been created as the result of the increased attention focused on educational policy in the mid-1960s. The report included a section calling for a large-scale experimental program of integrated comprehensive schools (Deutscher Bildungsrat, 1969: 21). Its timing was propitious, since it appeared a few months before Willy Brandt was able to form the first SPD-led Federal cabinet together with the Free Democrats. Both parties had encouraged the build-up of reform interest which developed in the wake of influential works by education reformers such George Picht (1964) and Ralf Dahrendorf (1968). They had helped to pass in May 1969 a constitutional amendment (Article #91b) which authorized the Federal government to share with the Laender the responsibility for educational planning and the financing of educational experiments. The Bildungsrat's goal of evaluating a large number of Gesamtschulen (comprehensive schools) by 1976 implied rapid activity, since in 1969 there were only ten such schools in all of the Federal Republic. In his 1969 government declaration, Chancellor Brandt explicitly gave education top priority among reform goals.

Because the Federal and Land governments share jurisdiction, the Gesamtschule-program had to be processed through a more complex set of decision-making institutions than was the case in Sweden two decades earlier. The first hurdle was the Permanent Conference of State Ministers of Education, which approved the program in November 1969 but made an important amendment. The Bildungsrat's integrated comprehensive school model approached the Scandinavian model, and was a more exacting one than that being generally applied in Britain or that being urged by advocates of the 'additive' or 'cooperative' model. The more conservative Land education ministers successfully insisted that the 'cooperative' model be also accepted within the experimental program.

Questions as to how the school reform thrust would fit into the overall program of the Brandt government arose when a non-party professor, Hans Leussink, a former head of the Wissenschaftsrat was appointed Federal Education Minister. Named as State Secretaries were the able Dr. Hildegard Hamm-Brucher, a fervent FDP advocate of comprehensivization reform who, however, lacked great administrative talents and Klaus von Dohnanyi, then a relatively junior SPD politician. The fact that no politically powerful Social Democrat was in the

Federal ministry limited the SPD's ability to channel and integrate the different vested interests represented by Social Democrats in Land ministries and the Federal and Land parliaments. However, the Ministry entered into the fray with gusto by developing an ambitious and comprehensive *Bildungsbericht 1970* as the Federal government's first contribution to a joint educational planning policy. It proposed extensive reforms in all educational sectors. One of its three major thrusts called for 'an overall internally differentiated system of integrated comprehensive schools, indicating an explicit break with the traditional tripartite school system'. The report strongly emphasized that the Federal Republic was lagging behind its neighbors and its goals constituted a 'maximum uncompromised program which succinctly brings together in a single package the most advanced official thinking on the future of education in the FRG' (OECD, 1972: 38).

A. The Reform Drive Falters. Government hopes that progressive opinion in the CDU Bundestag party might help overcome the resistance of their colleagues in the Land ministries were soon dashed. In a June 1971 Bundestag debate, Bavarian and other conservative parliamentarians advocated rejection of the report, and managed to couple emotional attacks on student radicalism with criticism of 'gigantic plans' to 'introduce untried new educational institutions' as an expensive cure-all mechanism (Deutscher Bundestag, 1971: 7268, 7282). In television debates CDU moderates like State Secretary Laurien stressed that recent studies had shown the working-class students had become somewhat more numerous in the Gymnasium, where now half of all students had fathers who had not finished Realschule, claiming that this showed that the existing system could effectively recruit for the new school milieu (Pro und Contra, 1971).[4]

The maximalist strategy pursued by the government strategists attempted to win endorsement in principle of a program of restructuring most educational subsystems and vastly expanding investment in education, from some DM 20 billion in 1969 to an estimated DM 100 billion in 1980. The difficulty of maintaining the momentum and high agenda position which education policy achieved in 1969, was due not only to the fear and envy of bureaucratic and other advocates of competing policy interests, but also to the unusually large number of decision-making sites in which opponents could rally opposition. Most important was the Federal-State Commission for Education Planning, or Bund-Laender Kommission (BLK), which sought to coordinate the initiatives received from the Bildungsrat and the Federal and Land ministries and legislatures. Within this body the representatives of the CDU-led Laender showed themselves adament against acceptance of the integrated comprehensive model as the long-term goal, its October 1971 Interim Report showed a clear disagreement on this question as well as that of the Grade 5-6 'Orientation stage'.

Harmful to the reformers was the fact that 'the figure of DM 100 billion became a political football . . . causing a widespread and un- fortunate exaggeration . . . of the true costs of school reform' (OECD, 1972: 39). It reflected, at the same time, the implementation strategy of a political shortcut, which some think led the reformers to engender a 'broad gap' between the level of their aspirations and available reform parameters (Naschold et al., 1972: 23). The bold projections of the Bildungsbericht alarmed the Finance ministers and gave the CDU a target against which it could mobilize many vested interests. Within the Federal-Land Commission, SPD members had earlier turned down a CDU motion to ask the government heads to lay down financial parameters for the reform. In January 1972, however the Land finance ministers took the initiative to call into question important assumptions of the BLK planners, especially as they related to the growth rate of the GNP and the share of the public sector investment that could go to education. Shortly thereafter, in March 1972, Minister Leussink re- signed, and after vainly scanning the horizon for a senior Social Demo- crat who would agree to become his successor, Chancellor Brandt elevated Dohnanyi to head the ministry.

The left-wing SPD parliamentarians, especially those on the Bun- destag education committee, were originally strong Gesamtschule sup- porters, but they came to feel the chilling effect of an increasingly skeptical position enunciated in most of the neo-Marxist educational literature being produced by graduates of the student movement. By 1971 a survey of left-wing educational criticism found that it had become 'exclusively criticism of reform efforts, and that criticism of existing conditions had almost ceased being articulated' (Nyssen, 1971: 34). The line generally enunciated sought to tag the comprehensive school as a mechanism for the training of workers who would prove maximally adaptable to the needs of the economy. As clearly stated in the Buehlow volume, 'the Left criticism of school reform in the Federal Republic has the important task of destroying the illusions, perpetuated especially by the SPD, that society can be changed through educational reforms' (Buehlow et al., 1972: 135).[5]

In this context SPD as well as FDP advocates of retaining the Gesamtschule impetus; and keeping general educational reform high on their parties' agenda,[6] fought a losing struggle during the build-up to the November 1972 general elections. Dohnanyi (1972: 7) blamed a 'massive conservative counter-attack' for helping to generate a false 'public impression that after two years of futile experiments the efforts for a long-term basic education reform had led to failure'. He sought SPD backing to resist CDU pressure to sacrifice structural reforms in the process of scaling down the Gesamtplan to what was economically feasible. The SPD-led Laender differed widely in the degree to which they had founded many new comprehensive schools. Hessen had taken the lead under its education minister, Ludwig von Friedeburg, but even he conceded in a *Der Spiegel* (1972: 40) interview that the prospects of the comprehensive school as a general model was limited by the fact that 'the wind is blowing in different strengths and from different directions' and that 'attitudes have been reversed here and there'.

At the Federal level, the SPD did not want to emphasize divisive campaign issues, which might affect attitudes already highly polarized by the Brandt government's Ostpolitik, confrontation over which led to the premature scheduling of the general elections. A possible campaign emphasis, reiterating the Bildungsbericht stress on the Federal Republic's backwardness in providing educational opportunities, clashed with the decision to build the campaign around the theme that Brandt and the SPD had led West Germans to the point where they could again be proud of their country.[7] After his victory, Brandt, in his January 1973 government declaration, pleaded for a 'new start' toward federal-Laender cooperation and did not mention comprehensive schools. Reformers protested that 'progressives' had lost out within both coalition parties (Der Spiegel, 1973: 23).

With the decline of Federal leadership, the main initiative returned to the Social Democratic Land education ministers, among whom comprehensivization priority had always varied considerably. The annual meeting of the pro-comprehensive association became increasingly gloomy. Those attending the May 1974 meeting were told that:

> 'the defences against the restorationist forces have been breached in several places . . . Apart from the strangulation of comprehensives in several CDU-Laender, there are signs of desertions in several SPD Laender . . . Political goals are being scaled down – and only in a few Laender, especially Lower Saxony and Hessen – is the reform being genuinely carried further! '[8]

Von Friedeburg told the meeting that Hessen was holding fast to its commitment to comprehensives, and that the intermediate assessment of comprehensive school development was positive. But the parents of

Hessian comprehensive school pupils complained that the parallel existence of Gymnasia, for which the majority of upper secondary pupils
were still opting, 'might lead to the final failure of the comprehensive
school'. Simultaneously the courts gave support to parents seeking to
block the transformation of a Gymnasium into an integrated Gesamtschule (Süddeutsche Zeitung, 1974 and Der Spiegel, 1974).

In Lower Saxony, Education Minister Peter von Oertzen tried to
handle the Gesamtschule complex gingerly in drawing up a new school
law which was passed by the Landtag in 1974. While anchoring the
Gesamtschule in Land legislation, and stressing that the integrated
version was the long-term goal, he in fact accepted the 'co-operative'
model as an alternative. He told the Landtag that 'the introduction of
the Gesamtschule as a standard model is not envisioned', and that the
fear that this law will destroy the Gymnasium is unfounded (Niedersächsischer Landtag, Protokolle, 1973). However the CDU rode the
crest of the spring 1974 backlash trend by having its speakers talk of
the immenent 'death of the Gymnasium' and by naming a Gymnasium
teacher as its prospective Education minister. In the light of the SPD's
leadership crisis in June 1974 Landtag elections received national publicity, and so did the fact that both von Oertzen and his State Secretary
were narrowly defeated in their constituencies. Although returned to
the Landtag via the SPD Land list, von Oertzen and his colleagues
decided that he should not continue as Education minister.[9]

Meanwhile within the CDU/CSU, the more progressive Land politicians, who had paid some lip-service to the Gesamtschule impetus in
the 1969-70 period, fell into line behind the anti-reform position laid
down by the strong, conservative education ministers of Bavaria and
Baden-Wuerttemberg, Rhineland-Palatinate, under CDU chairman
Helmut Kohl and education minister Bernhard Vogel, long had only
one comprehensive school in the entire Land. In the CDU-governed
Laender the few experimental comprehensive schools were supplied
with ample financial resources, which observers attributed to the desire
to demonstrate that, even if the comprehensives produced positive
educational results, these would be counter-balanced by high costs. In
Schleswig -Holstein, a CDU speaker in a 1974 education debate emphasized that the acceptance of the integrated Gesamtschule model
would bring about a 'complete change in our school system, and launch
us on a development which in Sweden has lasted twenty years'.[10]

On the Federal level the eighteen months of the second Brandt
cabinet witnessed a decline in the cohesion and morale of the politicians who were trying to hold the SPD to giving priority to educa-

tional reform and expenditures. SPD Bundestag members who in 1969 had eagerly competed for positions on the education committee, had by late 1972 to be assigned to fill the party's quota. Dohnanyi's relations with both the Bundestag Fraktion and the Land politicians deteriorated as it became evident that his political skill did not match his public relations flair, and as his ministry's legislative initiatives became bogged down. His efforts to push comprehensive schools on more economic-technocratic grounds were resisted by other Gesamtschule advocates. In April 1973 the SPD national convention failed to approve a Long-Term Program which would have committed the party to expand education's share of GNP from 4.5 percent in 1970 to 7.6 percent in 1985. In June 1973 the Bund-Laender Kommission finally ratified the fifth and reduced version of the *Bildungsgesamtplan,* only to have the Federal and Land finance ministers announce that they could not accept financing responsibility for even its reduced targets. At about the same time the Land Education Ministers Conference resolved to reduce the jurisdiction of and increase the bureaucratic dominance within the Bildungsrat, while the South German ministers even suggested its possible abolition in 1975.

The dissatisfaction with SPD reform policies, which formed part of the background to Chancellor Brandt's resignation in May 1974, was not uniquely linked to education policy. But the education sector became one of the most obvious targets when the new Chancellor, Helmut Schmidt, sought to demonstrate his willingness to drop some of the Brandt government's more far-reaching and expensive reform proposals. Federal education expenditures were cut back, and the lack of commitment to the financing targets of the *Bildungsgesamtplan* were made manifest, engendering bitter criticism from SPD and union educational spokesmen. Stung by the whip-lash of conservative voters' reaction, SPD leaders looked for sacrificial lambs, and found them all too conveniently among the maladroit educational politicians and jargon-spouting educational planners who, even within the party fold, had been unable to agree on reform models and priorities. None of the ministers were let go with less ceremony than von Dohnanyi, who was even the object of a parting rebuke from Federal President Gustav Heineman. The appointment of his successor, Helmut Rohde, a union politician who had served in the Labor ministry but was without any previous experience in the educational sector, seemed to signal a turn away from the goals and style of the academic educational planners. The right-wing CSU education spokesman, Anton Pfeiffer, was able gloatingly to state that 'the Schmidt government seems now willing to grant what its predecessor was not willing to admit . . . *namely that it has stopped giving priority to education policy* . . .' (CDU/CSU Press Release, 1974). He asked further to shift its support away from comprehensive schools, even while journalists noted low morale among their teachers and 'an inability of the Gesamtschulen to surmount the isolation of their founding stage' (Matthiesen, 1974).

IV IMPLEMENTATION INCENTIVES AND QUANDARIES

A. Bureaucratic Inertia. The problem of how to overcome and counterbalance the status quo preserving tendencies of established jurisdictions and bureaucracies was tackled most directly in Sweden. There administrative power was centralized in the National Board of Education, where holdover adherents of the tripartite system were gradually transferred away from sensitive policy-making decisions or encouraged to retire, then replaced by pro-reform successors (Wheeler, 1972). The actual operation of schools was in the hands of local communes. Status quo defenses there were undermined by a sweeping reform of local government jurisdictions, which in the course of a two-step process amalgamated some 2,500 communes in 1950 into some 280 by 1973. (See the chapter by J. A. Brand in this volume). The new, enlarged communities' ability to sustain comprehensive schools was one of the main criteria, and the promise of national financial support for better schools helped overcome resistance to amalgamation. In West Germany it was more difficult to upset the predominant centralized grip on education policy-makers held by bureaucrats at the Land level, who had so long resisted innovation. The strategy pursued since 1969 calls for co-ordinated intervention by both Federal and local governments. The latter had traditionally been quiescent in policy initiation, but the 'experimentation stage' presented them with the opportunity to utilize their jurisdiction over school building to launch initiatives calling for choices on behalf of the comprehensive option when new schools were being planned.

B. Experimental Programs. The Bildungsrat's initiative of 1969 followed the Swedish precedent of 1950 by proposing the creation of an experimental comprehensive program under which results obtained over an eight-year period, culminating in 1976, could be compared with those obtained in conventional schools. Even more than its Swedish predecessor, the German experimental program is an instrument for overcoming the deadlock resulting from a political confrontation, and for permitting different jurisdictions to proceed at different speeds (as indeed they have, with the SPD-led Laender setting up some 90 new schools in the following three years, while the CDU-led ones set up only a dozen). In Sweden the evaluation program helped push for broader-scale implementation, although the positive findings initially reported were much later challenged in some reanalyses of the data. In Germany the evaluation program soon showed signs of losing coherence, mainly because the different Land education ministries encouraged research which was considered irrelevant by others, since there was basic dis-agreement on the criteria of evaluation. The attempt of the CDU Laender to delay decisions until experimental results were in was criticized by the OECD team:

> The demands of some Laender for time to experiment is understandable, but in our view mistaken. The decision on whether to have comprehensive schools is inevitably a political one, to be taken primarily on social and political grounds.

(OECD, 1972: 75). At present the evaluation plans are scarcely opera-tive, since all attempts to establish a system of coordinated evaluation have failed. It is therefore almost sure that the end of the experimental period in 1976, which will be a Federal election year, will not bring about an agreement based on a consensus founded upon research findings.

C. Credentials and Laufbahn Symbols. Even the Bildungsrat recom-mendations did not refer to the question of eliminating the Abitur examination at the conclusion of Gymnasium study. In Sweden it had been abolished as part of a move to eliminate symbolic distinctions between academic and non-academic educational courses. The larger question of the Laufbahn system, which tracks young people in their school years, guiding them toward formal educational attainments which are specifically connected to their work careers, was regarded by the OECD examiners as a 'strait-jacket' reflecting the 'rigidities and inflexibilities that beset West German society' (OECD, 1972: 16, 109). They questioned whether or not Germany could adopt a schooling model which would eliminate hurdles and concluded that such a model 'does not appear to be practical politics in the Federal Republic of the 1970s', since few Germans could accept 'a system such as the Swedes are putting into operation, whereby a child goes from kindergarten to university without entrance or leaving examinations (OECD, 1972: 54). There might, however, be some question as to the degree to which the Swedish schools had indeed eliminated the competitive drive. The problem of academic unemployment should not have been as serious if the Swedes had eliminated Laufbahn characteristics as much as they claim to have.

D. The Adjustment Costs of Rolling Reform. When legislation, passed in 1962 set the basic pattern of the Swedish nine-year comprehensive school, sets of curricular alternatives for the higher grades were part of the package. Experience soon showed that the curricular choices of students departed radically from the distribution the planners had anticipated. This feedback helped shape the next stage of the reform, adopted in 1969, which affected a still wider ability grouping in the classes of grades seven through nine, requiring differentiated instruction within the same class. The Secondary teachers union, LR, won support of most teachers by its complaints that too many reforms were coming too quickly. Many teachers felt themselves overburdened by the higher demands in the classrooms, and in Germany similar complaints explain why even politically progressive teachers often did not support a more rapid adoption of the reform model. The Swedish changes initiated widespread press discussion about the breakdown of classroom discipline, as well as reports that the level of learning, especially in subjects like foreign languages, was declining.[11] The resulting parent dissatisfaction threatened to hurt the Social Democrats in the election campaign of 1973, but a few months prior to the election cross-national studies released by the International Association for Educational Achievement showed that pupils in the comprehensive Swedish lower and upper secondary schools were learning as well or better than comparable groups in other countries, or even than their age. peers in the more selective German Gymnasium.[12]

E. Losers in the Equalization Process. Reform goals aimed at keeping 85 percent of pupils in school voluntarily until age 18 were expensive when converted into buildings and teacher salaries, especially when, as in the Swedish case, prevailing standards and salary rates were high. In order to hold costs down, the salary advantages enjoyed by secondary teachers relative to elementary teachers and other professionals were reduced. Resistance against this trend led to two bitter strikes involving mainly LR in 1966, and then LR together with most other component members of the Swedish Association of Professional Workers (SACO) in 1971. The strike, which the secondary teachers initiated in 1966 when the government proposed narrowing the differential between them and the lower-level teachers by one pay grade, lost them much sympathy in Swedish public opinion. It was the spark that led to the popularity of the 'equalization' ideology which the Social Democrats subsequently used to develop an effective electoral theme in 1968-70 (Swedish Social Democratic Party, 1971). In 1971, the SACO strike strategy was met by an even tougher government strategy which involved both lockouts and unprecedented emergency legislation to end the strike.[13] In the aftermath, the LR-organized teachers who had utilized the earlier system to establish themselves among the more favored professions were among the hardest hit in the final salary outcomes and paid much of the cost of educational equalization. Other losers in the redistribution process were less educated people who were above 30 in 1970. The pre-reform system did not offer the changes that the youth were getting. This meant serious disadvantages for middle-aged workers who had to compete with younger ones. Partly to meet this increasing cleavage planners in the 1970s started to argue that investment in youth education should be shifted somewhat to recurrent education opportunities for adults.

V DETERMINANTS OF THE PACE OF REFORM

West Germany had about 120 comprehensive schools by the end of 1972, which enrolled about three percent of the pupils in the grades five through ten. These figures are comparable to those prevailing during the Swedish 'take-off period' around 1950. Contrasts between the successful Swedish comprehensive reform effort and both the initial West German record of non-reform, and the partially successful attempt at reform take-off during the 1969-72 period, should permit us to articulate some findings bearing on the different reform capacity of the two systems. Which political structures and institutions were able to play more successful reform-inducing roles in Sweden than in West Germany, and why? What socio-cultural factors blocked reform supportive values and iedologies from being as forcefully articulated in West Germany as in Sweden? What were the advantages of earliness and lateness in the context of European reforms?

The setbacks imposed on the German educational development by the Nazi era and reactions to it were not solely responsible for the West German lag. Incomplete secularization of the educational system, which reflected the lower level of socio-cultural homogeneity prevailing in Germany, also retarded both the elite and mass processes. Because most German Laender maintained Catholic and Protestant variants of each of the school types, the vested interests attached to particular sub-structures were for a long time much more numerous and diverse than in Sweden. Opposition to the denominational system was pronounced among most liberal and socialist elites, and challenges to it tended to structure the predominant educational issue in many areas of Germany into the 1960s. Educational reform had lower immediate appeal to the working-class sectors of the German mass electorate, to which the SPD catered most, because of the economic after-effects of the war era. In the shaping of family priorities, initial emphasis was predominantly given to regaining housing and other basic components of standard of living. The earning power of children was mobilized to these ends in a way less necessary in the more affluent and welfare-rich Sweden.

Education achieved and long held its strong agenda position in Sweden in the 1950s because large voter groups, mobilized not only by the Social Democrats, but also by the Agrarian and Liberal parties, could ideologically accept reform proponents' arguments that the educational system be used to achieve both goals of greater social equality and of greater economic growth. In Germany the ideological appeal of elitist institutions was stronger, and when, in the early 1960s, economic arguments for educational expansion and reform were brought into the general discussion, 'they went so much against the grain of German educational philosophy that there were violent reactions (Edding, 1967: 105).

When, by the late 1960s, reformers in the SPD and FDP were able both to create and staff the planning institutions which fed into decision-making processes, the favorable climate which had nurtured educational expansion throughout Europe in the previous decade began to turn. The student revolt and the growth of a neo-Marxist Left provided ideological ammunition for anti-reform elements, while the slackening of demand for academically trained manpower began to undercut the earlier optimistic assumptions that European systems could easily absorb almost all the highly-trained graduates which secondary schools and universities could turn out. The lateness of the West German takeoff on educational integration and expansion did favor the reformers who were able to utilize experiences in early countries like Sweden. However, it also helped anti-reform forces because they could use for propagandistic purposes negative consequences of educational reforms in other countries. Insofar as the comprehensive school became the special target of attack from both Left and Right, SPD educational leaders such as Dohnanyi have deemed it politic currently to de-emphasize this educational sector, and instead to focus reform dynamic on other educational sectors such as vocational training and the universities.

The relatively short-lived impetus behind the first phase of the post-1969 German comprehensive drive can, however, probably be primarily attributed to a much less productive inter-meshing of the reform efforts of the Social Democratic Party and the public bureaucracies. The advantages made possible by long-term continuity of party control are suggested by the case of Hessen, where the Social Democratic opportunity to reshape the Land bureaucracy had been almost as long-lived as in Sweden. This Land was, by 1973, operating almost as many comprehensive schools as the nine other Laender put together. Similar progress was not achieved in West Berlin, where intra-party factionalism impeded the kind of consensual mechanisms which served to smooth the way for reform acceptance in Sweden. In Laender where the Education Ministry was less continuously in SPD control, pro-comprehensive bureaucrats often struggled against conservative superiors in the hierarchy.[14] Rivalries between SPD Federal and Land ministers and bureaucracies made it more difficult for the German educational reformers to achieve a common front. The German education planners were supplied with plentiful financial resources and the reports they produced in a few years easily rivaled those of Sweden, but what was missing was the direction to channel this energy into a self-propelling 'rolling reform' process. This was provided neither by Chancellor Brandt nor by any of the half-dozen most powerful cabinet-party personalities.

Fundamental structural reforms in education require: large-scale mobilization efforts and the capacity to plan system change over a period of several decades. The SPD, due to the capacity of its party organization, to the instruments of its Long Term Program Commission which projected policy developments until 1985, and to the planning office created within the Federal Chancellery, seemed to command vehicles which were ideal for educational planning, which in fact was yielded pride of place. But both within the domestic policy area as a whole, and within the education sector, the planners sought to design too many sectoral reforms simultaneously. The 15-year framework chosen for the SPD planning effort was probably also too short to encompass completion of basic education reforms. It had potential for interweaving and coordinating the very diverse intellectual, trade union and bureaucratic interests which were essential components of the educational reform coalition – or for becoming the focus for fratricidal in-fighting between Left and Right factions. The fact that more of the latter developed can be attributed to short-circuits and unintended consequences of the mobilization effort. The penchant for Gesamtpläne was less evident in the Swedish case, probably to the benefit of reform implementation.

As Rainer Jochimsen (1974: 849) has noted:

> The 1970 *Bildungsbericht* raised the expectation that education reforms would engender an effort comparable to that which in the 19th century led to the development of social security as a 'solution' to the social question. Hopes were raised that Germany would within a few years be able to implement fundamental reforms for which other systems like Sweden, the US, and East Germany had introduced prerequisites many decades earlier.

Under these conditions the efforts to impose structural reforms on a previously rather autonomous sub-sector unleashed a cacophony of signals and a duplication of efforts which undermined the legitimacy of the education sector's claim to priority. The rapid swing from reform euphoria in 1969, to reform disillusionment and cynicism in 1974 had no parallel in Sweden or apparently in other comparable European situations.

VI CONCLUSION

The divergent fate of school reform in Sweden and Germany emphasizes that the dynamics of change can differ cross-nationally within the same area of public concern. (See Figure 1). In Sweden, the reformers sought to make progress in a linear fashion, increasing the proportion of young people in non-selective secondary schools each year. The reform generated its own momentum so that the proportion of Swedish young people in non-selective secondary education grew at an accelerating rate during the 1960s. Since the early 1970s comprehensive schools enroll nearly all Swedish adolescents. In this way, linear progress has resulted in a basic discontinuity from the old system of selective secondary education which was pervasive in Sweden until the reforms of the 1950s were initiated. In Germany, reforms had similar short-term and long-term aims. But the reform generated opposition to

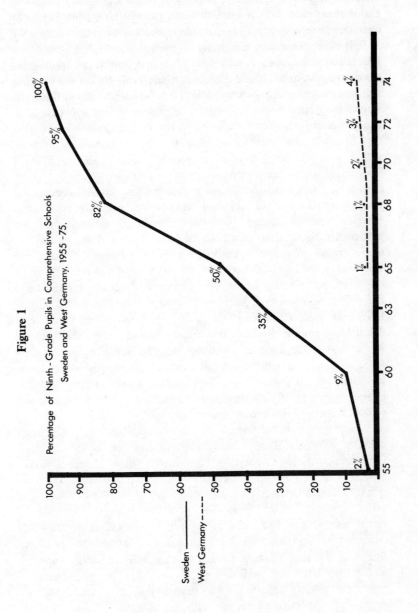

Figure 1

Percentage of Ninth-Grade Pupils in Comprehensive Schools
Sweden and West Germany, 1955-75.

Sweden ———
West Germany -----

change, rather than a readiness to accept new institutions at an ever increasing rate. As a result, the linear progress registered in the late 1960s appears to have levelled off, at a time when the proportion of German young people in Gesamtschule is very low in most Laender.

Will West Germany, launching a comprehensivization drive two decades after Sweden, be likely to achieve a fully comprehensive secondary system by 1990? Unless pertinent political variables change radically, it almost surely will not. Will it at least equal the British track record by having about half of its secondary school age groups in comprehensive schools by the mid-1980s? To achieve that goal in face of CDU/CSU resistance would mean that by then the Gesamtschule would have to completely replace Gymnasien in all the SPD-led Laender; that also seems very unlikely.

If these prospects should force the more ambitious SPD educational planners to admit to partial failure, what factors seem most responsible for the less impressive outcome? Structural factors, involving particularly the Federal allocation of jurisdiction and the role of the bureaucracies, obviously constituted a special German handicap, but one that was fully calculable at the start of the drive. The most important contributing factor for the reformers' decline of morale was the increasing need to fight a two-front war — simultaneously against Left and Right (Holger, 1973: 122-123). This proved particularly debilitating among the most strategically placed group, the teachers, which in turn engendered additional negative feedback effects. The force of conservative resistance fully utilized the established Land veto positions and redoubled the ardour and overtness of their counter-strategy when in 1972-4 they sensed a decline in the dedication and self-confidence of the reform alliance.

What does the overall German-Swedish comparison suggest about the capacity of Social Democratic parties to function as sponsors and producers of basic educational reforms? Other European cases, especially that of Britain, suggest that educational policy is not a sector in which Social Democratic parties have been at their most effective as prime agents of reform. Even more generally, it may be that educational reform is a task for which political parties are inadequately equipped to compete with bureaucracies and interest groups in influencing the flow of supports and resistances from service suppliers and clients. What the Swedish case shows is that they can effectively provide sustaining leadership under optimal conditons, i.e., continuity in power, supportive interaction with the bureaucracy, lack of socio-cultural obstacles, etc. In Sweden under the conditions of the 1950s and 1960s, mutually reinforcing mass and elite supports could be harnessed for consistent approaches to the final goal in a way which they could not in Germany, even in SPD-led Laender. What the German experience of 1969-74 seems to show is that high pressure attempts at 'take-off' can be accomplished if enough political instruments are under reformer influence, but that the thrust of the carry-through reform effort can all too easily be derailed as the result of resistance engendered by a 'maximalist' program and Opposition willingness to resist consensus solutions.

Some Conservative policy-makers argue that the Social Democratic and liberal proponents of comprehensives pursued ideological illusions and that their programs, even when implemented, represent not examples of linear progress, but of movement in the wrong direction. Thus the CSU Education Minister of Bavaria, Hans Maier, has asserted that the comprehensive school systems of Sweden and Britain constitute 'temporary regressions which are not likely to be able to maintain themselves against the differentiation and specialization tendencies of modern industrial society' (Löwenthal et al., 1972: 11). The toleration or reintroduction of some further differentiating elements within the British and the Swedish systems has been noted by those who question the feasibility of the goals of comprehensive schools. Will European school systems be able to alter fundamentally the relationships between schools' function in elite selection on the one hand, and their roles as instruments of social and cultural integration on the other? On this may depend whether comprehensive schools vindicate their advocates' goals by proving to be more than just a case of ideological-administrative reorganization.

If the German comprehensive program falters, it will constitute yet another instance of aborted discontinuity in German educational reform. This comparison has hopefully illustrated how such varying national system factors as centralism/federalism, the goals and intellectual-ideological infra-structure of educational planning and the commitment to social equalization within parties and political cultures have affected the pace of reform. What it also illustrates is that the dynamics of policy development differ not only between policy areas, but in relation to the dominant preoccupations of different time periods. Linear progress of the Swedish rolling reform was undoubtedly favored by the affluent, optimistic climate which prevailed when Sweden crossed vital threshholds in the late 1950s and early 1960s. The more restrictive prospects for educational policy development in the 1970s will probably impose greater limitations on both planners and the drafters of the party programs.

NOTES

1. 'Recognition of the parent's right to co-determination in the creation of school ordinances and curriculum development was established in Hessen after a 1958 court interpretation (of Article 56) of the Hessen constitution. Though this formal decision is unique in Germany, parents have been seen as potential political allies by educational interest groups to help push through their own goals. In 1968, Hessen teacher associations accused the Land parents consultative council of being an 'undemocratically elected, closed society which is hostile to reforms' ". In the North-Rhine-Westphalia parent's association, eighty percent of the Gymnasia but a much smaller percentage of the other schools were represented (Fischer, 1971: 43-44).

2. Several officials of the Board of Education have questioned Paulston's interpretation of which party provided the most initial reform support. (See Marklund, 1970: 396-399 and Isling, 1974).

3. The major concession to structural reform in Germany during the 1960s was limited to the introduction of an 'observation stage' to facilitate transfer opportunities during the first two years of the lower secondary cycle. Only isolated comprehensive schools were founded, mainly in Berlin and Hessen. In 1967 an author predicted that 'in most of the rest of Germany the traditional three-track system will operate for the foreseeable future' (Van de Graaff, 1967: 85).

4. CDU-controlled education ministries issued booklets giving graphic illustrations, based on the claim that overy eighty percent of existing schools would be closed if the comprehensive school model were adopted (Kultusministerium Baden-Wuerttemberg, 1972).

5. The OECD examiners felt constrainted to note: 'the danger that the new young teachers may bring to their tasks a new dogmatism, presently instilled by the more militant left wing factions within pedagogical seminars and institutes'. (See OECD, 1972: 104 and Merritt et al., 1971, 346-362). By 1974 Carl-Heinz Evers (1974: 46), the former Berlin Senator who led the Gesamtschule movement in the mid-1960s, acknowledged that he now believed that he and his fellow advocates of the first hour had chased 'the ideological illusion of compensatory education which assumed that it might be able to change consciousness even while not changing Being'.

6. By February 1971, Education (twenty-one percent) was third in a close contest with Environment (twenty-five percent) and Pensions (twenty-three percent) as issues which the population held to be the government's most important tasks. The weak position of Education was primarily due to lower support among the less educated (INFAS, 1971: 7).

7. A possible reflection: The German edition of the OECD Report on West German education was never published.

8. Texts of talks by Joachim Lohmann and Ludwig von Friedeburg (Gemeinnuetzige Gesellschaft Gesamtschule, 1974).

9. The Philologenverband reciprocated by mobilizing its members through

inflammatory slogans and massive propaganda. It produced what appeared at first glance to be a replica of the Education Ministry's information bulletin. The latter in contrast was in many schools withheld from circulation to pupils (*Schule and Ausbildung in Niedersachsen,* 1974: 1).

10. He asserted that the toughest evidence against the claim that comprehensives furthered equality of opportunity, was constituted by the fact that 'in Sweden the proportion of working-class youth at the universities has continously declined since the introduction of comprehensives, while here in the Federal Republic the number of working class students has continuously increased, and this through a differentiated school system'. Of course this constituted a blatant distortion of statistics, but it demonstrated that the Right was often able to make better use of the Swedish example than the Left (Schleswig-Holsteinischer Landtag, 1964: 3782).

11. Swedish teachers who visited German Gesamtschulen in 1972 noted classroom discipline problems not found at home. German teachers at the same time observed that Swedish teachers seemed to have a 'low tolerance threshhold' towards deviant student behavior, and that they dominated classroom discussions more than was usual in Germany. These and other interesting observations are contained in a report of a joint Swedish-German Commission on participation in school decision-making which was established in 1971 as a result of a suggestion made by the two heads of government. Larger political questions were outside its frame of reference, although it encountered some political problems of its own, one of which centered on the firing of a German Commission member because he was a Communist (Goldschmidt, 1973: 25, A27, A43).

12. For instance the IEA study of science learning, released in May 1973, showed that Swedish students' achievements at age 18 ranged ahead of those of the Germans. They ranked fifth in the national rankings compared to tenth of the Germans, even though the German sample was taken only from Gymnasium students (Comber and Keever, 1973).

13. On the 1966 conflict see the somewhat uneven study by Hight (1968). On the 1971 conflict see Nycander (1972) and Heidenheimer (1973).

14. This was the case for a while in the Education Ministry of Lower Saxony, which had been headed by a Christian Democrat up to 1970. When von Oertzen took over he was sometimes called 'the Red Baron'. In the struggle to shape policy images it may not have helped that the most well-known Social Democratic education ministers, at both the Federal and Land levels, had somewhat aristocratic-sounding names.

REFERENCES

BECK, R. H. (1971) 'A Contrast in European School Reform: West Germany and Sweden' in R. H. Beck (ed.), Change and Harmonization in European Education. Minneapolis: University of Minnesota Press.

BUEHLOW, G. et al. (1972) Gesamtschule Zwischen Schulversuch und Struktur-
reform. Weinheim: Beltz.

CDU/CSU Press Release (30 May 1974).

COMBER, L. E. and J. P. KEEVER (1973) Science Education in Nineteen
Countries. Stockholm: Almquist and Wiksell.

DAHRENDORF, R. (1968) Bildung ist Buergerrecht. Hamburg: Wegener.

DEUTSCHER BILDUNGSRAT (1969) Einrichtung von Schulversuchen mit
Gesamtschulen. Bonn.

DEUTSCHER BUNDESTAG (1971) Sitzungsberichte. 126 Sitzung (9 June).

DOHNANYI, K. VON (1972) 'Der konservative Gegenangriff', *Die Neue Gesellschaft* 19, 3.

EDDING, F. (1967) 'Educational Planning in Western Germany' in Bereday et al.,
World Yearbook of Education.

EVERS, C -H. (1974) 'Rueckblick auf die Gesamtschul – Idee' *betrifft: erziehung*
7, 3 (March).

FISCHER, A. (1971) 'Bundesrepublik Deutschland' in K. Schleicher (ed.) Elter-
nhaus und Schule. Dusseldorf: Schwann.

FUHRIG, W. (1969) 'West Germany' in A. Blum (ed.) Teacher Unions and
Associations. Urbana: University of Illinois Press.

GEMEINNUETZIGE GESELLSCHAFT GESAMTSCHULE (May 1974): mimeographed.

GOLDSCHMIDT, D. (ed.) (1973) Demokratisierung und Mitwirkung in Schule
und Hochschule. Braunschweig: Westermann Verlag.

HAGELIN, J. O. (1968) 'Enhetlighet eller mangfald? Studier i svensk enhets-
skolepolitik, 1950-61'. Licentiat avhandling. Statskunskap: Uppsala University.

HEIDENHEIMER, A. J. (1973) 'The SACO Conflict and Swedish Equality
Policy'. APSA, annual meeting.

HIGHT, B. (1968) 'Teachers, Bargaining and Strikes: Perspective from the
Swedish Experience'. *UCLA Law Review*, 15.

HOLGER, H. L. (ed.) (1973) Wirtschaftsriese-Bildungszwerg. Hamburg: Rowohlt.

HUSEN, T. (1971) 'Does Broader Educational Opportunity Mean Lower Standards? ' *International Review of Education* XVII.

–––, (1969) 'Responsiveness and Resistance in the Educational System to
Changing Needs of Society' *International Review of Education*, XV, 4.

–––, (1965) 'A Case Study in Policy-Oriented Research: The Swedish School
Reforms' *The School Review* (August).

–––, (1962) Problems of Differentiation in Swedish Compulsory Schooling.
Stockholm: Svenska Bokforlaget.

––– and G. BOALT (1968) Educational Research and Educational Change. New
York: John Wiley.

INFAS (1971) Aspekte der Schul- und Bildungspolitik (June).

ISLING, A. (1974) Vagen till en Demokratisk Skola. Stockholm: Prisma.

JOCHIMSEN, R. (1974) 'Staatliche Planung in der Bundesrepublik' in R. Löwenthal and H. P. Schwarz (eds.) Die Zweite Deutsche Republik. Stuttgart:
Seewald.

KULTUSMINISTERIUM BADEN-WUERTTEMBERG (1972) Bildungschancen
für Alle. Stuttgart.

LÖWENTHAL, R. et al. (eds.) (1972) *Schule '72. Schulkrise Schulreform und*

Lehrerbildung. Cologne: Markus.

MARKLUND, S. (1970) 'Review' *Comparative Education Review,* XIV, 3 (October).

MATTHIESEN, H. (1974) 'Die Fahne weht auf Halbmast' *Die Zeit* (31 May).

MERRITT, R. L. et al. (1971) 'Political Man in Post-war German Education' *Comparative Education Review,* XV, 3.

NASCHOLD, F. et al. (1972) Institutionelle Bedingungen von Partizipation ... im Bildungssystem. Berlin.

NIEDERSÄCHSISCHER LANDTAG, Protokolle (24 October, 1973).

NIXDORFF, P. (1969) The Pace of West German Educational Reforms as Affected by Land Politics. University of Florida: PhD dissertation.

NYCANDER, S. (1972) Kurs pa Kollisson. Stockholm: Askill and Karnekull.

NYSSEN, F. (1971) Schulkritik als Kapitalismuskritik. Göttingen: Vanderhoek and Ruprecht.

ORGANIZATION FOR ECONOMIC CO-OPERATION AND DEVELOPMENT (1972) Review of National Policies for Education: Germany. Paris.

– – –, (1969) Development of Secondary Education: Trends and Implications. Paris.

PAULSTON, R. G. (1968) Educational Change in Sweden. New York: Teachers College Press.

PICHT, G. (1964) Die deutsche Bildungskatastrophe. Olten: Walter.

POIGNANT, R. (1969) Education and Development in Western Europe, the United States, and the USSR: a Comparative Study. New York: Teachers College Press.

PRO UND CONTRA, Protokolle (1971) (14 January).

ROBINSOHN, S. B. and J. C. KUHLMANN (1967) 'Two Decades of Non-Reform in West German Education *Comparative Education Review,* XI, 3.

SCHEUERL, H. (1968) Die Gliederung des deutschen Schulwesens. Stuttgart: Klett.

Schleswig-Holsteinischer Landtag. *Protokolle* (1964) (7 May).

SCHMIEDERER, R. (1971) Bildungskrise und Schulreform. Frankfurt: Europäische Verlagsanstalt.

Schule und Ausbildung in Niedersachsen (1974) (February).

Der Spiegel (1 July 1974).

– – –, (8 January 1973).

– – –, (7 August 1972).

Süddeutsche Zeitung (15 June 1974).

SWEDISH SOCIAL DEMOCRATIC PARTY (1971) Towards Equality: The Alva Myrdal Report. Stockholm: Prisma.

TOMASSON, R. F. (1970) Sweden: Prototype of Modern Society. New York: Random House.

VAN DE GRAAFF, J. (1967) 'West Germany's Abitur Quota and School Reform, *Comparative Education Review,* XI.

WHEELER, C. (1972) Interest Groups in Swedish Politics. Columbia University: PhD dissertation.

Part Two

DYNAMIC PRESSURES

Chapter V

SOCIAL CHANGE, POLITICAL CHANGE AND PUBLIC POLICY: A TEST OF A MODEL

B. Guy Peters

Department of Political Science
University of Delaware

One clear example of linear progress has been the development of social programs in Western democracies. Year after year the amount of money spent on programs has increased, seemingly independent of political and economic forces. This paper is intended as a first step in the construction of a process model explaining the development of these social expenditures and services. It will be focused on one country — Sweden — usually taken as an archetype of the modern welfare state. This paper will present a causal model linking certain conditions in the socio-economic and political environments to these expenditures. If this causal model can be validated by the data, it should provide a parsimonious description of the policy process, reducing the blooming, buzzing confusion of the real world to a limited set of crucial variables predicting changes in policy.

In both the statistical manipulations and in the assumptions about relationships we are positing a model of linear progressive change. This does not, however, necessarily mean that expenditures in any one year will be a simple function, but rather that the *process* of policy formation is linear, progressive and stable. Transformations in the relationships between independent variables and the dependent variable of expenditures occur, but these changes are continuous and gradual.

The study is longitudinal, covering a long period of time: 1865 to 1967. With such time-series data one can discuss an aspect of causation which is usually avoided in cross-section causal models: the temporal sequence of influence. A second important question concerns the allocation of a limited number of resources available to the political system among a number of competing purposes. We know that all social expenditures in Sweden have increased markedly over time; we will also want to know why certain expenditures have increased faster at certain times than have others. This problem will be examined through the use of a linear programming model, based on the assumption of social rationality in decision-making (Nagel, 1974). If budgetary decision-makers conduct themselves in a socially rational manner, then changes in expenditures should be related across time to changes in objective conditions in the socio-economic environment indicating the need for those expenditures and services. For example, if health conditions in a nation should deteriorate, as evidenced by increases in infant mortality, then there is an apparent need for an increase in health expenditures. Thus, differential allocations in expenditures should be related to differential changes in the need for those expenditures. By using the changes in needs as the functional equivalents of prices in the economic model of linear programming, we can derive a set of socially optimal allocations of expenditures against which to compare the actual pattern of expenditures. This model could be classified as a 'response' model which will produce varying results dependent upon external conditions; with social expenditures this might produce constantly rising expenditures as the needs and demands rise.

With these two types of analyses of the growth of expenditures, we should be able to gain some insight both into the general processes of development and into the process of differential allocations of funds. It is believed that both of these processes are crucial to our understanding of why money is spent for any purpose, with the models developed being especially applicable to social service expenditures. Other types of expenditures, e.g., public works and agriculture, may be better described by cyclical models of the policy process.

I. A MOBILIZATION MODEL:
LINKAGES BETWEEN ECONOMIC CHANGE, POLITICAL CHANGE AND PARTY OUTPUTS IN SWEDEN

The basic assumption of this model is that the process of social mobilization is a crucial destabilizing force in changing a public policy. As Deutsch has pointed out:

> Social mobilization also brings about a change in the quality of politics, by
> changing the range of human needs that impinge upon the political process. As
> people are uprooted from their physical and intellectual isolation in their
> immediate localities . . ., they experience drastic changes in their needs. They
> may now come to need provisions for housing and employment, for social
> security against illness and old age, for medical care . . . They need, in short, a
> wide range and large amounts of new government services (Deutsch, 1961:
> 498).

Thus, we can expect that the process of social mobilization — to be
measured by the proportion of the population in non-agricultural
employment — is a crucial determinant of the pressures for improved
social services from the political system. This relationship has been
rather widely discussed with respect to Scandinavia in general and
Sweden in particular, and the rather long time-frame being used here
will allow for an examination of the effects of social mobilization in
moving a political system from a traditional state to modern conditions
(Bull, 1922; Galenson, 1949; 1952; Lafferty, 1971). Further, this time
frame will allow us to test whether the effects of social mobilization
persist even after the nation has attained a relatively high level of
development. We would hypothesize that these effects would, in fact,
diminish as a function of the proportion of the work force already
outside the primary sector, and also as a function of the movement
from the industrial to the service sectors of the economy. Thus, as
Sweden or another nation enters 'post-industrial society' the effects of
social mobilization are expected to wane rather rapidly (Heisler, 1974;
Huntington, 1968).

There may well be direct effects of social mobilization on the
development of social policy, but we hypothesize the major effects of
that influence to be transmitted through two more indirect paths. The
first is through the increase of demands to modify the political system
to allow greater inputs from those affected by the social mobilization
process — points 3 and 4 of Rose's process scheme (1973: 77-8). Social
mobilization is hypothesized to lead directly to an increase of political
mobilization of the working classes, with the purpose being both the
modification of the political system itself and the increase of social
benefits. In Sweden, this was indicated by pressures coming from the
working classes for the extension of the franchise, the introduction of
proportional representation, and the transfer of the executive powers
from the monarchy to a Prime Minister commanding the confidence of
the Riksdag (Verney, 1957: 159-73, 202-14). In terms of policy
changes, demands were forthcoming for a reduction of defense expendi-

tures and the inception of programs of social insurance (Verney, 1972). The beginnings of social insurance have, of course, been expanded to one of the more comprehensive social service systems in the world. For the quantitative analysis of this relationship, we will be using voting for parties of the ideological left – in large part the Social Democratic Party – as the indicator of political mobilization. This is a surrogate for the actual demands being placed on the system, but adequate to measure the demands for social service development and for the use of the public sector to redress grievances arising in the private sector.

The second direct effect of the process of social mobilization is economic development. In terms of Rose's process scheme, we can think of this as a lessening of the restraints on policy-making through the expansion of the resource base available for taxation. (1973: 78, point 5). The relationship between social mobilization and economic development is clearly reciprocal, but at least according to Deutsch may not be symmetrical (Deutsch, 1961: 498-9). Relatively large-scale movements can take place without a significant increase in the level of per capita national income, while changes in national income generally tend to produce further changes in the industrial composition of the population. More people are attracted away from traditional life-styles and occupations as the economy develops. However, in our initial analysis we will assume that the process of social mobilization is an independent influence upon the development of economic resources – measured by per capita Gross National Product – necessary for the production of large-scale social programs.

In terms of the political effects of social mobilization, we can hypothesize that political mobilization will have two direct consequences of interest here. The first is a direct effect of political mobilization upon the development of social expenditures and services; these effects appear rather well defined in the Swedish case (Verney, 1957: 206-14; 1972). A second effect of political mobilization will be the development of a strong governmental apparatus. One of the most consistent results of political change, especially when that change is directed toward the redress of difficulties created by the operation of the free market, is the growth of the government bureaucracy. As Deutsch points out:

> A rapid process of social mobilization thus tends to generate major pressures for political and administrative reform. Such reforms may include both a quantitative expansion of the bureaucracy and its qualitative improvement in the direction of a competent civil service – even though these two objectives at times may clash (1961: 499).

Huntington also emphasizes the importance of the institutionalization of political change (Huntington, 1968: 12-24). Political change without institutional development potentially leads to chaos. The development of a competent and comprehensive civil service is thus an important means of channelling the demands coming to the political system from its environment, and converting 'raw' demands into programs and services. Further, the institutionalization of the demand system, largely through the development of organized labor, has had a significant impact of the development of social programs (Peters and Hennessey, 1973: 20-25). This is likely to be especially important in a nation such as Sweden, with significant involvement of interest groups in the processes of policy-making providing a direct connection between institutions of interest articulation and those of policy-making (Castles, 1973; Foyer, 1961).

The growth of the public bureaucracy is, in itself, an important change in the form of government of a society (see Rose, 1973: 77, point 4). With this growth, administrators increasingly involve themselves in the policy process and begin to function as an interest group in their own right. They press demands not only for their own personal and professional interests but also for the interests of their agencies (Niskanen, 1971: Shapiro, 1973). Thus, we can expect the development of these 'bureaucratic entrepreneurs' to affect the growth of public expenditures. Further, Heidenheimer points out that the degree of reform and professionalization of the public bureaucracy is likely to affect popular willingness to accept large-scale public programs to be administered by the civil servants (1973: 324-327). This change in the style of policy-making in response to bureaucratic development can be expected to be less pronounced in Sweden than might be true elsewhere, given the long tradition of administrative involvement in policy-making and the relatively high status enjoyed for centuries by the public service there (Meijer, 1969). There should, however, still be a significant effect of civil service development on the growth of expenditures and services. In this analysis, the development of the civil service will be measured by the number of civil servants per capita. It would be useful to have measures of the qualitative aspects of administration as well, but such indicators are not readily available.

Finally, we come to the dependent variable: public expenditures for social services. We will hypothesize that expenditures will be a function of *both* the growth of public demands and institutions, *and* the growth of the resource base. Thus, unlike most studies attempting to explain levels of public expenditure, our methodology is not intended to eliminate one or another influence as significant, but rather to attempt to demonstrate that both are necessary for an adequate explanation (Peters, 1972a). In theoretical terms, we can argue that the development of expenditures are a function both of demands expressed through the political process and the availability of resources to meet those demands. If either of these causative factors is absent, then expenditures can be expected to grow more slowly if at all.

Thus, we hypothesize that social mobilization sets in motion a series of political and economic forces which will culminate in increases in social expenditures and services. We will be measuring only one aspect of the concept of social mobilization, but the results of this analysis should indicate the relationship between this type of social change and policy change. While a number of other important forces impinge upon policy change, the major influences can be parsimoniously presented in this fashion. Further, given the stable relationships between economic development and expenditures so often cited in the literature and the development of stable political institutions in Sweden, the development of social expenditures can also be described as linear progress reflecting the steady uninterrupted operation of persisting influences.

PROVISION OF SERVICES

We must also be concerned with the implementation of programs and the provision of services with the funds provided by those expenditures. There are at least four hypotheses to link the first portion of our mobilization model of expenditure with the provision of services. The *first* hypothesis is that services are a function of public expenditures for a functional area. While this is a seemingly obvious hypothesis at first glance, there are a number of possible difficulties with its acceptance. We can question it on the basis of our knowledge concerning the use and misuse of public funds in many governmental programs (Shapiro, 1973). Characteristics of the socio-economic environment can interact with the expenditure of funds to produce positive or negative multiplier effects (*Journal of Political Economy,* 1972). For example, virtually no amount of public health expenditure is likely to produce significant improvements in health conditions if the environment is not capable of providing adequate sanitation, diet and health information. Likewise, the ready availability of adequate diet, sanitation and the like (along with private funds which can be used for medical care) would make each dollar spent for health by the government more effective than would be expected on other grounds. What we are trying to say, therefore, is that it is not entirely clear that public expenditures are directly and linearly related to improvements in the level of service. This lack of a direct causal relationship has been supported to some degree in the literature. For example, Sharkansky found little systematic relationship between levels of service and levels of expenditure, rather than vice versa as has usually been assumed (1967: 26-28). Peters and Hennessey, however, find that services and expenditures are related across time, with changes in services preceeding changes in services (1973: 27). They argue that the development of service levels is a means for the 'bureaucratic entrepreneurs' to increase their budgetary allocations, rather than simply reflecting the increase of funds in prior time periods. Therefore, despite the relative simplicity and apparent logic of this first hypothesis, we have little expectation that it will be supported in the data.

A *second* hypothesis is that the demands expressed through the political system, and through public institutions such as the bureaucracy, are instrumental in the provision of public services. Again, there is some logic to support this hypothesis, as the actual contents of most expressed demands are not for so many dollars or crowns to be expended in a particular policy area, but rather for the improvement of certain types of services. To the degree to which these demands have been successfully put into operation — either by left-wing governments or by more conservative governments seeking to co-opt the working classes — they have been translated directly into policies and service. On the other hand, there is even a greater logical gap between political demands and services than between expenditures and services, with therefore even a greater number of possible intervening variables and conditions to limit the relationship. We will, however, test the degree of relationship between both political demands (left-voting) and political institutional development (civil service rate) and changes in the levels of service.

A *third* hypothesis is that socio-economic conditions particularly the resource base available to the society, will have a crucial determining role in the level of service. The environment can greatly affect the provision of services both by multiplying the effects of public expenditures and by making available through private means resources that might be provided through public means; the most obvious example is medical care in the United States. If we looked just at the levels of public expenditures in the United States, we would expect health conditions to be extremely poor; although they are not so good on the

average as those enjoyed by most European nations they are still good.
This is in large part a function of the high level of resources available to
Americans to purchase health care privately. Again, however, this
hypothesis has some rather important logical problems. The most
important of these is that the causal mechanism connecting resource
levels to service levels is rather unclear, especially outside the area of
health, and perhaps education. For many of the social programs we will
be discussing, the political system offers the only logical means of
allocating the resource base to the purposes desired. Despite this weakness in cross-sectional studies, there has been a significant relationship
demonstrated between the availability of resources and the provision of
services — both within the American states and cross-nationally
(Sharkansky, 1967, 1071-1072; Cutright, 1965). Further, the general
finding in the policy literature of the relationship of resources to levels
of policy, even when only measured as levels of expenditure, indicates
that this is a hypothesis which must be investigated (Dye, 1966;
Sharkansky, 1968; Hofferbert, 1966).

Finally, we can hypothesize that, just as with the explanation of
expenditures, no single-variable explanation will be sufficient for levels
of service. In particular, we will hypothesize that the combination of
public expenditures and resources will provide an explanation superior
to any single variable explanation; indeed, both of these variables will
have significant effects upon the levels of service independent of the
other. We will therefore be testing not only additive but also non-
additive combinations of these variables in order to attempt to explain
service levels.

The mobilization model with the four possible explanations of
service levels is presented graphically in Figure I. The arrows in this
diagram indicate relationships which are hypothesized to be statistically
significant. This model is a recursive model although it is abundantly
clear that in some cases there will be significant reciprocal relationships
among the variables. As well as testing the model for the entire time
period (1865-1967) we will also examine it in three shorter time
periods: 1865-1905, 1906-36, and 1937-67. By breaking the total time
period into smaller portions we will be able to assess the degree to
which the relationships found for the total time period are stable across
time. This type of information will be crucial in an attempt to construct a more process oriented model for the dynamics of policy
formation. Further, the three time periods selected represent important
developmental stages in the policy process in Sweden (Peters and
Hennessey, 1973, 9-14; Peters, 1972).

Figure I
The Mobilization Model for Development of Social Expenditures and Services

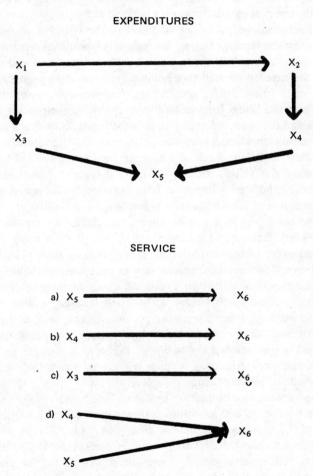

EXPENDITURES

SERVICE

a) $X_5 \longrightarrow X_6$

b) $X_4 \longrightarrow X_6$

c) $X_3 \longrightarrow X_6$

d) X_4
X_5 $\longrightarrow X_6$

X_1	=	Social Mobilization	X_4	=	Civil Service
X_2	=	Political Mobilization	X_5	=	Social Expenditures
X_3	=	Economic Resources	X_6	=	Services

The first period can be classified as a traditional period, encompassing the rather limited policy changes occurring up to the point of the beginnings of political reform. Further, the political system at this time was largely dominated by a traditional elite, although by the end of the time period the Social Democrats were beginning to attain significant representation in the Riksdag – to the point of forming a majority in coalition with the Liberals (Verney, 1957: 142).

The second period is one of major political reform as well as of major policy change. During this period proportional representation was introduced (1907), full manhood suffrage was introduced (1919), and the executive passed to a Prime Minister having a majority in the Riksdag (Verney, 1957; Tilton, 1974). This period also covers the time in which the Social Democratic Party acquired hegemony in electoral politics. As for policy changes, these include the initiation of a program of sickness insurance under the protection and later subsidy of the government (1910), the Poor Relief Act of 1918, a General Pensions Insurance Act (1913), the beginnings of a system of unemployment insurance, and some educational reforms in 1927. This period marked the inception of the welfare state in Sweden.

The third period is one of continuing domination by the Social Democratic Party, either in coalition or by itself, and the expansion and consolidation of the welfare state. It is further a period of increasing involvement of the public bureaucracy in policy-making, and the institutionalization of a co-optive and depoliticized manner of policy-making (Meijer, 1969; Heisler, 1974). This tendency toward the depoliticization of many important policy decisions, coupled with the development of 'post-industrial values' among the population has brought about the waning of Social Democratic strength in recent years, and some rethinking of their reliance on acquisitively oriented programs as a means of assuring electoral victory.

We expect our mobilization model to have some validity over the entire time span, but we will also expect some differing relationships among the three periods. In the first place, the influence of social mobilization should decline monotonically across time. During the first period, this form of social change should exert a quite pervasive influence over politics and policy, but after the initial dislocations this influence should wane as fewer and fewer people are left to undergo the process of uprooting and relocation.

A second significant difference across time is the influence of political mobilization on policy. This is expected to have its strongest relationship with policies – both expenditures and services – during the second time period, with relatively little direct relationship during either the first or last period. This is to be expected because of the high level of political agitation during the second period, with an altering of the patterns of budgetary allocation during the time (see Table 1). During the first period, the traditional basis of the political system and policy is expected to produce relatively little influence of political mobilization upon policy change, while during the last period the growth of administrative power should begin to supersede political mobilization as an influence on policy. Following from this, we expect the influence of the development of the civil service to be monotonically increasing across time, with little relationship in the first period and a very strong relationship in the third period. Finally, we expect the relationship of economic resources to policy to be relatively constant and statistically significant across time, with perhaps the strongest relationships occurring in the first time period. However, these changes in relationships are not discontinuous — social expenditures have increased linearly across time. A graphic presentation of these relationships is presented in Figure II.

TABLE 1
Changes in Budgetary Allocations
(percentage of total spending)

	1865	1905	1936	1967
Defense	41	39	16	14
Education	10	11	18	15
Health	5	0.6	11	14
Social Welfare (including pensions)	4	2	26	20

RESULTS OF THE ANALYSIS

For the total time period and for each of the shorter periods, we will seek to answer the two rather important questions concerning the relationships among these variables. First, are the temporal patterns among the variables consistent with our hypothesized recursive model? this question can be answered through an examination of the cross-lagged correlations among the variables. The second question is whether the significant effects of the independent variables on the dependent variable of expenditures are also consistent with those hypothesized in

Figure II
Hypothesized Strength of Independent Variables in Explaining Expenditures Across Time

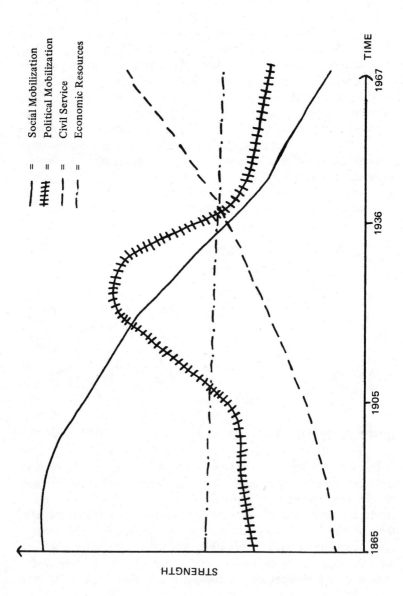

the model? This information will come largely from the path analysis.

TABLE 2
Cross-Lagged Correlations for Total Time Period

Social Mobilization

	Polit. Mobil.	Econ. Resources	Civil Ser. Rate	Health Expend.
Independent Lagged	.66	.07	.62	.29
Dependent Lagged	.64	.05	.59	.25

Political Mobilization

	Civil Ser. Rate	Health Expend.
Independent Lagged	.45	.26
Dependent Lagged	.24	.24

	Econ. Resources Expend.	Civil Ser. Rate Expend.
Independent Lagged	.76	.75
Dependent Lagged	.73	.73

Results in the Total Time Period[1]

Our assumptions concerning the temporal ordering of the variables receives quite strong confirmation for the total time period (see Table 2). Each variable hypothesized to be causally prior to another variable did in fact meet that assumption. However, the differences between the correlations in most cases are not statistically significant and in most cases are quite small. We must therefore exercise caution in interpreting these results. The results from the path analysis are also quite supportive of the hypothesized model. Figure III shows the path diagram with all significant coefficients included. The values of R_i are the values of a residual path from all variables not included in the model to that particular variable, indicating the degree to which the variables included in the path model are also functions of exogenous and unmeasured variables; this residual path is equal to the square-root of the coefficient of alienation (Land, 1969: 12). The values of the path coefficients along the paths hypothesized to be significant in the model are quite

---

[1] For statistical methods used see Appendix A, page 138.

Figure III
Results of Path Analysis in Total time period

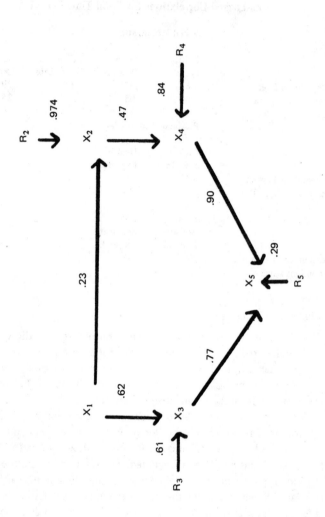

strong, with the exception of the statistically significant but relatively weak effect of social mobilization on political mobilization. It is especially important to note the strong influences that both the availability of economic resources and the development of political institutions had on the development of policy. Likewise, there are no direct effects of social or political mobilization on expenditures, with the influences being channeled through economic resources and political institutions. In addition, despite the hypothesis advanced by Deutsch, there is no statistically significant direct effect of social mobilization on the development of the bureaucracy (1961: 499). Thus, we have some rather strong support for the model outlined in Figure I.

One of the important features of path analysis is the ability to calculate the indirect effects of antecedent variables upon dependent variables. We are especially interested in the indirect effects of social mobilization on the development of social expenditures and the public bureaucracy. Those indirect effects have been calculated and are presented in Table 3. The calculation of those indirect effects is somewhat complicated by changes in the sign of the coefficient for social mobilization and expenditures when all variables are included in the equation. However, it can be said that the majority of influence of social mobilization for the total time period is carried through the development of the economic system, and that the stronger direct effects of political institutions on expenditures have relatively little to do with transmitting the influence of social mobilization. This would appear to indicate that a number of other factors impinge upon political change, and especially upon political mobilization. Thus, although there is a statistically significant relationship between the particular indicator of social mobilization and the indicator of political mobilization, there is relatively little influence of social mobilization transmitted along this path. This is in part a function of the complexity of the concept of social mobilization, so that no single indicator can capture its full influence on political change. Other possible indicators of social mobilization, such as urbanization, literacy and mass media exposure, also have significant effects on political change relatively independent of the relationships of industrialization and political mobilization (Deutsch, 1961; 503). With a more complete set of social mobilization indicators, therefore, we might be able to demonstrate a more important indirect effect of social mobilization on expenditures through the political system. Much the same can be said for the relationship of social mobilization and the development of the public bureaucracy, with significant indirect effects, but little occurring through political mobilization.

TABLE 3
Indirect Effects of Social Mobilization on Expenditures and Civil Service Rate

Variable	Total Indirect Effects	Through Economic Resources	Through Political Variables
Expenditures	−.39	−.48	.09
Civil Service	.10	−	.09

Thus, the model of the entire time period does receive some validation, with the important caveat that social mobilization makes itself felt on expenditures for health largely through economic change rather than political change. This is not to say that political measures are unimportant for the total period, because indeed they have quite large direct effects on policy change. Rather, this is to indicate that political mobilization and the development of the public bureaucracy does not rest entirely or even primarily upon social mobilization. A number of other factors must be taken into account in order to obtain an adequate explanation of political mobilization for the entire time period. Perhaps the most obvious explanation for political mobilization comes from Huntington's work concerning the relative rates of change of social mobilization, economic development, and opportunities for mobility. (1968: 53-55). The argument is that political mobilization and participation are not a direct function of social change, but rather a function of the ability of other aspects of the social system to absorb the socially mobilized individuals, allow them social mobility and reduce the frustrations and dislocations resulting from social mobilization.

Results in the First Time Period (1865-1905)

The results for the first time period also confirm our assumptions concerning the temporal ordering of influences. In each case, the correlations of the variables hypothesized to be antecedent lagged one year were stronger than those of the variables hypothesized to be dependent lagged one time period (see Table 4). Again, the majority of the differences in correlations were slight and statistically insignificant, but the pattern of relationships does support our assumptions.

The results of the path analysis did not, however, confirm our expectations concerning the changes in these patterns of relationships across time (see Figure IV). More specifically, social mobilization did not exert the dominant influence on changes in public policy and the

Table 4
Cross-Lagged Correlations for First Time Period

Social Mobilization

	Polit. Mobil.	Econ. Resources	Civil Ser. Rate	Health Expend.
Independent Lagged	.61	.32	.55	.33
Dependent Lagged	.56	.21	.53	.22

Political Mobilization

	Civil Ser. Rate	Health Expend.
Independent Lagged	.43	.95
Dependent Lagged	.42	.91

	Econ. Resources Expend.	Civil Ser. Rate Expend.
Independent Lagged	.24	.07
Dependent Lagged	.08	−.08

growth of the public bureaucracy which we had hypothesized. The path coefficients from social mobilization to each of these two variables were quite small and statistically insignificant. Furthermore, there was no significant relationship between the development of economic resources and the growth of expenditures once the effects of other variables were controlled. Thus, the first time period appears to be much as we would have expected the second period to appear. There is a very strong effect of political mobilization on both the development of social expenditures and the development of the civil service, and the civil service has some significant relationship with the growth of expenditures, even after the effects of political mobilization are taken into account. Social mobilization has a very strong relationship with political mobilization and a reasonably strong relationship with economic development, but its direct effects on expenditures and the public bureaucracy are almost entirely mediated through political mobilization. Thus, it appears that the direct political consequences of social mobilization are more immediate than we had hypothesized and that these political consequences, i.e. political mobilization, likewise began to have direct policy consequences earlier than we had anticipated. Some of this relationship in Sweden may be attributed to the now proverbial spirit of compromise which has been used so often as an explanation for the moderation and evolutionary change of Swedish politics (Rustow, 1955; Anton, 1969). From this data, it appears that when the Social Democratic Party began to press demands on the political system, even very early in their development, they did receive a hearing and some success in producing actual policy change, at least in terms of growing expenditures.

Results in the Second Time Period (1906-36)

The results for the second period are almost an exact replica of those of the first; again the major influences on expenditures come directly from the political system, both through the public bureaucracy and directly from political mobilization. In the second period, however, the effects of political mobilization were even stronger than in the first, and the indirect effects through the development of the public bureaucracy were lower. Thus, the second period can be classified as a period of direct impact on policy by political mobilization. In this period there is also a stronger relationship between social mobilization and political mobilization, but again no significant direct impact of social mobilization on either expenditures or the development of the bureaucracy. Further, during this period there were no direct relationships between social mobilization and economic growth — in part a function of the occurrence of the Depression in this period — or between economic growth and expenditures. The second period is one of political effects on the development of policy, with political mobilization transmitting a large indirect effect to the development of expenditures through bureaucratic growth. This confirms our prior expectations that this would be the period during which political mobilization and change would have the largest direct impact on policy, and politics would be the dominant force explaining policy change.

Results in the Third Time Period (1937-67)

During this period, our general assumptions concerning the temporal ordering of the variables continue to be applicable (see Table 6), albeit with one significant exception: social mobilization apparently becomes a dependent variable of economic growth. This would appear to be a function of an economy moving into a very high level of development; instead of increasing industrialization driving up production, increases in production may in fact be pulling more people from agricultural positions to industrial or service positions.

Figure IV
Results of Path Analysis in First Time Period (1865-1905)

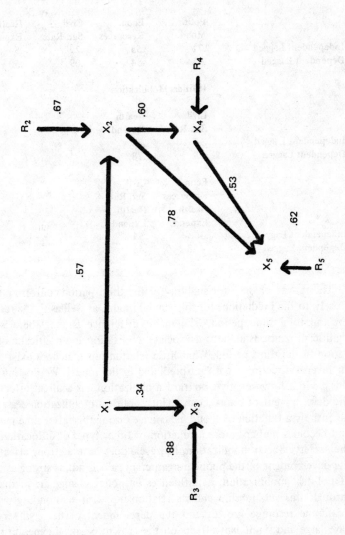

TABLE 5
Cross-Lagged Correlations for Second Time Period

Social Mobilization

	Polit. Mobil.	Econ. Resources	Civil Ser. Rate	Health Expend.
Independent Lagged	.71	.55	.29	.54
Dependent Lagged	.61	.54	.09	.50

Political Mobilization

	Civil Ser. Rate	Health Expend.
Independent Lagged	.13	.81
Dependent Lagged	.08	.78

	Econ. Resources Health Expend.	Civil Ser. Rate Health Expend.
Independent Lagged	.06	.54
Dependent Lagged	−.28	.48

The results of the path analysis for the third period conform rather closely to the predictions for the general model, as well as to the results for the total time period. The major difference is that there is no significant relationship between social mobilization and political mobilization in the third period. What little relationship that does exist is in an inverse direction from that predicted in the model. We do find for this period, however, that political mobilization has a direct effect on the development of bureaucracy. Thus, political mobilization ceases to be entirely a function of economic change during this latter time period and becomes perhaps more a function of other types of disloeations in the society. Social mobilization, however, does have a strong effect on the development of the public bureaurcracy, albeit not as strong as that of political mobilization; its influences on policy change are mediated through this relationship and its relationship with economic growth. Economic resource growth and the development of the civil service have large and significant effects on the growth of social expenditures, with both transmitting approximately equal indirect influences from social mobilization.

Figure V
Results of Path Analysis in Second Time Period (1906-1936)

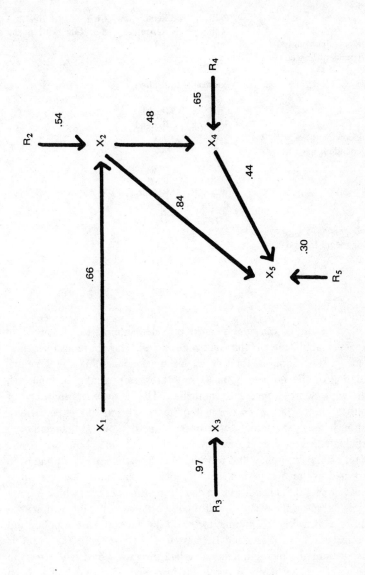

TABLE 6
Cross-Lagged Correlations for Third Time Period

Social Mobilization

	Polit. Mobil.	Econ. Resources	Civil Ser. Rate	Health Expend.
Independent Lagged	−.05	.84	.76	.54
Dependent Lagged	−.01	.86	.56	.52

Political Mobilization

	Civil Ser. Rate	Health Expend
Independent Lagged	.62	.50
Dependent Lagged	.22	.44

	Civil Ser. Rate Health Expend.	Econ. Resources Health Expend.
Independent Lagged	.58	.57
Dependent Lagged	.55	.54

Summary

The results of our analysis have provided support for the model as generally applicable to the total time period. They have also provided some general support for our assumptions concerning the temporal ordering of the influences on expenditures, as presented in Figure II, but with some important anomalies. The actual relationships of political mobilization conformed quite closely to our expectations, although they were somewhat stronger in the first period than had been anticipated. Likewise, social mobilization did not show the strong direct effects on policy and bureaucratic development which had been expected in the first period. In fact, social mobilization had very little direct impact on expenditures in any of the time periods, which is quite important given the discussion of the importance of the institutionalization of political and economic forces on the development of policy and political stability (Peters and Hennessey, 1973: 7-12). In line with this observation, the public bureaucracy had the most consistent effect on the development of policy, and this increased over time as had been hypothesized. The effects of economic development, on the other

Figure VI
Result of Path Analysis in Third Time Period (1937-1967)

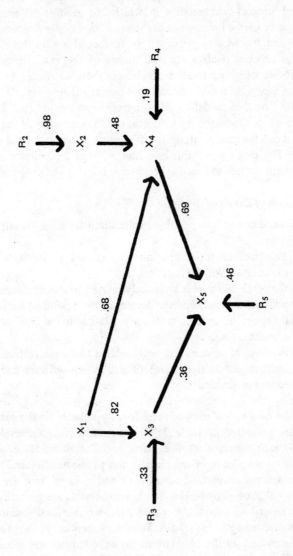

hand, did not display the stability anticipated, and were in fact almost totally absent during the second period. This variable did, however, have significant effects in the third time period and the total period. With this information on the sequencing of influences, we can begin to construct process-type models in which the relative influence of a variable is in part a function of the relative state of development of the variable and the whole system. If we further elaborate the model to take into account relative rates of change of the variables and some sensitivity to other parameters of change, then we should be able to construct a process model for this one country (Klingman, 1973). The application of that model to other national and sub-national data sets will then allow the further specificiation of the generality of the model, and the need for modification in different socio-economic and cultural settings. The findings for this one case are that the policy process in Sweden with respect to social expenditures is linear and progressive.

Explanation of Levels of Service

We have advanced four possible explanations for service levels:

- a). the level of services is directly related to levels of public expenditure for the function;
- b). the level of services is directly related to the advancement of political demands and the development of political institutions;
- c). the level of services is directly related to the level of socio-economic resources;
- d). the level of services is directly related to the interaction (either additive or multiplicative) of public expenditures and socio-economic resources.

The results of a test of each of these four hypotheses for the total time period are presented in Table 7. Four measures of public services are included, each representing one major social service area: education, economic security, care of the elderly, and public health (see Table 8).

There are two important conclusions to be drawn from the results for the total time period. The first is that services are generally more strongly related to expenditures than has been previously assumed on the basis of cross-sectional studies. With the exception of the provisions of relief services, all the correlations for expenditures and services are statistically significant across time, and that for the pension rate is quite large. There is also some support for the hypotheses concerning political factors and economic resources being related to services, but

TABLE 7
Explanations of Service Levels in Total Time Period

	Expend.	Polit. Mobil.	Civil Ser. Rate	Per Cap. GNP	Interactive Add.	Multip.
School Rate	.20*	.16	.28*	.25*	.37*	.41*
Relief Rate	.18	.19	.29*	−.17	.36*	.39*
Pension Rate	.81*	.21*	.02	.48*	.82*	.89*
Doctors/Capita	.47*	.16	.35*	.34*	.49*	.98*

* Statistically significant at the .05 level

TABLE 8
Variable Listing

	Services	Needs
Education	*School Rate* = total number of pupils in elementary and secondary schools as a percentage of all children 5-15 years	Number of children 5-15 years of age
Health	Number of physicians/capita	Infant mortality rate
Pensions	*Pension* Rate = total number of old age pensioners as percentage of population 65 or older	Percentage of population 65 years or older
Welfare	*Welfare Rate* = Recipients of Public Welfare/Capita	Percentage of work force unemployed
Labor	*	Percentage of work force receiving its income from agricultural employment

* We have not included a measure of the services rendered for labor benefits. The rather thin line between public and private in things such as accident and sickness insurance makes this quite difficult and we have little confidence in our data.

the strongest relationships by far occur for the interaction of expenditures and resources, especially when those factors are multiplicatively combined. This multiplicative interaction is especially pronounced for the health service measure, as might be expected given the large quantity of economic resources required in the training and maintenance of physicians, as well as the strong relationship of governmental expenditures and medical services in Sweden. Thus, our second conclusion is that the provision of social services across time appears to involve the interaction of several forces, with public expenditures and economic resources being one set of interacting forces producing close fits with these data, as well as having some sound logical and theoretical justification.

In the three shorter time periods (see Table 9), there is an interesting pattern of development somewhat paralleling the pattern found for the explanation of expenditures. We can first note that the relationships of political mobilization with policy follow the curvilinear pattern noted earlier with respect to expenditures, with quite strong relationships in the second period and little or no positive relationship during the other two periods. Likewise, the availability of economic resources shows a pattern of increasing relationship across time. The relationships of expenditures to services are generally stronger in the second time period, although their relationships were significant in each time period. Especially interesting in this regard is the development of a pattern of interaction among the variables. This interaction is generally increasing across time, with the development being especially pronounced for the multiplicative form of interaction (Strouse and Williams, 1972). This interaction is very strong in the third period, which would tend to substantiate our earlier findings of the necessity of including one political parameter and one economic resource measure when attempting to explain policy. If we regard expenditures as a product of political decisions — albeit influenced by economic considerations — then much the same conclusion may be reached with regard to the provision of services.

The findings for the shorter time periods also point up some interesting differences between policy areas. First, it is more difficult to explain the relief rate than any of the other service variables. Especially interesting in this regard is the negative relationship found between the relief rate and per capita GNP, indicating some reaction of political decision-makers to needs created by economic recessions. In general, therefore, we could argue that the relief rate is an example of a self-steering or 'cybernetic' policy which is determined more by changes

TABLE 9
Explanation of Service Levels in Three Time Periods

| | **First Period Hypotheses:** | | | | |
| | A | B | C | D Interactive | |
	Expend.	Polit. Mobil.	Civil Ser. Rate	Per Cap. GNP	Add.	Multip.
School Rate	.63*	.10	.61*	.26	.66*	.69*
Relief Rate	.26	.09	.24	−.44	.47*	.21
Pension Rate	.47*	.04	.37*	.14	.51*	.26
Doctors/Capita	.10	.03	.43*	.03	.19	.69*

| | **Second Period Hypotheses:** | | | | |
| | A | B | C | D Interactive | |
	Expend.	Polit. Mobil.	Civil Ser. Rate	Per Cap. GNP	Add.	Multip.
School Rate	.74*	.80*	.36*	.46*	.78*	.59*
Relief Rate	.60*	.41*	.06	−.16	.66*	.65*
Pension Rate	.81*	.74*	.62*	.60*	.83*	.62*
Doctors/Capita	.83*	.70*	.27	.57*	.86*	.84*

| | **Third Period Hypotheses:** | | | | |
| | A | B | C | D Interactive | |
	Expend.	Polit. Mobil.	Civil Ser. Rate	Per Cap. GNP	Add.	Multip.
School Rate	.63*	−.04	.73*	.89*	.91*	.96*
Relief Rate	.16	−.11	.40*	−.60*	.64*	.74*
Pension Rate	.77*	−.34	.60*	.79*	.83*	.91*
Doctors/Capita	.59*	−.27	.58*	.85*	.87*	.90*

* Statistically significant at the .05 level

in environmental conditions than by overt attempts of the political system to manipulate it (Deutsch, 1963; Rose, 1973: 468-469). This particular process might therefore be better described as cyclical rather than linear.

We also note that generally higher levels of interaction occurred for the health variable than for any of the other policy measures, although education also did display a high level of interaction of the independent variables. These two policy areas can be seen, on theoretical grounds as well as on the basis of this empirical analysis, as the two social policy areas requiring the highest levels of support from the socio-economic environment (Heidenheimer, 1973). This is quite clear for health, with the need not only for economic resources for the maintenance of the personnel and physical plant but also for adequate diets, sanitation and leisure for the population. In the training of medical personnel, the long period of time required necessitates either private personal wealth or strong public support (or both) to allow the individual to acquire medical skills. For education, the relationship is somewhat less clear, but a relatively enriched social background is apparently crucial both for the desire of education and the willingness of the population to support educational programs (*Journal of Political Economy,* 1972; Himmelweit, 1954; Martin, 1954). The relationship between social backgrounds and the success of public educational programs becomes even clearer when one moves from the quantitative aspects of educational policy into the qualitative aspects.

In summary, we have found first that expenditures and services have a considerably stronger relationship across time than has been found to be true in cross-sectional studies (Sharkansky, 1968). As strong as these relationships are, however, superior explanations can be obtained if expenditures are not considered singly but are rather used in combination with a measure of economic resources. Thus, again we reinforce our basic assumption that the explanation of policy formation, in both the statistical and theoretical sense, is not so simple a task that any one variable or type of variable can be considered sufficient to provide the explanation. Rather, we should seek to find some parsimonious set of variables which can be used to provide a stronger explanation. Further, we should attempt theoretically and empirically to judge the dynamics of interaction among those variables in order to obtain some more useful description of the processes involved in public policy formation.

II SOCIAL RATIONALITY AND THE OPTIMAL ALLOCATION OF EXPENDITURES

Our analysis to this point has concentrated on explaining a single category of public expenditure: health expenditures. We could extend this analysis to include other categories of expenditure and compare the results with those for health, but this analysis might still avoid an important point in the policy process. Decisions on expenditures are not made in isolation, but rather are made comparatively. Given relatively restricted revenue sources, a decision to spend more money for one purpose implies a decision to spend less for some other purpose(s). The classic dichotomy of 'guns and butter' is certainly applicable, but decisions must also be made among various categories of both guns and butter. Thus, even within the relatively homogeneous category of social policy, there are choices which must be made between expenditures on health, education and social security. Thus, when we look at comparative rates of change, policies which appear linear and progressive may in fact be better described as cyclical or counter-cyclical, e.g., welfare.

Our question now becomes how we can measure and evaluate this type of allocative decision-making. Perhaps the easiest manner is to begin with an assumption of rationality on the part of the political decision-makers. That is, we will begin by assuming that decision-makers will act to maximize some value, working within the constraints of limited information and limited resources. For this analysis, we will posit that decision-makers act to maximize the objective social welfare of the population (Sharkansky, 1971). In other words, the decision-makers have some information concerning changes in objective conditions in the socio-economic environment, and will attempt to match policy changes to the needs created by the environmental changes. For example, an increase in the infant mortality rate would indicate a need for an increased allocation of resources to health care, while an increase in the rate of unemployment would signal a need for increased allocations for welfare and labor benefits.

The social rationality model is not one of several possible alternative models of rational behavior which could be applied to the same decisions. The most obvious competitor would be a model of political rationality in which political decision-makers manipulate the budget in order to maximize their probability of re-election (Williamson, 1967; Peters and Winters, 1974). In this case, we would be interested in measuring the changing demographic composition of the electorate as an indication of the 'needs' for a reallocation of expenditures among various purposes. This would have to be weighted by the level of mobilization and intensity on the part of those demographic elements.

To test a model of rationality such as this requires some method of judging optimal allocations of resources to competing purposes. The method for making such judgments in this case will be linear programming. Linear programming assumes that all variables are linearly and additively related; it maximizes or minimizes a numerical function of those variables subject to certain constraints. In doing this, it requires the input of three types of information. The first are activity vectors. These are the relationships between the particular commodity and the desired output. For example, in the classic diet problems, the activity vectors are the amount of protein, carbohydrates, fats and vitamins which would be supplied by one unit of any food (Dorfman, et al., 1958: 9-13). The second type of input is the cost of the commodity per unit. The final input is a set of inequalities. For example, in the classic diet problem, the inequalities are set at the minimal requirements of a human being for protein, etc. These three pieces of information can then be used to provide a desired output at a minimum of cost.

In the case of public policy, we will be interested in the optimal allocation of resources among competing governmental purposes. The commodities, instead of being different foods, will be budgetary allocations to different functional areas of government. The activity vectors will be defined by the relationships of these expenditures to service variables. These will be the standardized regression coefficients of each independent variable (expenditure) with each dependent variable (service) resulting from the iteration process for the removal of serial autocorrelation described in the appendix. The costs will, in this case, be negative costs or benefits. These benefits will be related to changes in certain measures of need for services of a particular type. For example, for expenditures for labor benefits, the best indicator for changes in the services provided will be the rate of unemployment (See Table 8 for a listing of the measures of need). As this fluctuates, so will the need of the government to spend on services to workers, especially unemployment benefits. Finally the inequalities will be simply that the government will spend more in year *t* than it did in year *t-1*. This is a fairly accurate description of the ratchet effect which is built into most spending programs (Peacock and Wiseman, 1961: 26-27). In addition, the total change in expenditures should not exceed the total changes in revenue and legal limits of indebtedness. (This may be a meaningless constraint in real life, in that debt limits are usually raised to meet expenditures. It will, however, place some reasonable limits on the results in our analysis.)

The above anlysis will provide a measure of the optimal allocation of expenditures among the competing uses available to a decision-maker — in this case five categories of social expenditures. These results can then be correlated with the actual patterns of expenditures to determine the degree of apparent rationality employed by the policy-makers. Further, the total period can be broken into smaller periods to determine if there have been changes in the budgetary style of the Swedish decision-makers. Finally, the residuals of the correlation between optimal and actual expenditures will constitute an interesting dependent variable in themselves, and we will use these to attempt to explain deviations from rational allocations by the policy-makers. Due to the constraints within which we were working, we have performed the linear programming analysis for every fifth year within the sample of 103 years, giving a total of 21 observations. These 21 observations will allow some preliminary investigation of the overall patterns of policy-making over the time period. Perhaps the first finding which should be reported is that feasible solutions could be found for the linear programs. Thus, even though there were a number of competing uses for the resources, and a rather complex set of interrelationships between the expenditures and services, the problems were solvable. In several years — mainly those since 1936 — these solutions required the introduction of slack variables but a feasible solution was possible (Dorfman, et al., 1958).

Beyond the simple observation that there were feasible solutions, we also found high longitudinal correlations of the absolute values of the expenditure variables developed by the linear programs with the actual values of those expenditures (see Table 10). This is to be expected, given that there was a strong pattern of increasing expenditures across time. Thus, even after the effects of time were removed through the iteration procedure, the general pattern of increases produced strong positive correlations. A more difficult test of these relationships is to correlate the sectoral allocations among the five expenditure categories. These correlations were also significant, with the exception of educational expenditures, although these correlations were not as high as those of the absolute values of expenditures. In a more specific sense, we find that for both types of expenditure variables the relationship of actual educational expenditures with the predicted expenditures were the lowest, while those of health were the highest. An examination of the residuals of the regressions indicate that there was a rather persistent overspending for education on the part of the government during the early portions of the total period. Although not as pronounced, there was also an underspending for labor, welfare and pensions during the early periods and some overspending during the later portions.

We also computed rank-order correlations (Spearman's rho) for the changes in expenditures derived from the linear programs and changes

TABLE 10
Correlations of Expenditures Derived from Linear Programs and Actual Expenditures

Absolute Values

Health	Education	Welfare	Pensions	Labor
.67*	.46*	.54*	.60*	.59*

Sectors

Health	Education	Welfare	Pensions	Labor
.53*	.22	.49*	.45*	.44*

* Statistically significant at the .05 level

in actual expenditures among the five functional expenditure categories. These rank-order correlations were not as strong as those found for the longitudinal analysis. The only years in which these correlations were significantly greater than zero were from 1906 to 1936. Before and after that time the correlations were quite low and in several cases were zero. Thus, the marginal adjustments made by decision-makers in the short-run do not demonstrate the level of correspondence to environmental change found in the longitudinal correlations.

When we again examine the patterns found for individual expenditure categories, we find corroboration for our earlier finding that decision-makers tended to greatly overspend for education during earlier portions of the 103 year period, and at the same time they tended to underspend for health and labor benefits. In the later portions of the period they tended to overspend on pensions and social welfare and to underspend for educational purposes. Further, despite the low overall values of the correlation coefficient of unemployment and labor expenditures reported above, the changes in labor expenditures here corresponded rather well to the changes which would be expected from an optimal linear solution.

These deviations from optimality do correspond quite well with what might have been expected from a knowledge of the characteristics of the political elite during the several portions of the total time period. The middle and upper class elite which dominated Swedish politics prior to the beginnings of reform in 1907 might have been expected to be more willing to spend money on public education than on any other social function. Not only might their own children be expected to derive benefits from those expenditures — especially since the secondary schools were filled almost entirely with children from these classes — but also a better educated workforce might be expected to pay economic dividends to the entrepreneurs as well as the nation as a whole. Likewise, the Social Democratic elite which has dominated Swedish politics since 1936 might be inclined to spend more than would otherwise be expected on social welfare and public pensions. However, unlike our assumptions in an earlier portion of this paper, it is not at all evident that these Social Democratic elites have been inclined to overspend for benefits to labor. Thus, the attempts of the Social Democrats to use the public budget as a means of satisfying their natural constituency have gone more in the direction of providing general social benefits rather than programs which might more directly benefit organized labor.

This brings us to question why the relatively brief period of 1906-36 should be characterized by such apparently high levels of social rationality in budgetary decision-making? There are several possible explanations. The first is that this was a period of great adjustment among a number of competing political and economic forces. The relative equality among these competing factions may have produced a greater degree of moderation in decision-making than might have been found otherwise. In a similar vein, although rather simple-minded, is the argument that this period of transformation was simply a period of transition from one type of overspending to another. During this brief period neither side was capable of producing the type of overspending they might have desired. A third possible explanation is that the Liberal Party, which was rather intimately involved in governing Sweden during this period of transition, was an important moderating force in decision-making. They were faced with a number of internal schisms which in turn may have aided in their ability to appreciate the larger schisms in the society. Thus, they may have been better able to balance the competing needs of a number of segments of the society to a greater degree than the preceeding or succeeding elite groups. Especially important also is their curtailing of defense expenditures and a consequent rechanneling of funds into social programs (Verney, 1972: 57).

These findings contitute a preliminary analysis of an exceedingly complex question. To attempt to assess the degree of social rationality exercised by decision-makers over such a long period of time is perhaps logically impossible. If, however, we can establish a strong degree of correspondence between optimal (in relationship to needs) allocations and actual allocations, we can also establish a strong presumption of social rationality. We have indicated that at least during some portions of the time period under investigation there was a correspondence between the optimal expenditures and actual expenditures which can not be attributed solely to random chance.

A further point to be made from this analysis is that political as well as social rationality must be taken into account in assessing the allocational quality of budgetary decisions. We have been assuming to this point that the patterns of budgetary allocations should correspond to patterns of social need. However, we must obviously take into account not only what society may objectively need, but also what it *believes* it needs. It is especially important that we take into account these needs as perceived by the decision-makers. Thus, the degree of rationality can perhaps be better assessed in relationship to needs as they are perceived by political actors. It is expected that the comparison of the politically optimal and the socially optimal allocation of expenditures will illustrate a good deal concerning the differences between politics as practised in Sweden (or any society) and the political sterility of the 'cybernetic state' (Schick, 1971).

SUMMARY AND CONCLUSIONS

We should first note that the model for explaining the development of social expenditures across time does receive some confirmation from the data. This confirmation is not as strong as we might like, but the basic structure of the model appears to be a usable means, at least in the short-run, of describing policy change at a macroscopic level. Social mobilization appears to trigger a series of events resulting in some eventual changes in social policy outputs. This confirmation exists only in a single society and testing is obviously needed in other settings. In terms of the basic models outlined at the outset of this volume, the dynamics of change are linear with respect to the set of independent variables included in the analysis.

Even more important are the results from each of the three smaller time periods. These findings have considerable importance for our understanding of the dynamics of policy change. Furthermore, they have importance for the development of more precise theoretical explanations of those changes. The most basic finding across these time periods is that there has been a decline of the direct influence of political mobilization on policy outputs and a concommitant increase in the influences of political institutions (Peters and Hennessey, 1973).

Along with the increasing influence of institutional factors in the political system is an increasing influence of economic resources, especially evident in the third period. On this basis, we can argue that there is a pattern that policies appear to follow during the course of their development. They begin as the products of direct political mobilization efforts and as the products of the classical demands being placed on the political system by the public. This period of mass mobilization is hypothesized to be crucial for defining the basic parameters of policy. Following the period of mass mobilization, the politics of policy becomes more incremental, more determined by internal bureaucratic politics, and more directly influenced by the availability of resources (Peters, 1972a). This policy cycle can, in fact, serve as a possible explanation for both the findings of the incrementalists and for the consistent findings of analysts of American state politics that policy is incremental and largely determined by the characteristics of the socio-economic environment. That is, once the basic parameters of policy are set, change will tend to be slight and related to changes in resources. The findings of incremental change by Davis et al. (1966), and of relationships with the economic environment by Dye (1966), Sharkansky (1967) and others would conform to our expectations of policy formation after mass mobilization. The choice of different time periods, or of different policies (e.g., civil rights or environmental protection in the US) would be expected to produce different results.

It is also interesting to note at this point that these findings are obviously influenced by historical developments common to all aspects of the political system and in fact most developed political systems. The above theoretical description of the policy process could also be taken as a description of the 'End of Ideology' as it applies to public policy (Rejai, 1971). While we certainly do not accept all the assumptions or conclusions of that body of literature, it is at least partially descriptive of political life in post-industrial political systems. In particular, there has been a decline of the traditional input mechanisms of the political system — especially of ideological political parties — and the development of a more institutionlized and regularized means of access to decision-making (Heisler, 1974). Thus, further research must focus on the degree to which our findings are descriptive of the policy process in general, as opposed to the extent to which they are a function of the time period of analysis, even one as long as this.

As we move from these findings toward a process model, there are several obvious places at which to begin to explore the greater complexities of the policy process. The first of these is an attempt to specify a threshold value at which social mobilization will begin to spill-over into changes in political mobilization and changes in policy. The regression models used above assume that any changes in any of the independent variables will have a direct and linear effect upon the dependent variable(s), and this assumption may not be supportable in reality. Relatively small changes in any of the indicators may not have any appreciable effects on the other variables in the model. In the short-run, however, the regression weights will serve as useful parameters with which to begin the construction and evaluation of a process model.

The second important modification of the model is the inclusion of both reciprocal causation and interaction more directly in the explanation. The mathematical methods suggested by Blalock offer one interesting means of beginning to specify the reciprocal effects and the conditions for stability (Blalock, 1969: 100-140). These methods can be further extended by the use of linear systems models and state-space analysis to deal with the interrelationships among the variables as analogues of physical systems (Timothy and Bona, 1968; Schwarz and Friedland, 1965). While our work with such models is still quite rudimentary compared with that of physical scientists, this analysis can be an important mathematical extension of our verbal conceptualizations of social and political phenomena as systems.

Finally, we must note the need to move from the analysis of policy development using a single dependent variable at a time to the study of policy development as an allocational process. We have already presented some evidence of the feasibility of such analysis, and further extensions and refinements are certainly possible. However, in terms of the construction of a process model, the allocation problem serves as an excellent means through which to link our knowledge of macro-level policy characteristics to our knowledge of micro-level political behavior. We can conceptualize the macro-level policy process as setting general parameters within which decisions are made concerning differential allocation of funds. Using a process model, we can plug in differing assumptions concerning the decision-making behavior of elites in the allocational process, always working within the broad parameters set by the general growth of economic resources and the influence of political mobilization and institutions.

APPENDIX A: METHODOLOGY

THE DATA

The data used for these tests of the assumptions of this model come from a compilation of statistics for Sweden prepared by the author and donated to the Inter-University Consortium for Political Research. The major sources are official statistical publications and records, these were cross-checked with several secondary sources. The major sources of data are:

Sveriges officiella statistisk, *Sammandrang.* (Stockholm: Kungliges Boktryckeriet, 1867-1914).
Statistiska Centralbyran, *Statistisk arsbok for Sverige* (Stockholm: Kungliges Boktryckeriet, 1914-1970).
Statistiska Centralbyran, *Historisk statistisk for Sverige,* I, 1, (Stockholm: Kungliges Boktryckeriet, 1968).
Statistiska Centralbyran, *Bidrag til Sveriges officiella statistisk: Valstatistisk* (Stockholm: Kungliges Boktryckeriet, 1872 to present).
Finans department, *Riks-stat och intilldess nasta statsreglering vidtager* (Stockholm: Kungliges Boktryckeriet, 1866 to present).
Erik Lindahl, Einar Dahlgren and Karin Koch, *National Income in Sweden 1861-1930* (Stockholm: P. A. Norstedt och Soner, 1937).

The data is taken on a year by year basis, covering a period of 103 years. The use of annual data presented no problem for the expenditure and policy data, which generally occur annually. For most political measures which might be used in this analysis, however, there are no annual observations. The most obvious example is voting data which is available only for election years. Two options are open in an analysis which is intended to be on an annual basis. The first is to use the value of the most recent event as the value of the variable in subsequent years. For example, there was an election in Sweden in 1914 and another in 1917. The number of voters and the number voting for the various parties would be used as the value of these political indicators in the years 1914, 1915, and 1916. This has the effect of reducing the variance of these indicators and therefore of reducing the levels of intercorrelations of these indicators with other variables. It further makes the unrealistic assumption that political feeling and predispositions do not change between elections. The second option for dealing with the non-annual data, which we have employed here, is to use a linear interpolation of the values from one event to the next. Assuming that the dynamics of change over the time between elections or other non-annual events were linear, we calculated a value of the variables for each time period. If our assumption of linearity is correct, then little bias will be introduced by this operation. This is further aided by the presence of relatively frequent elections (at most three successive annual values had to be calculated) and by a very large number of elections during periods of political stress, e.g., 1907-20 in Sweden. This provides more closely spaced observations during periods in which it is likely that political variables could be changing at exponential rather than linear rates.

STATISTICAL ANALYSIS

The basic means of testing these models is the use of linear correlation and regression. The results of that analysis will then be used in causal models using path analysis. In addition to the usual problems which that methodology may present, the use of time series data offers not only some more difficulties, but it also offers some unique opportunities. The additional problems which are presented have to do with the relationships of the variables to time and to other unmeasured variables which produce significant patterning of residuals, and the assumption that the error terms of the equations are not unrelated as is assumed by the statistical model. This is the problem of serial autocorrelation. The opportunities are those of being able to assess something more concerning causation given the presence of time series data and the ability to lag both independent and dependent variables to determine if indeed our assumptions of the temporal ordering of causation are accurate. We will deal with these two questions in order.

In any series of data across time, independent and dependent variables may be related not only by function of their true relationships, but may also share some joint relationship with time itself. Thus there frequently are very high intercorrelations of the variables which are not a true function of the relationship of the variables. In such a situation, the assumption (usually untested) that the residuals of the regression equation will be randomly distributed will be violated, and there will be a distinct patterning of the residuals across time. In such a situation, it is difficult to tell what portion of the variance explained in any regression equation is a result of systematic relationships with the independent variables (experimental variance) and what portion is a result of the systematic relationship with time (extraneous variance).

In order to correct for the problems of *serial autocorrelation* it must first be detected, and then the bias may be removed from the equation. There are several standard means of detecting the presence of autocorrelations, but we will rely on the most commonly used of these − the Durbin-Watson statistic. This statistic is used to test a null hypothesis of no serial autocorrelation, with values below the significance points allowing the rejection of the null hypothesis of no significant positive autocorrelation. Assuming that a significant value of the Durbin-Watson statistic is found, we must then proceed with a process for elimination of the bias. This again can be accomplished through several means, but perhaps the most efficient of these is the iteration technique proposed by Durbin. The residuals of the regression are first used to compute a new regression in the form:

$$u_t = q(u_t - 1) + e$$

The resultant regression coefficient q is then used to compute a regression in the form:

$$(Yt - qYt - 1) = (Xt - qXt - 1) + e$$

If the autoregressive structure is of the first order, the above regression should yield a randomly distributed set of residuals. If it is of a higher order, then successive iterations can be used to eliminate the patterning of the residuals, and to provide a true estimate of the relationships between the variables. We have used this procedure here and the values reported are for the first iteration without significant autocorrelation.

Cross-Lagging. One of the assumptions of a causal relationship is that changes in the assumed independent variable should precede change in the assumed dependent variable. In a cross-sectional analysis, this type of assumption cannot be directly tested. Given the long time span of our data, however, we can examine such relationships directly. This can be done through examining the degree of relationship between variables with first the independent variables in the direction hypothesized, the relationship with the independent variable lagged should be stronger than that with the hypothesized dependent variable lagged. In our analysis, the time lags can only be for integral values of years, and this will therefore involve an important assumption that these are appropriate intervals for the effects of causation to become apparent. This assumption is certainly questionable for most mass political events, where a shorter time lag appears appropriate, but in dealing with matters of public policy it is more acceptable. Most policies are made in an annual ritual, with the most important example being the annual budget. Likewise, the administration of most public programs also tends to work on an annual cycle. Thus, we feel relatively comfortable with the assumptions of an annual lag for determining temporal relationships among this set of variables. There are other techniques, most notably spectral analysis, which can be used to isolate patterns of temporal relationships, but the method of cross-lagging would appear more appropriate for the problems encountered in this data.

Path Analysis. Path analysis has by now become a sufficiently common technique of causal analysis in the social sciences that relatively little needs to be said by means of explanation, but perhaps a few words should still be said as an introduction to its use. In general, path analysis is a means of assessing the direct contribution which each independent variable makes to the statistical explanation of the dependent variable. A path coefficient is therefore directly interpretable as a measure of the influence which that independent variable has on the dependent variable, adjusting for the influences which the other independent variables included in the model may also have had. In that sense, the path coefficient is mathematically and logically equivalent to the beta weight in regression analysis. Path analysis, however, provides a means of linking a set of regressions together in order to construct an interpretive system, thus serving as a mathematical extension of verbal theory, as well as a means of testing that theory. Further, path analysis allows the computation of the indirect effects of each variable assumed to be causally prior to each dependent variable, and to compute the proportion of that effect which came through any one of several possible paths. For example, in our analysis, we will be able to ascertain

The raw material for the path analysis will be the results of the iterative regression analysis discussed above. Thus, each of the regressions used has the extraneous variable resulting from time-series relationships removed, at least to the point that there is no statistically significant trend among the residuals. We can therefore have some confidence that the assumption of uncorrelated error terms is not severely violated as it might be otherwise in time-series analysis.

Finally, we should note here that we will be extending the path analysis only so far as the level of social expenditures, and that indeed the test to be presented will be for a single type of social expenditures: expenditures for public health services. This was done because of the complexity of dealing with a large number of possible relationships within the context of the model, and the consequent confusion resulting from the presentation of an extremely large number of coefficients. The hypotheses concerning the levels of service will be tested through the presentation of results from time-series regressions.

REFERENCES

ANTON, T. (1969) 'Policy-Making and Political Culture in Sweden', *Scandinavian Political Studies* **4**, 88-102.

BLALOCK, H. (1969) Theory Construction. Englewood Cliffs, N.J.: Prentice-Hall.

BULL, E. (1922) 'Die Entwicklung der Arbeiterbewegung in der drei Skandinavischen Landern', Archive fur die Geschictedes Sozialismus und der Arbeiterbewegung, **10**, 329-361.

CASTLES, F. (1973) 'The Political Functions of Organized Groups: The Swedish Case', *Political Studies* **XXI**, 1 (Spring), 26-34.

CAULEY, J. and R. B. SHELTON (1973) 'National Defense and Legislative Decision-Making', Paper presented at Conference on Comparative Public Policy, University of Denver, Denver, Colorado (November)..

CUTRIGHT, P. (1965) 'Political Structure, Economic Development, and National Social Security Programs', *American Journal of Sociology* **70**, 4 (March) 537-550.

DAVIS, O. A., M. A. H. DEMPSTER, and A. WILDAVSKY (1966) 'A Theory of the Budgetary Process', *American Political Science Review* **60**, 3 (September) 529-547.

DEUTSCH, K. (1961) 'Social Mobilization and Political Development', *American Political Science Review* **55**, 3 (September) 493-514.

DEUTSCH, K. (1963) The Nerves of Government. New York: The Free Press.

DORFMAN, R., P. SAMUELSON, and R. SOLOW (1958) Linear Programming and Economic Analysis. New York: McGraw Hill.

DURBIN, J. (1960) 'Estimation of Parameters in Time-Series Regression', *Journal of Royal Statistical Society,* Series B, 22, 139-153.

DURBIN, J. and G. S. WATSON (1950) 'Testing for Serial Correlation in a Least-Squares Regression', *Biometrika,* **37**, 409-15.

DYE, T. (1966) Politics, Economics and the Public. Chicago: Rand McNally.

EASTON, D. (1965) A Systems Analysis of Political Life. New York: John Wiley.

FISHMAN, G. (1969) Spectral Methods in Econometrics. Cambridge: Harvard

University Press.

FOYER, L. (1961) 'Former för kontakt och Samverkan Mellan Staten och Organisationerna', Statens Offentliga Utredningar 1961: 21. Stockholm: SOU.

FRY, B. and R. WINTERS (1970) 'The Politics of Redistribution', *American Political Science Review* 64, (June) 508-23.

GALENSON, W. (1952) 'Scandinavia', in W. Galenson (ed.), Comparative Labor Movements. New York: Prentice Hall.

———, (1949) Labor in Norway. Cambridge: Harvard University Press.

GRILICKES, Z. and P. RAO (1969) 'Small Sample Properties of Several Two-Stage Regression Methods in the Context of Autocorrelated Errors', *Journal of the American Statistical Association* 36, (March) 253-72.

HEIDENHEIMER, A. J. (1973) 'The Politics of Public Education, Health and Welfare in the USA and Western Europe: How Growth and Reform Potentials Have Differed' , *British Journal of Political Science* 3, (July) 315-40.

HEISLER, M. (1974) 'The European Polity Model', in M. Heisler, et al., *Politics in Europe*. New York: David McKay.

HIMMELWEIT, H. T. (1954) 'Social Status and Secondary Education Since the 1944 Act: Some Data for London', in D. V. Glass (ed.), *Social Mobility in Britain* (London: Routledge and Kegan Paul), 141-159.

HOFFERBERT, R. (1966) 'The Relation Between Public Policy and Some Structural and Environmental Variable in the American States', *American Political Science Review* 80, 1 (March) 73-82.

HUNTINGTON, S. P. (1968) Political Order in Changing Societies. New Haven: Yale University Press.

INGLEHART, R. (1971) 'The Silent Revolution in Europe: Intergenerational Change in Post-Industrial Societies', *American Political Science Review* 65, 4 (December) 991-1017.

JOHNSTON, J. (1972) Econometrics Methods (2nd Edition). New York: McGraw-Hill.

JOURNAL OF POLITICAL ECONOMY (1972) Special Issue on 'Investment in Education: The Equity/Efficiency Quandry'.

KLINGMAN, C. D. (1973) 'Economic Development, Political Labor Movements and Public Policy: A Quantitative Comparison of Time-Series Indicators from Norway and Sweden', Unpublished Ph.D. Dissertation, Department of Political Science, Michigan State University.

LAFFERTY, W. M. (1971) Economic Development and the Response of Labor in Scandinavia: A Multilevel Analysis. Oslo: Universitets forlaget.

LAND, K. C. (1969) 'Principles of Path Analysis', in E. F. Borgatta (ed.), Sociological Methodology 1969. San Francisco: Jossey Bass.

MARTIN, F. M. (1954) 'An Inquiry into Parent's Preferences in Secondary Education', in D. V. Glass (ed.) Social Mobility in Britain. London: Routledge and Kegan Paul.

MEIJER, H. (1969) 'Bureaucracy and Policy Formation in Sweden', *Scandinavian Political Studies* 4, 103-16.

MILLER, W. L. and M. MACKIE (1973) 'The Electoral Cycle and Asymmetry of Government and Opposition Popularity: An Alternative Model of the Relationships Between Economic Conditions and Political Popularity', *Political Studies* XXI, 3 (September) 263-79.

NAGEL, S. (1974) 'Minimizing Costs and Maximizing Benefits in Providing Legal

Services to the Poor', *Sage Papers on Administrative and Policy Sciences.*
Beverly Hills: Sage.

NISKANEN, W. A. (1971) Bureaucracy and Representative Government.
Chicago: Aldine/Atherton.

PEACOCK, A. J. and J. WISEMAN (1961) The Growth of Public Expenditures in
the United Kingdom. Princeton: Princeton University Press.

PETERS, B. G. (1972a) 'Political and Economic Effects on the Development of
Social Expenditures in France, Sweden and the United Kingdom', *Midwest
Journal of Political Science* 16 (May) 225-238.

---, (1972b) 'Public Policy, Socioeconomic Conditions and the Political
System: A Note on Their Developmental Relationship', *Polity* 5 (Winter)
277-284.

---, (1974) 'The Development of Social Policy in France, Sweden and the
United Kingdom', in Martin Heisler (ed.), Politics in Europe. New York: David
McKay.

---, and T. M. HENNESSEY (1973) 'Political Development and Public Policy in
Sweden, 1865-1967', Paper presented at Conference on Comparative Public
Policy, Denver, Colorado (November).

---, and Richard F. WINTERS (1974) 'A Rational Theory of the Budgetary
Process', unpublished paper, University of Delaware.

REJAI, M. (1971) Decline of Ideology? Chicago: Aldine/Atherton.

ROSE, R. (1973) 'Models of Governing', *Comparative Politics* 4 (July) 465-96.

ROSE, R. (1973a) 'Comparing Public Policy: An Overview', *European Journal of
Political Research,* J, 1 67-94.

RUSTOW, D. (1955) The Politics of Compromise. Princeton: Princeton University Press.

SCHICK, A. (1971) 'Toward the Cybernetic State', in D. Waldo (ed.), Public
Administration in a Time of Turbulence. Scranton, Pa.: Chandler.

SCHWARZ, R. and J. B. FRIEDLAND (1965) Linear Systems. New York:
McGraw Hill.

SHAPIRO, D. L. (1973) 'Can Public Investment Have a Positive Rate of Return?'
Journal of Political Economy 81, 2 (March/April) 401-13.

SHARKANSKY, I. (1967) 'Government Expenditures and Public Services in the
American States', *American Political Science Review* 61, 4 (December)
1066-77.

---, (1968) Spending in the American States. Chicago: Rand-McNally.

---, (1970) 'Environment, Policy, Output and Impact: Problems of Theory and
Method in the Analysis of Public Policy', in I. Sharkansky (ed.), Policy
Analysis in Political Science. Chicago: Markham.

---, (1971) 'Economic Theories of Public Policy: Resource Policy and Need-
Policy Linkages Between Income and Welfare Benefits', *Midwest Journal of
Political Science* 15 (November) 722-40.

STROTZ, R. H. and H. O. WOLD (1960) 'Recursive and Nonrecursive Systems:
An Attempt at Synthesis', *Econometrica* 28 (1960) 417-27.

STROUSE, J. C. and J. O. WILLIAMS (1972) 'A Non-Additive Model for State
Policy Research', *Journal of Politics* 34, 2 (May) 648-57.

TILTON, T. (1974) 'The Social Origins of Liberal Democracy: The Swedish Case',
American Political Science Review, 68 (June) 561-571.

TIMOTHY, L. K. and B. E. BONA (1968) State Space Analysis. New York:

McGraw Hill.

VERNEY, D. (1957) Parliamentary Reform in Sweden 1866-1921. Oxford: Clarendon Press.

———, (1972) 'The Foundations of Modern Sweden: The Swift Rise and Fall of Swedish Liberalism', *Political Studies* **20** (March) 42-59.

WILLIAMSON, Oliver (1967) 'A Rational Theory of the Budgetary Process', *Papers on Non-Market Decision Making* **2** Charlottesville, Va.: Thomas Jefferson Center.

WRIGHT, S. (1960) 'The Treatment of Reciprocal Interaction With or Without dog in Path Analysis', *Biometrics* **16** (September 423-45.

Chapter VI

FOREIGN WORKERS
AS A SOURCE OF SOCIAL CHANGE

Ernst Gehmacher

Institute for Empirical Social Research,
Vienna

Industrial growth in every Northern European nation in the 1960s
brought with it a stream of Southern European immigrants from
low-wage lands extending from Portugal and Spain to Greece and
Turkey. In host countries, they were welcomed because they reduced
the problems of labour shortage. In the countries of emigration, their
move was welcomed because they sent back a portion of their earnings
and often brought back new skills to their native land. In short-run
terms, the increase in foreign workers followed a path of linear progress
upward. An economist viewing the problem in the longer term might
expect a pattern of cyclical change, as the proportion of foreign
workers rose and fell with the ups and downs of the host economy, and
with the relative advantages of working at home or abroad. This is also
more or less the official view taken of the problem in the host
countries. Yet from a social perspective, the arrival of large numbers of
workers alien in many respects – language, religion, customs and, not
least, in their lack of citizenship – meant that the host society would
be subject to a fundamental discontinuity, either through becoming a
multi-racial society by the integration of workers from a different
cultural background, or by becoming a society dependent, in part, upon
an 'underclass' recruited from abroad and potentially vulnerable to
removal.

In short, population movements commenced for the simplest and
narrowest of economic motives have major implications for the social

system of both emigrant and host society. From a systemic perspective, changes in one part of the economy can lead to unexpected and significant changes in society or in the polity. The purpose of this study is to examine rigorously and from a variety of points of view the chief pressures created by foreign workers upon the social system, and to consider alternative scenarios arising from different choices affecting the future employment of foreign workers, especially the alternatives of integrating foreign workers (and their families) as against a policy of rotating foreign workers to avoid the problems of integration. While the study[1] draws primarily upon Austria for examples and data, the problems and relationships depicted are common to many Northern European nations and, in some, such as Germany, a major magnet for foreign workers in the 1960s, even more intense and important.

The overall system of foreign manpower comprises the national social systems of the Central European host countries and of the Mediterranean countries of origin. Although allowance must be made for diversity, the host countries are without exception social systems subject to the economic processes of a by-and-large free economy, but whose political mechanisms seek to maintain the distribution of costs and benefits within a given social field and to preserve a consensus within the society.

Within this overall system foreign manpower employment has the following immediate effects — and up to now it has also been primarily motivated by these effects, since mutual relationships very often function as control mechanisms:

i)   The free influx of manpower allows the development of production without bottle-necks in the labour supply, thus permitting maximum economic growth.

ii)   Regional differences in economic development potential and favorable location are exploited in the cheapest short-term way through the migration of manpower to areas of greatest economic utility.

iii) To the degree that incoming foreign workers enter the lowest social class and fill socially undesirable jobs which could otherwise be filled only with great difficulty, foreign manpower employment favors constant upward mobility, which is deeply anchored in the ideology of competitive industrial society and the realization of which confers a strong sense of purpose permitting all kinds of stress to be more easily endured. Foreign workers make it possible for more natives to rise socially and their foreignness makes this rise especially visible.

iv) By migrating into growth centres foreign workers reduce the basic problem of the developing regions they leave, where inequitable economic and social conditions exist — how to respond to the pressure of a semi-industrial population growing due to medical and hygienic progress? If there was not the safety valve of emigration, political stability would be threatened.

It is interesting to note that this migratory movement deeply anchored in long-term processes and part of the continuing boom of the last two decades in European industrial nations has been regarded as a temporary phenomenon. This attitude is neatly expressed by the German designation for foreign worker, *Gastarbeiter,* which literally means 'guest worker'. This assumption derives from the increased ease of movement back and forth between countries; it also reflects a latent uneasiness at having committed oneself to intensifying concentration at a time when the strongest apprehensions about the tendency to concentration of an economically directed society were making themselves heard. For a long time the fiction was maintained that foreign workers were only a stop-gap and could be sent home again at any time.

Today it has generally become clear that employment of foreign manpower would not cease even in an economic crisis, since native manpower would no longer be willing to fill the socially undesirable jobs now held by foreign workers. Because of this situation foreign workers are very quickly becoming a structural component of the economy in areas of economic growth. If the employment of foreign workers is controlled by economic relationships alone, a nation can attain very high growth rates and also a very high proportion of foreign workers in the work force before it reaches limits immanent in these mechanisms.

One basic limit to foreign workers is the profitability of foreign labour. The additional economic value created by the foreign workers provides an advantage for the native population only as long as the foreign workers do not themselves consume all of the extra resources they create. This condition is fulfilled for the entrepreneur by the profit margin from the employment of foreign manpower and from the market growth resulting from consumption by foreign workers, and for native unskilled workers by higher job status in relation to the foreign workers.

This latter point means that native unskilled workers benefit from the employment of foreign workers only as long as the foreign workers hold low status socially undesirable jobs. If all less skilled jobs, as far as is practically possible, are held by foreign workers, and if foreign workers start taking over highly skilled jobs, then individual competition develops with the native worker. At this point a limit for this social group has been reached beyond which the employment of foreign workers becomes directly disadvantageous.

Limits upon foreign workers are directly operative in the existing socio-economic system: there is no need for specific planning — the social control mechanism could be sufficient. If the influx of foreign manpower is greater than the need created by economic growth and the development of the population, unemployment is the result. This will affect the natives and can not be eliminated by simply sending away less skilled foreigners. In such a situation, however, the influx of foreign workers would be curbed and the employment of foreign manpower would at least be stabilized if not reduced. Likewise, resistance to further expansion of foreign manpower would reach its full impact as soon as foreign workers began to compete with natives for better and more highly skilled jobs: this would be the case when all less skilled jobs are held by foreign workers and the influx continues.

The control mechanisms are based on a directly visible infringement of the interests of the unskilled native labour force. They presuppose, therefore politically efficient representation for native employees in the host countries. This does in principle exist, although the effectiveness of this representation varies from case to case.

In addition to the basic control mechanism demonstrated here, there are a series of other effects caused by foreign manpower employment. At the present time these effects are not so crucial because they produce results only in the long run; their cost-benefit structure is difficult to estimate; and they affect interests which are of little or no immediate effect in the overall system.

The following relationships may be viewed as effects of this kind:

i)   Foreign manpower delays or prevents changes in the economic structure which would result from a reduced supply of less skilled manpower in areas of concentration. *(Structural effect)*

ii) Foreign workers reduce marginal technological rationalization which would only be profitable where manpower is scarce.[2] *(Rationalization curb)*

iii) Foreign manpower employment has an anti-egalitarian effect because it creates a socio-economic lower class in areas of growth. It increases income and status differences, depresses wages in the low-wage sector and drives up wages in the high-wage sector. *(Equality curb)*

iv) Likewise, in the countries of origin, changes in the structure of the labour market and in the composition of labour skills produce effects dependent to a high degree on the economic and social development tendencies in countries of immigration. *(Development effects in countries of origin)*

v) Like all rapid increases of population, the influx of foreign workers entails significant longer term infrastructure and social costs. Since foreign workers initially create relatively low costs — they arrive in their best working years and for the time-being make fewer demands on the host country than native workers — increased infrastructure and social costs fall due later. *(Long term social costs)*

vi) Foreign manpower required mutual adjustment of the host population and the foreign workers. A variety of assimilation and integration phenomena occur in this process. The most serious effect might be the formation of new minorities and subcultures within the overall system. This effect could only be minimized through a foreign manpower strategy of complete integration or of pure rotation. Such absolute foreign manpower strategies seems, however, to be most unlikely. *(Minority formation)*

vii) The presence of foreign workers alters the entire social structure and the political system. The prejudices and aversions of the native population in the host areas interact with the ideas and values that integrated foreign workers bring to their new homeland. On a long-term basis foreign workers could profoundly influence the historical development of the host countries. Parallel to this development, political pressures must also be expected from returning emigrants to their countries of origin. *(Political effects)*

In turn, each of these complexes affects the overall system. Population change, for example, affects the quality of life, economic concentration, and the political balance of power. The economic differentiation effect (equality curb) cuts deeply into the way of life and into the political decision-making process; in some cases, it can also influence the social costs resulting from increased stress or criminality.

BASIC CONTROL MECHANISM

The basic control mechanism can lead to a large linear increase in the number of foreign workers over a period of time. If the economic growth potential of a national economy allows an annual manpower increase of three percent, whereas the national labour market produces only one percent additional labour per annum, the remainder will be filled up by foreign workers — if growth potential is the only steering force of the system. This would raise — as Table 1 shows — the foreign workers rate to nine percent within six years, and to 31 percent within 20 years. This may seem an extreme assumption, but up to now the Austrian rate of increase is not far from such a figure. (Table 1).

TABLE 1

Theoretical growth of foreign manpower, given economic growth of 6 percent, productivity increase of 3 percent and natural growth of the domestic work force of 1 percent

Years	Total force	Native workers	Foreign workers	Foreign workers %	Proportion of foreign workers actually in Austria	
					Year	%
1	100,000	100,000	Nil	Nil		
2	103,000	101,000	2,000	1.9	1969	2.6
3	106,090	102,010	4,080	3.8	1970	4.0
4	109,270	103,030	6,240	5.7	1971	6.8
5	112,550	104,060	8,490	7.5	1972	7.4
6	115,930	105,100	10,830	9.3	1973	8.7

Such a growth of foreign manpower, which other considerations would make impossible in larger regions, might very well become a reality for single cities or regions. Accordingly, in the final analysis, the critical value in the basic control mechanism is not the growth potential of the economy but the filling up of lower skilled jobs — and the accompanying threat of competition for the natives. Statistics in hand indicate that in Austria the filling up of less skilled jobs has already reached an advanced stage. (Table 2).

TABLE 2

Unskilled workers by economic sectors (Austrian enterprises sample survey 1973)

Nr.	Enterprises with 15 or more employees	Total unskilled workers	of which foreigners	foreigners %	enterprises with more than 50 employed %
031	Foods and beverages	20,954	4,751	22.7	
033	Textiles and textile products	37,656	12,995	34.5	
039	Musical instruments, sporting goods and toys	3,045	953	31.3	46.3
052	Metal processing, steel and light metal construction	5,539	2,114	38.2	
053	Fabricated metal products	18,646	7,136	38.3	
054	Machinery	14,722	4,427	30.1	46.1
058	Transportation equipment	11,542	2,433	21.1	
059	Precision instruments and related products	3,082	1,112	36.1	
061	Construction	50,565	17,051	33.8	50.3
078	Hotel and food service	9,480	4,259	44.9	49.6

1 *Structural Effects*

Technological obsolescence of jobs and of entire enterprises occurs in an expanding and technologically progressive economy. When a job becomes unprofitable at given wage levels, since workers are on the look-out for better paid jobs and find them, it must either be made more productive through rationalization, shifted to an area with a lower wage level, or be given up. If foreign manpower can be got at lower wages, then the job can continue. This represents a profit for the economy and for the enterprise since they can prolong use of existing investments. Such preservation of less productive jobs becomes questionable when new investments are undertaken in less productive low-wage areas, inhibiting an increase in economic productivity. A consumption pattern, particularly in service trades, is perpetuated which relies strongly on cheap labour, as foreign domestic servants, shop personnel, street vendors — and thus impedes the development of more rationalized service forms; the command over 'personal servants' may grow quickly into a habit contrary not only to productivity but also to democratic ideals.

Stagnation of technological development as the result of employing cheap foreign manpower occurs first in economically backward areas with a less mobile work force. The surest way to prevent negative structural effects of the kind described is an active wage policy on the part of labour. Negative structural effects can also be combatted by measures to promote mobility and by a regional policy which aims at improving the economic structure by encouraging industrial relocation. In general, foreign workers are very mobile. They seldom remain in decidedly underpaid jobs and migrate quickly to growth centres with a more promising job market. They linger at their first place of work under unfavorable conditions only as long as they pledged themselves to do so at the time they were recruited in their country of origin. Therefore, the higher the rate of rotation, the greater will be the opportunity to employ foreign manpower at low wages.

Even structural effects which do not yet seriously endanger the progressive increase of productivity can lead to the preservation of sectors of the economy which would otherwise migrate to other countries or yield to a more modern technology. As Adrian H. Gnehm has shownn,[3] in Switzerland the primary and secondary sectors must be depleted by migration to the tertiary sector. Because of the possibility of replacing migrating workers in the production of goods with foreign manpower, the shifting between the sectors of the economy slows down, and slows down more as the number of immigrating foreigners increases.

TABLE 3

Employed Persons in Austria as of 31 July 1950 and 1970

| | Employed (in thousands) | | Percent | |
	1950	1970	1950	1970
Primary economic sectors (agriculture, forest products, mining)	292	129	14.8	5.3
Secondary economic sectors (manufactures)	923	1,131	46.7	46.5
Tertiary economic sectors (commerce, transportation, services)	763	1,173	38.5	48.2

The employment of foreign manpower in Austria has helped the manufacturing sector — and most foreign workers are employed in this sector — to increase its production considerably. (Table 3). In Germany and in Switzerland this development is even more strongly marked, because in Austria foreign workers are also playing a significant role in the hotel and food service industry.

Accordingly, there is no question but that without the employment of foreign manpower an essentially different economic development would have resulted. The socially undesirable jobs in the manufacturing sector and in the service industries would have become significantly more difficult to fill, and more expensive. Some jobs might have disappeared as a result of automation and others through plant relocation to developing countries.

The employment of foreign manpower also causes basic price relationships and consumption patterns to shift. The provision of long-term consumer goods, which in the course of a few years has also created acute problems of transportation, environmental protection, energy supply, and scarcity of raw materials in Austria, would hardly have taken place so quickly if it had not been possible to maintain the cheapness of the secondary sector of the economy. In comparison with manufactures, many more services and goods based on highly skilled workmanship would have remained relatively low-priced were it not for the structural effect of foreign manpower employment.

The structural effects of foreign manpower employment have also encouraged a strongly materialistic orientation to life. Without foreign manpower employment autos, fancy goods, technical gadgets and mass-produced articles would be more expensive, but restaurants, school instruction, books and handmade art objects would be relatively cheaper than they are today.

After the shock of the 1973 oil crisis, it is no longer necessary to explain that a strengthening of qualitative growth would create fewer problems and be more favorable to the quality of life than an increase of purely material growth.

2 Rationalization Curb

The effect of foreign manpower on rationalization is closely connected with structural effects. It can also be viewed apart from this, for foreign manpower also produces certain effects on technological development under average (not marginal) conditions.

Critical values for the rationalization curb occur only at the level of individual firms; that is, within the framework of an enterprise or of a division of an enterprise. A given number of foreign workers in an economy can therefore at a given time produce an effect promoting rationalization, but at another time can act as a strong curb on rationalization. A strictly observed sectoral quota system – as is provided for in Austrian foreign manpower policy – can at least reduce the more massive structural effects and work against the continuation of low-wage output, when it is supported by an efficient regional policy and by an effective wage policy on the part of labour.

This means, however, that where a strong labour wage policy and an efficient regional policy (possibly supported by measures to promote investments) exist, the critical zone of the rationalization curb need not yet have been reached, even when foreign manpower is employed almost to the limit of economic growth potential. The creation of efficient political and economic mechanisms to deal with foreign manpower is of greater importance than determining the critical limits of foreign manpower employment.

3 *Equality Curb*

Closely connected with the structural effects of foreign manpower is its curb on equality. Foreign workers hold socially undesirable jobs and therefore occupy the lowest class in the social hierarchy. They are willing to do this because even the lowest position on the scale of the host country can still signify social advancement for them within their own social reference group, e.g., the village community or the extended family (clan) in their home country. As long as foreign workers are not socially integrated into the population of the host country, they compare themselves primarily with their own countrymen. Accordingly, apart from the small percentage who integrate quickly or who push their way to a higher social position by virtue of a special skill or special ability, foreign workers form a lower social class.

Foreign manpower employment clearly retards the formation of the relatively egalitarian social structure, which is typical of all more highly developed industrial nations. Such an egalitarian social structure is characterized by the presence of ever smaller remnants of a real lower class and by increasing pressure on the upper classes to conform to the competitive ethos and to the life style of the broad middle classes.

The gradual levelling process of technological society would only slowly free the native lower class by degrees from their disadvantaged situation. The influx of foreign workers into socially undesirable jobs raises them into the middle class much more quickly and with perhaps fewer demands on their capacities. But this occurs only as long as significant numbers of foreign workers are not able to penetrate the lower ranks of the middle classes and compete with socially mobile natives. When that occurs, the basic control mechanism is activated. The critical limit of relative tolerance coincides with the filling up of socially undesirable jobs by foreign workers: real competition could produce massive aggressiveness.

In the presence of an immigrant minority, the lower middle classes strongly regard the lower class of foreign workers as primitive and less cultivated and keep aloof from them. This behavior, in turn, reinforces the readiness of the lower middle classes to acknowledge the superiority of an elite. The self-esteem which in an egalitarian society does not permit recognition of the dominance of an upper class, now finds expression in contempt for the foreign workers. The upper middle class would have no interest in the formation of a new lower social class since even in a strongly egalitarian society it would still command sufficient status and has correspondingly less feelings about foreign workers.

The patterns of prejudice correspond to class interests: the upper middle class proves to be more tolerant and benevolent toward the foreign workers than the lower middle class but is sooner prepared to dispense with foreign manpower employment altogether.[4] The white collar employee and the skilled worker are contemptuous of foreigners, but nonetheless consider them necessary and useful.

This explanation of prejudices on the basis of class interests is in complete accord with the theory of prejudices. Indeed, prejudices and stereotypes are simplified group judgments against entire social categories which ignore the very great differences among individuals. Such group judgments may not in fact correspond to the real interests of the group but they reflect at least their imaginary interests.

It is not our purpose to determine what the objective interests of foreign workers themselves may be. For this purpose too little information about the life chances of foreign workers in their home countries is available. It may very well be true that the majority are better off belonging to the lower class of a modern industrial society than to the lower class of an over-populated, technologically underdeveloped agricultural society. However, whether this conjecture would also be valid for their children, who may have become rootless between two cultures or who grow up in broken families, is another matter.

If it is assumed that deficient socialization would only cause every tenth child to become gravely anti-social (criminal or unable to perform normal work because of personality disturbances) and that only children who grew up in the host country would be affected then, based on present conditions, within approximately 10 years every 100 foreign workers would generate five anti-social persons; in 30 years, 15 (since it must be taken into account that anti-social persons will burden society for at least 30 years). If the proportion of foreign workers remains constant at 10 percent of the population, the deficient socialization of foreign workers' children would burden the population with an additional 1.5 percent of anti-social persons; where the proportion of foreign workers is 20 percent however, the proportion of anti-social persons in the population would jump up by 3.0 percent.[5]

Finally, the functional requirements of society in the host country must be taken into consideration. The gradual levelling of social hierarchies represents a higher cultural development. This higher development can only take place in conjunction with economic progress, growth of productivity and improvement of the educational level. As long as the necessities of life remain scarce and most work is regarded as an unpleasant burden, functionally determined inequalities will become evident, even when political equality has been ordained by decree. Without the intellectual ability to participate in the decision-making processes, formal equality can not be transformed into equality of influence. The progress of equality is therefore closely connected with the progress of productivity, with the development of skills and with improvement of the cultural level.

A modest influx of foreign workers could step up this positive progress — by consolidating economic progress and by intensifying the challenge to the educational system, especially within the framework of a culturally integrative foreign manpower policy — which provides ample provisions for the education of foreign workers' children. However, the formation of a large culturally isolated lower class would clearly reverse the trend to equality. The critical limit might very well be reached when foreign manpower filled approximately half of all socially undesirable jobs.

4 *Country of Origin Effects*

In the overall system of manpower migration, effects on countries of origin play a decisive role. At the present time all countries of origin are interested in mitigating their labour problems by exporting manpower. This will continue to be the case until stepped-up economic development in countries of origin increases domestic manpower needs and/or countries of origin discover that by exporting migrant labor they are creating difficult social problems for themselves.

Countries of origin hope to speed up their own economic development with the help of returned migrant workers who bring know-how and an industrial work morale home with them. To what degree these expectations will be fulfilled cannot yet be fully foreseen. Those Mediterranean countries of origin which have been exporting manpower longest are beginning to fear that the best workers, and many more than was expected, have been permanently lost to the host countries. This development jeopardizes to a certain degree the value of the substantial amounts of foreign exchange remitted by workers abroad; in the case of Yugoslavia, for example, this is greater than foreign exchange receipts from tourism.

It must be reckoned that the resistance of countries of origin to exporting manpower will grow considerably with the passage of time. Especially in the case of a pronounced rotation strategy, this could imply significant problems for the host country. Let us assume, for example, that countries of origin take sweeping political measures which suddenly reduce the influx of foreign workers by half, and that a quarter of all foreign workers – those who have been in the host country for less than five years – are called home. (It would probably not be possible to influence foreign workers who have been in the host country for more than five years.) This is a very simplified example of an event which could one day occur on approximately such a scale. Under the conditions noted below such a situation would produce a potentially significant contraction of the work force. (Table 4).

Only an intensive integration policy would secure a host country from the dangers of the acute tightening of the manpower situation resulting from sudden changes in the migration policy of the countries of origin. This would be especially true if all or most of the countries of origin acted jointly on the basis of a fundamental reappraisal of their own interests. While a functioning political community might still be able to adjust to a sudden increase in manpower requirements of one to two percent (though not without massive inflationary tendencies and difficulties in low-wage enterprises), the sudden loss of four to five percent of the entire work force – affecting above all socially undesirable jobs – would lead to a genuine economic crisis, which could only be countered by government intervention. It is difficult to avoid comparison with the situation at the end of 1973 when the threat of a decline in the energy supply triggered emergency measures everywhere in Europe.

In a climate of international understanding where common interests in the extended economic region exist, such extremely restrictive

TABLE 4

Estimates of the Effects of Different Migration Policies

Proportion of foreign workers to total work force	Contraction of the total work force assuming	
	Rotation policy %	Integration policy %
5 percent	1.9	0.6
10 percent	3.7	1.2
15 percent	5.6	1.9
20 percent	7.5	2.5
30 percent	11.2	3.7
Definition of assumptions	**Rotation policy**	**Integration policy**
Average length of stay	2.5 years	10.0 years
Yearly replacement rate as a percentage of foreign workers present in host country	40 percent	10 percent
Proportion of foreign workers who have been in the host country for less than five years	70 percent	30 percent

measures may very well not come from countries of origin. But it must be expected that countries of origin will endeavor to get as high a price as possible for their manpower.

This price might take the form of direct compensation for manpower procurement (manpower leasing, compensatory charges for training received in the country of origin, etc.) but it might also take the form of requests for support of the economy (industrial relocation to countries of origin, technical advice, return of well-trained skilled workers to the developing industries of the countries of origin, etc.). This could develop into an independent control mechanism. The more expensive foreign manpower becomes as the result of such return services — in a free economy the costs would be apportioned to enterprises employing foreign manpower — the less foreign manpower would be taken on. A slowly operating control mechanism of this kind could avoid the crises which might otherwise be expected from arbitrary changes in the foreign manpower policy of countries of origin. Even in the case of such continuing adjustment processes, however, a host country is much less susceptible to crises the more its foreign manpower policy favors integration and the lower its proportion of foreign workers may be.

Tolerably clear rules for avoiding critical limits emerge from these considerations. If, in the interest of its economic development, a region aims at (or can not avoid) a proportion of foreign workers of more than 20 percent, it should pursue a positive integration policy — as indeed traditional countries of immigration have always done. If a proportion of foreign workers under five percent is desired, a pure rotation policy with strong fluctuation and control of the influx seems justifiable. For intermediate goals a mixed strategy seems to be adequate.

5 *Long-term Social Costs*

Foreign workers are especially profitable manpower insofar as they give rise to few infrastructure costs. If a corresponding number of native workers were to be procured by raising the birth rate it would be necessary to make immense investments in the form of child and family welfare payments, kindergartens, and schools, public health and medical services, housing, etc. Foreign workers arrive in the host country as prefabricated manpower.

It must, however, be borne in mind that the majority of these infrastructure services will have to be provided later on. The costs are only shifted into the future, when foreign workers begin sending their children to kindergartens and to school or when, with increasing age, they begin to demand medical and social services, housing, and various other community services for themselves. These delayed infrastructure costs can become very great, especially with an increasing number of foreign workers and with increased family relocation. Under these conditions the original economic profitability of employing foreign manpower can be jeopardized.

In 1973 IFES carried out a cost-benefit analysis of these delayed costs up to the year 1990 for the Vienna City Government.[6] The same procedure was also used for Salzburg to estimate the delayed social costs resulting from foreign manpower employment (compared with the value-added created by foreign manpower) which would accrue for the years 1980, 1985 and 1990, if a proportional increase in the number of employed of one percent (restrictive growth) or of three percent (expansive growth) were to be maintained by means of foreign manpower.

On the basis of explicit cost and benefit assumptions the two different strategies produced the economic cost and benefit values described in Table 5. The estimates are only as valid as the assumptions they contain. On a few points, depending on the measures taken, reactions of the foreign workers, and economic development, considerably different values could be arrived at. The model could easily accommodate very different assumptions in order to test the consequences of various conditions and strategies. A single case is presented here to illustrate how the model functions.

TABLE 5

Results of the cost-benefit analysis of the economic profitability of employing foreign workers

Work force growth rate	Number of foreign workers	Benefit demand per foreign worker in AS 1000	Cost (Value 1970) AS 1000	Balance per foreign worker AS 1000
Rotation policy *Vienna*				
1985 zero growth of foreign workers	97,000	200	134	66
1990 zero growth of foreign workers	97,000	206	138	68
Salzburg				
1985 1 percent	21,500	216	145	71
1990 1 percent	25,300	218	146	72
1985 3 percent	48,500	203	138	65
1990 3 percent	62,200	213	143	70
Integration policy 1985 zero growth of foreign workers	97,000	220	159	61
1990 zero growth of foreign workers	97,000	229	162	67

These computations clearly show that from an economic point of view the employment of foreign manpower is unquestionably worthwhile for the host country even when delayed infrastructure costs are taken into consideration. An integration policy produces more economic benefit but requires greater social expenditures; on balance, the rotation policy would be slightly cheaper.

6 Minority Formation

Foreign workers with different cultures and languages form

minorities in the host country. Only complete integration ends membership of a minority group. A few studies of the ability of foreign workers to integrate and of the process of integration in the German-speaking countries, and in Austria in particular, are now available. They indicate that the integration of foreign workers, who by and large plan to return to their homeland and to whom no specific integration aids have been offered, takes place more slowly than is the case with traditional immigrants. To be sure, this is the case only for the foreign workers themselves. The children of foreign workers, if they go to school in the host country and make social contacts, have many more changes of integration. The children of foreign workers who do not succeed in adapting linguistically and socially have much to endure. They do not become properly socialized in either culture and remain excluded from both: the crime and neurosis rate among such people is above average.

It is difficult to determine critical size limits for a minority. Basically, there are none. There are many historical examples of various cultures and peoples living closely side by side in one territory and, indeed, under the most varied conditions – as rulers and ruled; as different castes and vocational groups; in the most favourable circumstances as equals in completely separate settlements; or in the melting pot of large cities. Minorities can be accepted and, regardless of their size, live in a country without causing destructive tensions. But two kinds of danger constantly threaten the stability of such arrangements:

a) Social and political groups may use the minority as a scapegoat and make it a target for frustrations and tensions caused by completely different problems *(incited aggression)*.
b) In striving to attain a better place in society the minority may infringe on the interests of other groups and thereby generate conflicts *(reactive aggression)*.

It would be necessary to spend considerable sums for effective measures to prevent such negative developments. Foreign manpower would have to be burdened with financing continual educational and public information campaigns as well as of other purposeful measures. The prevention of serious social tensions belongs to the necessary long-term costs of foreign manpower.

Education and information alone will not suffice to prevent reactive aggression against the rapid and marked access to power of a foreign worker minority, especially in critical situations with intense competitive pressure. A sensible and well-balanced foreign manpower policy must ensure that on the one hand ambitious and adaptable foreign workers will be integrated individually and as quickly as possible but that foreign worker minorities on the whole will remain sufficiently linked to their homelands so that they can return there; and that on the other hand, as an alternative for advancement, the possibility remains open to them (after successful training in the host country) of finding a good job in their country of origin.

7 *Political Effects*

At the present time potential political effects of foreign workers can be estimated only with great difficulty. Only a few studies are available which permit inferences about political attitudes and behaviour of foreign workers. The following relationships must be taken into account:

(a) Until they are naturalized, foreign workers by and large have little or no chance to engage directly in the politics of the host country by voting. In Austria exceptions are elections to the Chamber of Workers and Employees and to the works council..

(b) Foreign workers can, however, indirectly exercise political influence in the host country inasmuch as they form a lower class which enables the natives to enjoy relative social advancement. The question arises, however, whether such subjectively mobile persons tend to vote conservative or left.

(c) Under certain conditions, foreign workers expose socialist parties and labour unions to internal tensions. On the one hand these organizations, because of their humanitarian and egalitarian philosophy, are concerned about equal rights for foreign workers, but on the other hand they have to take sides in conflicts of interest between foreign workers and native workers.

(d) If foreign workers acquire citizenship only as individuals and after personal adjustment to conditions in the host country, they tend to strengthen the conservative side in politics because they also want to dissociate themselves from the foreign worker lower class.

(e) If foreign workers acquire citizenship in larger groups as the result of political settlements, they tend to strengthen labour movements since they regard themselves as a collective upward striving lower class.

(f) By their absence foreign workers reduce political demands in their homeland; if they return to their homeland they bring with them ideas which have in part been acquired abroad.

These political effects of foreign workers' employment will only become strongly felt on a long-term basis.

By making explicit the future implications of recent linear trends in the employment of foreign workers in Austria, it can be shown that a simple persistence hypothesis is unlikely to lead to a situation properly described as linear progress. The dynamics of change induced by the introduction of foreign workers involve greater uncertainty. For example, economic recession in the host country or political pressures from the homeland may abruptly alter established patterns. It is equally important to emphasize that not all of the effects would be regarded as benign. For example, neither foreign workers nor Austrians wish foreign workers to raise families (whether in Austria or in their native land) with a dis-proportionate number of disturbed children and potential adult delinquents. The systemic implications of the introduction of large numbers of foreign workers imply discontinuities, e.g., in the manpower resources of low wage industries or of low status occupations, in the social status of poorly paid workers and, not least, in the political relationships within the host nation, and between the countries involved as senders and receivers of labour, and those workers who move back and forth between them.

NOTES

1. These research studies are recapitulated in the book *Gastarbeiter − Wirtschaftsfaktor und soziale Herausforderung* (Vienna, Europa-Verlag und Wirtschafts-Verlag, 1973).

2. On the other hand, in other areas the growth tendency resulting from foreign manpower employment may encourage re-equipping the means of production with progressive technology.

3. (Ausländische Arbeitskräfte − Vor und Nachteile für die Volkswirtschaft, Bern, 1966).

4. See *Gastarbeiter-Wirtschaftsfaktor und soziale Hereausforderung,* ed. Ernst Gehmacher, Wien 1973, Europa-Verlag und Wirtschaftsverlag.

5. In 1968 the number of criminals in the United States was estimated to be 1.0 to 3.0 percent of the total population. This produced a murder and manslaughter rate which was four to twelve times greater than in other industrial nations such as Japan, Canada, England or Norway and an armed robbery rate nine times greater than in England.

6. Cost-Benefit-Analyse Gastarbeiter Wien, IFES-Studie für die Magistratsabteilung Wirtschaftliche Angelegenheiten der Stadt Wien).

Chapter VII

THE BREAKDOWN OF GOVERNABILITY
IN IRELAND, 1919-1921

Tom Bowden

Manchester Polytechnic, England

INTRODUCTION

This paper concerns the climacteric of Anglo-Irish relations, the Irish War of Independence 1919-21. Its central concern is the decline and breakdown of governability in Ireland, the ultimate political discontinuity. Overall, it is a study of the morbid, violent and chaotic world of *sub rosa* politics occurring in the eye of a bitter revolutionary war. The events leading up to the collapse are viewed from the perspective of the British Government and its field agents – the Irish Office in Dublin Castle and the Royal Irish Constabulary. They were the institutions trying to maintain order under the authority of the British Crown, in the face of political violence and armed rebellion aimed against their authority.

The intelligence function of police units are among the most critical elements opposing a challenge to a regime's authority. One aspect of a government's responsibility in the sphere of the maintenance of public order – its intelligence system – holds the key to the tactics of the government in an insurgency situation. Without detailed information about the organization, personnel, aims and strategies of militant subversive groups, the incumbents have to act 'blind'. Lacking insight into events, without a measure of empathy with the rebels, government becomes reactive rather than curative or preventative. By infiltration and the use of informers it is possible to know where, when, how and by what means the insurgents are acting. This style or mode of pre-

ventive policing was at the centre of the maintenance of British control
in Ireland during most of the 19th century. Indeed, the history of
Ireland throughout the 19th century clearly demonstrates that an
efficient intelligence service, in the shape of the 'G' Division of the
Dublin Metropolitan Police and the Special Branch of the Royal Irish
Constabulary, was quite capable of controlling or diverting putative
rebellion (see Bowden, 1973 a). However, in the 1880s, during the
Land League agitations in particular, it became increasingly apparent
that the Royal Irish Constabulary had begun to go into decline. It was a
decline that reflected the general malaise then beginning to infect the
whole of the British Administration in Ireland. At this time policies of
political expediency and financial stringency began to be applied
rigorously to police work. The outcome was that rebels and subversives
prospered whilst the police, demoralized, could only watch. Eventually,
well prepared and ably led by Michael Collins, the rebels attacked in
1919 using targetted political assassination as the tactical edge of a
protracted guerrilla campaign. It was a different species of warfare to
that exhibited by the Irish rebels during the failed Easter Rising in
Dublin in 1916. The assault in 1919 was not a 'once and for all' attack
to seize Dublin Castle but consisted of an assault directed at the already
ailing police structure. By the winter of 1920 that police structure was
broken. With that, not only the police but the British regime, based on
Dublin Castle, went into abeyance.

The subject matter of this paper provides a case study in one of the
most, if not *the* most controversial and important areas of policy
formulation – the maintenance of political control and the preservation
of a regime's claim to compliance with its laws and allegiance to its
overall authority. The content of this study thus goes some way
towards vindicating the assertion that,

> Order is a collective good. When the agents of the law fail to provide what the
> citizens wish – public order – they cannot expect to retain popular con-
> fidence. As disorder becomes a collective evil, citizens become very intense in
> their wants and direct in their readiness to secure them. When the power of
> the law is limited, then something stronger will prevail. (Rose and Miller,
> 1972: 19).

The preservation of public order can therefore be regarded as one of
the vital 'defining activities' of the state – a collective good for which
the state makes a monopoly claim. (Rose and Miller, 1972: 7). In
Ireland, as we shall see, the alternative underground Republican government with its Parliament, Dail Eireann and army, the Irish Republican

Army, had by the winter of 1920 become far more effective than the Dublin Castle Administration in maintaining public order and the full range of governmental activities in many of the Irish localities.

THE DYNAMICS OF THE
IRISH CRISIS

Historically Ireland was dogged by a tradition of equivocation on the part of English politicians, whose policy toward Ireland continually oscillated in cyclical fashion between conciliation and coercion. A detailed assessment of Anglo-Irish relations 1880-1921 reveals two clear schools of thought. First, one can identify the advocates of *coercion:* men like Chief Secretary Sir Hamar Greenwood or the anti-Fenian Chief Secretary 'Bloody' Balfour; they believed that sufficient coercion would bring about a static policy of order. The *conciliators,* best typified by Chief Secretary Augustine Birrell, had a more optimistic view of political man; they hoped for linear progress from conciliation to benign events leading towards a permanent and consensual solution.

Neither conciliation nor coercion was resolutely pursued. The Irish developed a matching duality of protest. Irish resistance to English rule was made up in equal parts of constitutional agitation and re-volutionary violence. The balance was in favour of constitutionalism until the opening years of the 20th century and the demise of the Irish Parliamentary Party as a force in Ireland's affairs during the First World War. From 1867 onwards, through the example and organizational stimulus of the Fenian movement, Irish sedition passed slowly through a series of tactical changes. Though both wings of the Irish opposition sought separation from England, there developed in Ireland from 1867 onwards a growing belief that 'England would never concede self-government to the force of argument but only to the argument of force'. (Moody, 1968: 103). During the last decades of the 19th century the Irish group favouring discontinuity increasingly moved towards coercion as a means to achieving that end.

Thus on the Irish side the equivalent of English conciliation and coercion was negotiation and rebellion, a cyclical pattern beginning with the rising of 1689 and continuing through the rising of 1798, the Fenian disturbances and into the 20th century. During the 19th century Irish violence had been dealt with in a swift and hard manner by the police and the Dublin Castle Administration. The Fenians in particular were broken by Royal Irish Constabulary infiltration. Yet in reacting to the increasing Irish violence emerging between 1916 and 1921 the British opted for a policy of *systematic coercion* late in the day. It was not until the summer of 1920 that the containment of rebels was replaced by a policy aimed at the physical eradication of the leading cadre of the Irish politico-military opposition. In the short-term, such a course of action seriously escalated the level of violence within Ireland. By 1920, for His Majesty's Government, thoroughgoing coercion had replaced conciliation. In the light of this commitment to victory through coercion, the granting of major rebel demands by the Truce of 1921 appears all the more dramatic. What process and factors induced the members of the British Coalition Cabinet to make a reversal of policy which Churchill described as more sudden and complete than any in modern times? Was it calm choice? Or was it all desperate improvisation in response to a political and military situation increasingly without any semblance of effective control?

This study seeks to understand not only the discontinuity represented by the 1921 recognition of Irish independence but also the move from conciliation to coercion and back again, in terms of the nature and extent of the breakdown of governability in Ireland.

IRELAND – THE BACKGROUND TO BREAKDOWN

(a) *The Political Will*

At the hub of Anglo-Irish affairs 1880-1921 lay a battle of political will. Britain had at first held the initiative since the majority of the Irish, whilst voting for Home Rule, were prepared to await a constitutional solution, and accordingly remained faithful to Ireland's colonial administration down to 1916 and the Easter Rising. However, Britain's initiative was fading before 1916. The reasons for this decline in British authority are not difficult to see.[1] In the main they were the product of a mood of conciliation which characterised British policy from 1880 down to the Easter Rising. The Land League agitation from 1879 to 1882 excepted, the period 1880-1916 was unusually quiet on the surface. In a country noted for political turmoil the calm was misleading. The underground of Irish politics was passing through a crucial transition. There was little concrete evidence of it since the predominant activity was, as yet, intellectual. Nevertheless, this was the time of the inception of the Gaelic Athletic Association and the Gaelic League, which were later at the heart of a widespread spiritual regeneration of 'Irishness'. More important, it was a period which saw the end of agrarian-centred protest. This style of protest had been little more than a complex type of peasant banditry, lacking an ideology, provoked by local grievances yet producing on occasions cross-local organizations. This was especially the case during the period of Land League agitation in the 1880s. Irish peasants supported the Land League cause out of self-interest. Having achieved the alleviation of their grievances through parliamentary legislation, they moderated their violence which itself had come out of a live tradition of non-constitutional action against the British Crown. By 1890 a more sophisticated ideology of revolutionary Republicanism had taken the place of burning haystacks. In the 1890s a European mode of violent protest, selective political assassination, was adopted and justified as legitimate. Dublin, Belfast, and Cork became the new centres of political agitation.

These qualitative tactical changes occurred without the British administration being initially aware of them. At the height of the revolutionary guerrilla war of 1920 the tactics of the control force, the Royal Irish Constabulary, were still dominated by the outmoded lessons learned from the fight with the Fenians in 1867. Whereas the Irish Administration marked time and then regressed, the Irish revolutionary underground evolved from riot through rebellion to people's revolutionary war. The inadequacy of the Irish administration helped the revolutionary zealots to mobilize.

If the superficial quiet in Ireland conditioned the British non-response, what were the critical elements that led to the long-term downward trend in governability? First, there was the effect of political expediency regarding public security work. During the 1880s and 1890s the British desire to avoid political crises was fueled by the ability of the Irish Parliamentary Party to instill anxiety in the government of the day at the House of Commons. Its political opposition in 1906 was sufficient to induce the discontinuation of the 1881 Peace Preservation Act (Arms Act), the one unambiguous legal power which the Dublin Castle Government possessed for controlling the use and importation of arms.[2] The Act of 1881 had been passed at the height of a rash of agrarian disorders. Amended and continued by an Act of 1886 for one year, it was extended a further five years by the Criminal Law Procedure (Ireland) Act of 1887 and afterwards continued from year to year. A major debate ensued in 1906 about whether to retain the Act or not. The Resident Magistrates and police administrators advised retention of the Act. The British Cabinet was divided on the issue. The law, however, was quietly allowed to expire. It was expedient to do nothing

— at least in Britain. The move resulted in a massive influx of arms into Ireland. The only remaining legal powers to control the importation of arms were an ancient and inadequate Riot Act of the disestablished Irish Parliament (27 George III cap 15) and a Gun Licence Act of 1870, which could not be enforced by police officers, only by the Customs and Excise Department (Crime, Special Branch Report April 9, 1913). Quaint distinctions were also made in the quality of illegally imported weapons which were detected. From amongst a large file of legal opinions on the powers of police to seize arms, one police document stands out. A note reporting that seven cases of guns had been found in the Imperial Hotel, Belfast, March 13, had the following rider attached: 'As the police have satisfied themselves that these are only cheap shotguns I do not think the matter requires any special attention'. (Crime Special Branch March 6, 1913).

In pursuing conciliation, successive British Governments refused to take a stand over controversial Irish issues — especially those related to policing. What few teeth the police still possessed were effectively drawn by political expediency. Colonel Edgeworth Johnstone of the Royal Irish Constabulary reported,

> I have this force under my command . . . . . and I have a free hand as regards discipline — practically a free hand as regards discipline so far as ordinary breaches of the law are concerned, but in cases where there is a political tinge of any kind, everything has to be referred to the Under Secretary . . . . . . Anything that would involve, for instance, the arrest of any of those Sinn Feiners or anything of that sort, I mean, in a case of that kind I daren't move on my own initiative. (Macready 1924: 179a).

The police in particular were affected by such a conciliatory policy posture. Major-General Sir Neville Macready, later to have command of the security forces during the 1919-1921 conflict, wrote of the Royal Irish Constabulary in 1920:

> This once magnificent body of men had undoubtedly deteriorated into what was almost a state of supine lethargy and had lost even the semblance of energy or initiative when a crisis demanded vigorous and resolute action. The immediate reason was not far to seek. If an officer of whatever rank took it upon himself to enforce the law, especially during the faction fights which are the popular pastime of the Irish, this action would as often as not be disavowed by the authorities at Dublin, on complaint being made to them by the Irish politicians by whose favour the government held office. This is no idle assertion on my part. (Macready, 1924: 179b).

The intent of such a conciliatory stance was never matched by its impact. Ireland was to be kept quiet at all costs. The law, should it be thoroughly enforced, would be provocative. The solution was simple: the law was not enforced. Yet the outcome was more rather than less political violence. Indeed, in sensitive operations the police had no guarantee of government support. One incident should suffice to demonstrate this point. On July 26, 1914, arms were illegally landed at Howth, near Dublin and collected by the Irish Volunteers, who then proceeded ostentatiously, to march back to Dublin bearing the arms. The police naturally intervened, shots were fired and the Volunteers disarmed in Bachelor's Walk, Dublin. Many on both sides were wounded though there were no fatalities. In Irish terms the whole incident was little more than a fracas. However, its implications for the Irish Office vis-a-vis the police were serious. The commanding Royal Irish Constabulary Officer involved in the Bachelor's Walk incident, in less sensitive times and under a government less overtly concerned with crisis management through conciliation, would have been commended for his stand in the face of an armed mob. He was, however, dismissed from the force,

> sacrificed to popular clamour in circumstances which shook the confidence of the Royal Irish Constabulary in the government to its foundations. The police perceiving that they could not be sure of its support in emergencies and would be made scapegoats completely lost heart and every officer of the force realized that if he got into conflict with political movements he imperilled his position, so with this feeling of nervousness and insecurity prevailing in the police force the Sinn Fein movement was nourished and took root, and they continued their operations under the eyes of the police. (Robinson, 1923: 220).

Such treatment of the police, the dominant control force in Ireland, was in itself indicative of the loss of political will to hold Ireland. Special Branch activities were reduced even after the 1916 Rising showed that not only had the search for stability through conciliation failed, but also that a government could not safely ignore all warnings of its police and intelligence services. The Commission of Inquiry into the 1916 Rising reported:

> The main cause of the rebellion appears to be that lawlessness was allowed to grow up unchecked and that Ireland for several years had been administered on the principle that it was safer and more expedient to leave the law in abeyance, if collision with any faction of the Irish people could thereby be avoided. (Cd 8279, 1916: 12).

If political expediency influenced the decline of governability in Ireland a further factor was the application of financial stringency upon police work. The general trend of economy in all departments of state was applied with particular vigour in Ireland. (C.O. 904/172/2, 1895). Beginning in the 1890s financial retrenchment was compounded by the survival of laissez-faire attitudes of governing, in essence the belief that time would heal Ireland. Again the police suffered. The Royal Irish Constabulary in particular was cut back because of grumblings in the British press and constituencies about the cost (C.O. 904/174/1: 1895). As late as 1919 the extra allowance to the Royal Irish Constabulary Special Branch was cut altogether. Sir Ormonde Winter, later to command a rejuvenated British intelligence apparatus in the summer of 1920, stated that it was 'the parsimony of Birrell', Chief Secretary of Ireland, 1907 to 1916, that, 'had resulted in the decline of the secret service organisation' (Winter, 1955: 290).

Taken together, financial stringency and political expediency led to a very low profile police force. Little surveillance was maintained of those organizing a violent overthrow of the British Government. Accordingly Irish affairs appeared inordinately quiet. The Irish office drew the erroneous conclusion that since all was quiet there was little danger. The result was that additional cuts were made in security expenditure, beyond those implicit in the standard policy of economy on the security front for many years. The consequences debilitated the police force. Because of economies fewer police were recruited. In Ireland police strength was cut back whilst population, especially in the cities continued to rise. The figures of police strength 1912 to 1919 (below) clearly indicate the decline in the capacity of the force to fulfill its multiplicity of tasks.

TABLE 1

Royal Irish Constabulary Strength 1912-1919 (H.O. 184; 35; 36; 1919)

Year	Police Strength
1912	10,412
1913	10,259
1914	10,181
1915	9,668
1916	9,456
1917	9,452
1918	9,275
1919	7,609

Hence in quiet times and for normal duties the police apparatus was short staffed. Police reserves were fewer. When disturbances commenced, reinforcements were not available.

(b) *The Nature of the Control Force, the Royal Irish Constabulary*

Historically it is possible to detect two broad styles of policing (Chapman, 1970), one based in Common Law and the other stemming from the Roman law tradition. English policing, where the policeman serves as a representative of the citizenry, best exemplifies the Common Law mode of enforcement. In countries adhering to this approach there has tended to be a narrower conception of the functions of government and certainly a less intrusive police apparatus. By way of contrast, the Roman law tradition has historically led to a more 'positive' or interventionist state apparatus. Government and its agencies are far more pervasive and paternalistic. The police represent the regime, not the citizenry. The police of continental despots, and European police forces since the 18th century have all operated within this tradition. It is something of a paradox that the Royal Irish Constabulary, created in what was then 'English' Ireland, can be placed firmly in the European Roman law style of policing.[3]

The police in Ireland resembled the European quasi-military gendarmerie for more than they did the civilian police forces of their parent country. In Ireland of course the police operated under greater pressure from subversives than did the police in Scotland, Wales or England — hence their overt concern with public security, the suppression of anti-regime propaganda and subversion. The Irish police were a control force. They were concerned with political regulation and control. An anonymous pamphleteer writing in the late 19th century reported that the,

Royal Irish Constabulary, being free from any local or any Irish control whatsoever, the police have, in the past habitually conducted themselves — no doubt in accordance with the orders of their superiors — not as the servants but as the masters of the public. A village sergeant and constable is a little king or emperor. Is it any wonder if, under these circumstances, the police have not been popular in the past? The extent to which the police make themselves felt in Ireland would, no doubt, astonish most Englishmen. They attend, fully armed, every public meeting . . . . The present writer had occassion to attend some twenty meetings in Dublin County in the years 1883, 1884, 1885 for the sole purpose of securing the registration of nationalist political voters, and at almost every one of them a police reporter was in attendance and ostentatiously took a report of the proceedings. (Sundry Tracts: 19).

Yet, though they were conceived, trained, structured, equipped and recruited as a paramilitary Roman law force, the Royal Irish Constabulary, because of the cyclical movement between the *conciliators* and the *coercers*, was never consistently allowed to act in that capacity. The role-definition of the Royal Irish Constabulary was never satisfactorily resolved either prior to or during the War of Independence. Chief Secretary Birrell, referred to the Royal Irish Constabulary as,

> an ambivalent force . . . . . . some people say they are much better soldiers than policemen . . . . . People who do not like them say that they are much better policemen than they are soldiers (Cd. 8279).

Indeed, between 1912 and 1915 there was an earnest debate about the status of the police. The Dublin Castle administration held to the belief that 'military service is quite distinct from constabulary service. We think it quite clear that the Royal Irish Constabulary are not a military force' (C.O. 904/174/2 part 1, 1915). The British War Office, however, preferred to see them as part of the armed forces in Ireland. It is hardly surprising that, confined to a frustrating limbo between action and inaction, the police went into decline. An editorial in the *Constabulary Gazette* of 1916 suggested 'The Royal Irish Constabulary may be likened unto a noble mansion of the early Victorian era, still occupied but showing visible signs of decay' (*Constabulary Gazette* 29, No. 7; 4/9/1916). In 1918, the force was described as 'a wooden velocipede — a marvellous invention fifty years ago'. (*Constabulary Gazette* 41, No. 2, 10/8/1918).

The decline of the Royal Irish Constabulary had been underway since the 1880s with only periodic attempts made to face the resultant escalating lawlessness and the growing failure of the judicial arm as well. Difficulty was found in enforcing the law about minor matters as well as against political crimes. This failure escalated, and with it the inability of the police to enforce prosecutions for both politically motivated and anti-social crimes. The total number of offences prosecuted consistently fell from 1898 onwards; almost certainly the number of offences actually committed also rose. The decline in prosecutions coincided significantly with the retrenchment in the administration and particularly, the stringencies imposed upon the police. The government and the police in Ireland increasingly failed to enforce law and order. Crimes involving violence against property rose from 174 in 1900 to 630 in 1901. Even more alarming for the government was the increase in the number of what His Majesty's Government itself defined as 'Crimes against the State'; these rose from 249 in 1915 to 880 in 1919

(Cd. 1746; 2218; 2632). Violence was being targetted upon the British administration as security, protection of citizens and the government's agents, and the vigorous prosecution of the law, were in decline. There was an especially dramatic fall in the number of people receiving police protection between 1887 and 1916 and a further steep decline in the aftermath of the 1916 Rising. This state of affairs was in itself indicative of the reduced efficacy of the police.

(c) *To the Brink of Revolutionary War*

From the 1880s onward, as a result of declining British political will and of policies of political expediency and financial stringency, the governability of Ireland declined. In the first instance the failure of the control force allowed Irish rebels to organize and then become operational. The Easter Rising of 1916 provided ample evidence that events and forces in Irish society were moving out of the grasp of the Castle administration and its police. However, after the temporary coercive response to the Rising, the return to conciliation within a year allowed the underground forces shattered in the aftermath of 1916 to regroup. Committed and dedicated men already planning 'the next time' were released from internment in August 1917.

British policies might have sustained the regime had they not coincided with a major tactical reorientation in the methods of Irish protest, which reached maturity by 1919. Previous Irish risings of 1793, 1803, 1848, 1867 and 1916 itself had revealed a revolutionary idée fixe in Irish revolutionary thought − the quest for an immediate victory achieved through a frontal assault on Dublin Castle. It was the Irish Nationalist Invincibles, a radical offshoot of Fenianism, who ended this Bastille mentality and took the first practical step towards a change (Corfe, 1968; Tynan 1894). Their example of systematic targeted assassination of the officers of government became the leading theme of the IRA guerrilla campaign under the leadership of Michael Collins. Selective assassination came to form the core of a war of attrition in 1919-1921. Resurgent nationalism, fostered and led by the Gaelic Athletic Association and Gaelic League, provided the sacrificial ideology motivating revolutionary activists to kill and die for Ireland. Except in Ulster, no comparable ideology sustained British forces.

THE WAR OF INDEPENDENCE 1919-1921
AND THE END OF BRITISH AUTHORITY
IN IRELAND

(a) *British Policy and the War — the changing emphasis*

It was this guerrilla struggle, waged by small, mobile groups from a popular base conducting their operations in the clandestine manner, which caused the British Government to re-examine its policy of conciliation. It should also have stimulated tactical rethinking because the police, housed in barracks, were trained and equipped for static, formal engagements employing set routines. The IRA fought by emphasising flair and inventiveness; under Collins theirs was a campaign of inspiration and attrition. In response to the escalation of violence triggered by the onset of the IRA campaign the prevailing mood in the Coalition Cabinet significantly changed from conciliation towards coercion. Thomas Jones records in an entry in his *Whitehall Diary* during 1919 that,

> considerable differences of opinion within the Cabinet became manifest, but upon one point every member of the Committee (Cabinet Committee on Ireland) was agreed, namely that as a preliminary to proceeding with government policy . . . . . it was first necessary that the new Irish Administration should restore respect for government, enforce the law and, above all, put down with a stern hand the Irish-German conspiracy which appears widespread in Ireland. The Committee were unanimously of the opinion that until this had been done neither branch of the government's party (conscription and self-government) had any chance of success. (Jones, 1971: 9).

Although the prevailing mood moved towards coercion, it was never systematically employed during the Irish rebellion. Examples of this curious half-way-house are legion in the British prosecution of the war. The police, for instance, were never sure of their precise role during the war. At the height of the war an individual police officer wrote to ask the *Constabulary Gazette's* legal column for advice on,

> how to act if an armed band attacked one's barracks. Should one use the baton first and then, if forced by circumstances to fire, should the riot act now be read first? (*Constabulary Gazette* **40,** No. 47; 21/6/1919).

Again, at the height of the crisis the British Government declared Martial Law in only four counties of Ireland despite the fact that the Chief Security Officer, Major-General Sir Neville Macready, had made it abundantly clear that,

There was only one possible way by which order could be restored, although I did not realize it myself until I had been in Ireland for some months, and that was to declare Martial Law throughout the whole country, North and South, to be applied as might be deemed necessary, and to treat the restoration of order as a purely military operation without interference by civil elements on either side of the Irish Channel. (Macready, 1924: 448).

As the struggle reached a pitch the military as well as the police felt restricted in carrying out their security role by the political expediency of Dublin Castle and Westminster. Some sixteen years after the end of the Irish War the British administration in Palestine, when facing similar disturbances among the Arabs and casting round for a solution to the dilemma of declining governability, revived a government paper which had assessed the policy in Ireland with regard to the application of martial law. That paper clearly indicated the reasons for military dissatisfaction when it observed that,

The declaration of martial law in four counties only had great disadvantages. In the first place it seemed probable that in order to avoid the penalties incurred by carrying arms in the martial law area, parties of rebels would make their way to adjoining counties. To prevent that it would be necessary to guard the boundaries and there were not sufficient troops to do this. Secondly, the demand for the surrender of arms was not likely to be complied with in the martial law area where extremists were in a majority and the morale of the IRA was therefore such as to encourage defiance of that order; whereas in areas less terrorised such an order might have produced the desired result and gradually spread . . . . Had martial law been proclaimed throughout Ireland the control of all Crown forces would have been centred on one head – the Military Governor General. This would have ensured coordination of effort and unification of policy. Whereas martial law led to the anomalous position of the police in the proclaimed counties being under the local Military Governor while divided control existed throughout Ireland . . . . Again two separate forms of trial were necessary. In the martial law area trials were by Military Court, whereas in other areas they were by Court Martial (instituted under the crisis measure, the Defence of the Realm Act) and a similar offence was liable to a death penalty in one place and not in a place a few miles away. (C.O. 735/315).

Sir Mark Sturgis, a leading Castle administrator throughout the Irish War, summarized not only the changing mood but also the dilemma induced by uncertainty whether conciliation or coercion should be adopted when he wrote, 'If we aren't to treat, we must hit damned hard. Why does some hideous fate make all politicians love half-measures which of all so-called policies is the only surely fatal one.' (PRO 30/59; August 3, 1920).

(b) *The Breakdown of Governability*

In this environment of indecision, failing will and administrative malaise the IRA began to concentrate severe pressure upon what they regarded as the vital component in the preservation of British rule in Ireland, the Royal Irish Constabulary. The result in purely military terms was impressive. From January 1st, 1919 to October 2nd, 1920, 109 policemen out of a total force of some 10,000 were assassinated by the IRA under Michael Collin's direction. A further 174 were injured, 484 Royal Irish Constabulary barracks destroyed and some 2,861 raids for arms made, primarily upon police stations. (Cmd. 1025; June 1920). The overall goal of the IRA was to break the intelligence sections of both the Dublin Metropolitan Police and the Royal Irish Constabulary. In addition to assassination, a boycott was rigidly enforced against the police and their families in every town or village where there was a police station. The IRA made abundantly clear their intention with regard to the police. Typical of the warnings given was the following IRA leaflet issued by order of its Dail, declaring,

We hereby proclaim the South Riding of Tipperary a military area with the following regulation. A policeman found within the said area will be deemed to have forfeited his life, the more notorious police being dealt with as far as possible first . . . . . Every person in the pay of England – magistrates, jurors who help England rule this country will be deemed to have forfeited his life. Civilians who give information to the police will be executed, shot or hanged. (Hansard 129, 20/5/1920: 1721).

Increasingly the police became cut off from their sources of information. Isolated in their sand-bagged barracks and allowed out only in fours with a military escort, both the Dublin Metropolitan Police and the Royal Irish Constabulary ceased to function as a control force. The 'G' Division or Special Branch of the Dublin Metropolitan Police was broken first. Then the Royal Irish Constabulary were subjected to terror tactics at a more intense pitch. The inherent weaknesses of the Royal Irish Constabulary and its intelligence section were soon exacerbated by boycott and terror. Table 2 indicates the scale of lawlessness resulting from the decline of both police forces.

The police were chosen as the target of IRA activity not just because they were the symbolic representatives of government but because in very real terms the police were the government's controlling force. Attack on the paternalistic politicized police was also a more or less direct assault on the governmental structure. The IRA attack had the military utility of immobilizing the control force plus challenging the authority of the government by assaulting its representatives in society. Paradoxically whilst the IRA perceived the importance of the Royal Irish Constabulary as a control force and symbol of governmental authority, His Majesty's Government did not. They were anti-Fenian but not pro-Royal Irish Constabulary. It was by attacking and defeating the police that the IRA demonstrated the ineffectiveness of the incumbent government to the local populace.

The impact of this campaign of terror against the police is captured nowhere better than in one document of 1920 — a plea from the Ballinasloe police to the Chief Secretary — urging him to disband the force.

> We consider it is almost an impossibility to carry out our function as a civil police force under the present circumstances. The strain on the force is so great, by the daily assassination of our comrades who are ruthlessly murdered and butchered by the roadside without getting a chance to defend themselves and by the boycotting and threats against us, against our families, our relatives and our homes, that the agony of a long suffering force cannot be much further prolonged . . . . men are resigning in large numbers and the old ranks of the RIC are growing thinner daily. These men are not resigning through cowardice but because there was no adequate protection for their lives . . . We are now useless as a civil police force. We are simply trying to defend our lives — every day we are being more alienated in platform and press, and even the moderate section of the community are so terrorized or apathetic that not even a voice of sympathy nor ray or hope comes from any side . . . men are separated from their families — their wives and children left behind in hostile localities. There is no provision made for houses or homes for married members of the force . . . . No policeman will get a house or accommodation, and even where a house may be found the possibility is that it is generally blown up or burned to prevent occupation by policemen . . . . The dead bodies of our murdered comrades are even insulted, booed and jeered and there is the greatest difficulty getting them to their last resting place — in short there is no such thing as sympathy or charity today for a policeman dead or alive . . . . Our functions are now being carried out by others and our jurisdiction is dwindling daily. We as a body are not able to restore law and order in this country today nor is there any hope on the horizon for a changed order of things when we could do so . . . We consider the best thing to be done is to wind up the force. (C.O. 904/188/97).

Increasingly, responsibility for enforcement of the law — at least the law of the underground Dail Eireann — was taken up by local Sinn Fein cadres and officers of the IRA. The records of the Dublin Brigade IRA reveal, especially by the summer of 1920, increasing demands placed upon the IRA, 'owing to the destruction of the alleged 'police' force of the enemy and the rapid development of the civil side of Republican Government' (IRA GHQ 19/6/1920 Ms 900 Dublin National Library).

TABLE 2

The Monthly incidence of crime and violence, Ireland
June 1920 – July 1921

1920	June	July	Aug.	Sept.	Oct.	Nov.	Dec.
Murder	2	9	14	14	18	19	8
Wounding	2	16	33	13	19	38	24
Robbery	12	99	121	194	186	104	86
Highway Robbery	9	22	21	50	42	50	42
1921	**Jan.**	**Feb.**	**March**	**April**	**May**	**June**	**July**
Murder	25	28	18	22	46	29	21
Wounding	67	44	26	74	68	57	48
Robbery	173	128	105	309	324	494	445
Highway Robbery	69	76	65	238	333	342	328

Realizing the gravity of the situation and the impending collapse of the Dublin Castle Administration, the British Government under Lloyd George made a concerted effort not only to reconstitute that administration but to end conciliation and move vigorously to a coercive policy against the IRA and Sinn Fein leadership. The decision appears to have been taken at some point in the spring or summer of 1920. By that time the British Government had begun to organize a counter-insurgency campaign against the IRA. By that time too the whole of the British Administration in Ireland was in a perilous state.[4] The Fisher Committee of Inquiry, hastily convened to assess how severe was the decline of governability and the debility of the Dublin Castle administration, recommended immediate and widespread reforms (see Wheeler-Bennett, 1963). Just how far governability had declined by the summer of 1920 can be seen from the report of Sir John Anderson, one of the bureaucrats dispatched from Whitehall in the wake of the Fisher Committee to revivify the Castle administration. In what he described as, 'a few brief notes upon the Irish position looked at from the standpoint of a civil servant whose concern is with administration rather than high policy', he reported,

i) the ordinary machinery of civil administration in the Chief Secretary's Office . . . was practically non-existent . . . business that was not urgent was not being attended to and business which had become urgent was disposed of in very many cases without proper consideration. The general state of this office, on which the whole civil administration of the country should really incredible.

ii) The police were in a crucial condition. The morning I arrived in Dublin the Inspector General of the RIC stated in my presence that he was in daily fear of one of two things, either, of wholesale resignations from the force or his men running amok. Either, he said, would mean the end of the RIC. They had practically no motor transport and were stationed in many cases in indefensible barracks without means of securing aid in the event of attack. Many important questions in regard to their pay, allowances and pensions were long overdue for settlement. The all important matter of intelligence and secret service had been entirely neglected. (C.O. 904/188/1a).

Anderson also found the prisons to be very poor, most insecure and inadequately staffed. The military too he felt were present in insufficient numbers whilst the rank and file were inexperienced and quite raw, 'and for the immediate purposes of giving support to the civil authority in the task of maintaining law and order throughout the country, almost useless'. (C.O. 904/188/1b). Similarly, he reported that Major-General Sir Neville Macready, in overall charge of security, had said that Chief Inspector Marrinan of the RIC had told him,

in strict secrecy that the RIC were now half informers to Sinn Fein and the other half prepared, owing to the strain, to become assassins – in fact the force is on the verge of break-up at all events in the South. (C.O. 904/188/1c).

Anderson later added in his diary:

The Royal Irish Constabulary have been paralysed by the murders of their comrades. Anyone passing by a police barracks with its locked doors and seeing the constables looking out through barred windows will at once realize that no body of men could preserve its morale under such conditions . . . . At present the policeman in Ireland is never free from the dread of being murdered. (C.O. 904/188/1d).

Indeed in the 82 weeks from January 1919 to 31 July, 1920, 73 policemen were assassinated. The local government officers serving the Crown were subjected to similar pressures. Anderson found them to be 'profoundly disaffected' and the local civil service, composed entirely of Irishmen to be 'politically alienated and exposed as it is to every kind of pressure and in many places intimidation, cannot be relied upon in the execution of a vigorous policy'. (C.O. 904/188/1e). Thus the machinery of government had, by the Spring of 1920, broken down (cf Table 2).

To remedy the situation, coercion was once again adopted in

Ireland. From the spring oof 1920 the change from conciliation to coercion was dramatic. Lloyd George, almost overnight it would appear, was converted from conciliation to a Cromwellian policy of 'thorough'. To bolster the breaking Royal Irish Constabulary, the Black and Tans and Auxiliary police were recruited and despatched to Ireland.[5] The Tans, ill-disciplined and operating as vigilantes, proved less effective than the Auxiliaries, who were hardened officers with World War I experience. Together, they operated a policy of reprisal against Sinn Fein and the IRA with the very highest governmental backing. The policy probably originated either from Lloyd George himself or from Field Marshall Sir Henry Wilson, Chief of the Imperial General Staff. Wilson, a senior member of the Orange Order, was a noted advocate of harsh methods having declared his preference to 'shoot all the Irish leaders by roster'. Wilson himself records Lloyd George's commitment to counter-terror in his diary, writing that the Prime Minister 'continued to be satisfied that a counter-murder association was the best answer to Sinn Fein murders'. (Callwell, 1927, Vol. II: 25a). Or perhaps the initiative came from Sir John Anderson, who wrote to Wilson,

> I have been in close communication with the GOCs (of) the four areas in this country and as a result I must reiterate that if the present state of affairs in this country continues, some steps must be taken, and taken very shortly, to regularize reprisals for outrages committed on troops .... It is a fact that where reprisals have taken place, the whole atmosphere of the surrounding district is changed from one of hostility to one of cringing submission? (C.O. 904/188/1f).

That reprisals were officially sanctioned as part of the new emphasis on coercion is affirmed by Anderson later in an order to the effect that 'Reprisals should be undertaken only by order of officers not below the rank of Brigadier General .... and by police Divisional Commissioners or Chief Inspectors' (C.O. 904/188/1g).

To uphold and apply this coercive policy in Ireland, a new Chief Secretary, a military man and noted 'hawk' on the Irish issue, Sir Hamar Greenwood, was appointed. He established a Propaganda Department in Dublin Castle whose job was to minimize criticism of this far more vigorous policy. Simultaneously, the statements of Cabinet members became far more belligerent. In Cabinet Churchill observed,

> What strikes me is the feebleness of the local machinery. After a person is caught he should pay the penalty within a week. Look at the tribunals which the Russians have devised. You should get three or four judges whose scope

should be universal and they should move quickly over the country and do summary justice. (Jones 1971 b: 19).

Lloyd George replied that he considered hanging Irishmen a necessity.

The Irish aims were viewed by British Cabinet members in the same light as a tribal revolt in India and the Boer Rebellion. Churchill in fact compared Sinn Fein to the Wafq Party and Zaghul in Egypt. The Cabinet were to learn, to their cost, that the Irish rebel leaders had more stature and were far more determined and sophisticated, both politically and militarily than peasant rebels. Lloyd George believed that the Crown security forces were combatting a small murder gang composed of roughs and corner boys, the dregs of Irish society. He was quite mistaken. By 1920 the Irish were a people in arms, committed to the IRA, itself a highly disciplined guerrilla army.

This fundamental misconception, existing from the onset of the Anglo-Irish War, in 1919 affected not only the overall British policy but also the specific methods by which the IRA was opposed. It was felt by the British that a brief campaign would defeat the group of wild boys. A protracted war of attrition was not envisaged. The IRA was far from being a bandit coterie. It possessed a 16 man executive, an army council, a general headquarters staff and a brilliantly conceived intelligence organisation (Bowden, 1973b). The whole struggle was masterminded by the guerrilla leader, Michael Collins, who had built into IRA operations a very high degree of planning and preparation.

As late as July 1921, the ignorance among Cabinet Ministers of Sinn Fein leaders was great. Cabinet policy was often formulated on hearsay evidence and guesswork. In a crisis situation, prompt and pertinent responses were of the utmost importance. Such policy requires sound information. The decline of the intelligence gathering unit, the police Special Branch, denied such information to the Irish Office and the Coalition Government when they most needed it.

The commitment towards coercion was most evident in the British Government's choice of a policy of assassination of Sinn Fein and IRA leaders. The central battle of the war had now quite clearly become one of intelligence and counter-intelligence tied to the 'removal' of critical personnel through assassination. Late in the day the British Government was adopting Collins' tactics – only in reverse. Collins, the guerrilla leader, had indeed written,

England could always reinforce her army. She could replace every soldier that she lost. But there were others indispensable for her purposes which were not so easily replaced. To paralyse the British machine it was necessary to strike at individuals. (Collins, 1970: 70).

The British policy, in time, followed suit. As we have seen already, Wilson, Chief of the Imperial General Staff, had recorded that Lloyd George 'continued to be satisfied that a counter-murder association was the best answer to Sinn Fein murders'. (Callwell, 1927; Vol. II 25b). Accordingly in the summer of 1920, a bureau was formed to recruit British intelligence specialists capable of carrying out such work. In all some 60 agents were recruited, trained and sent to Ireland (Winter, 1955: 296). Once in the field these men spearheaded the British counter-offensive. The IRA began to experience difficulties. Collins and his men could no longer bicycle around Dublin with impunity. The new security offensive appeared to be having effect. Collins wrote in 1920,, 'I have had some severe hunting . . . closer and closer it has been, but yet they have not had the ultimate success . . . things have been harder than anybody knows'. (Forester, 1971: 188).

With the influx of Black and Tans and Auxiliaries, the security forces were able to sustain the pressure on the IRA. During the period August to November 1920, 1,745 arrests were made in the Dublin district alone. Similarly, from 16-28 August, 1920, some 716 were made under curfew by the Royal Irish Constabulary and the military (W.O. 35/70; 10 October — 31 December, 1920). The assassination of leading Republicans began. The police were encouraged to shoot at anyone they suspected. Smyth, Divisional Commissioner of the Royal Irish Constabulary for Munster, informed men of the police barracks at Listowel, County Kerry, in the presence of the most senior police officer in Ireland, General Tudor, that,

> If the persons approaching you carry their hands in their pockets, or in any way look suspicious, shoot them down. You may make mistakes occassionally and innocent persons may be shot, but that cannot be helped and you are bound to get the right parties sometimes. The more you shoot, the better I will like you and I assure you, men, no policemen will get into trouble for shooting anyone.[6]

With such encouragement of violence, the tactic of reprisal grew. Whereas there had been only one indisputable authorized fatal reprisal by Crown forces in May and three in June, 1920, there were 15 in July, 11 in August and 18 in September. In the first weeks of November 1920, 23 fatal reprisals were carried out by Crown forces (Irish Bulletin, Vol. 3, No. 56, 19/11/1920). This British security offensive became a serious setback for Collins. The Republican cause was suffering, for the British offensive began to induce a marked decline in allegiance to the IRA and the Republican cause. Special Branch reports from various RIC headquarters in the Irish Counties indicated that the boycott of the police was breaking down (C.O. 904/113, November 1920). Special Branch reports also indicated that many former IRA adherents had renounced the organization and were now providing the police with information. If the RIC Special Branch had sensed the change in mood, one can be sure Collins' more efficient intelligence network would have relayed the alarming message from the countryside back to Dublin. It was at this point in time that Collins conceived and then carried through the assassination of the core group of British intelligence experts who were directing the British counter-terror policy.

(c) *Bloody Sunday, 21 November 1920*

On 21st November, 1920, in the quiet of a Dublin Sunday, six groups of IRA gunmen began the systematic assassination of British intelligence specialists. (see Bowden, 1972). The attack was deliberately and coldly calculated to destroy at one stroke the vanguard of the British policy of coercion. Collins himself observed, 'Those fellows who were put on the spot were going to put a lot of us on the spot, so I got in first'. (Winter; 1955: 321). The method for each of the assassinations was very similar. One or two men would knock at the door, gain entry and others would follow, usually shooting their victims in bed or in the bedroom. The scale of attacks, their precision and the number of gunmen involved made the exercise a major undertaking with seven assassination groups varying in size from 12 to 20 men. Six groups were detailed to carry out the assassinations. When they had finished their work 13 intelligence specialists were dead, six injured and two auxiliary policemen, who stumbled upon one of the assassination squads, also killed. The action was a devastating success. By this one act Collins broadcast the IRAs military capabilities and its resolve. On the propaganda level it reinforced the Irish will to carry on the struggle. Above all he had effectively nullified the British policy of coercion. After November, 1920, short of declaring all-out war on Ireland, the British forces on the ground had little hope of breaking the IRA in the immediate future. British intelligence, the crux of the counter-insurgency operation and coercive response, had been nullified at one blow. It would have required a year to rebuild that structure and more time before a new unit bore fruit; this was too far ahead for the Coalition Government. Total repression, given Britain's liberal traditions and democratic ethic, as well as the post-Versailles international climate, was the very last option available to the British. After November, 1920, the IRA attacks increased dramatically as the data below reveals.

Collins then proceeded to hammer home the IRA's advantage. On 28 November 1920, the Cork Brigade IRA under Tom Barry killed all of a group of 20 Auxiliary police at Kilmichael. The war was also carried to England. A massive fire at Liverpool docks was the work of the IRA, as was a thwarted attempt to blow up key installations in Manchester.

TABLE 3

Attacks on British Security Forces and monthly casualties inflicted by the IRA January 1920 – May 1921

Month	Number of Attacks	Killed and Wounded
January 1920	13	4
February	11	7
March	13	12
April	15	23
May	15	24
June	24	20
July	30	54
August	32	69
September	32	27
October	42	86
November	57	94
December	50	76
January 1921	97	102
February	79	95
March	122	158
April	211	158
May (first 14 days)	102	92

(Source: *Irish Bulletin* Vol. 4, No. 93, May 20, 1921).

After November 21, 1920, British counter-insurgency floundered. Without efficient intelligence the British were no longer able to evaluate the impact of their policy of coercion or gain a feedback of information to evaluate on-going policies. Nevertheless, without the special intelligence group and without information about efficacy, coercion continued in increasingly disjointed and wayward fashion on through 1920 and into 1921. It is quite likely that the continuance of this policy

turned upon the faulty military assessments of the Irish situation given
to Lloyd George and the Cabinet. Consistently, the military affirmed
that the 'rebels' would be under control by May 1921, in order that
elections could be held under the new Government of Ireland Act.
(Jones, 1971: 53). However, March and April 1921 proved to be two of
the bloodiest months of the war. Governability declined further. One
commentator observed that Ireland had been

> converted into a cross between a medieval Italian city where hired bravoes
> worked at street corners to stab a foe in the dark, and a more modern Balkan
> state, where brutalised soldier-peasants made whole countrysides reek with
> atrocities. (*Blackwoods Magazine*, No. 212, December, 1922: 165).

In the aftermath of Bloody Sunday, November, 1920, the stark
policy alternatives open to the British Government were simply to
negotiate or wage all-out war – the constraints increasingly forced the
government towards negotiating with underground Irish government.
The Chief Security Officer, Major-General Sir Neville Macready, had
already written to the Chief Secretary, Sir Hamar Greenwood urging
that he saw,

> no reason to deviate in the least from the opinion I originally formed of the
> position here, and indeed, am every day strengthened in that opinion, and that
> the state of affairs in this country has been allowed to drift into such an
> impasse that no amount of coercion can possibly remedy it. (C.O.
> 904/188/1h).

Similarly, in 1921 a Labour Party Commission reported that, 'Things
are now being done in the name of Britain that must make our name
stink in the nostrils of the whole world'. (Jones, 1971; 11a). This type
of criticism, incessant in the liberal press, drove the Chief of the
Imperial General Staff, Wilson to urge that the British must 'go all out
or get out'. (Jones, 1971: 11b). On April 8, 1921, General Crozier, who
had already resigned his command of the Auxiliary Police in protest
against their activities, wrote to *The Times* urging a truce. The division
within the Irish Administration and the Cabinet and the shift in the
mood back towards conciliation under the force of circumstance was
becoming greater. Sir Mark Sturgis, a Dublin Castle Administrator
noted,

> The more I see of it (the Anglo-Irish War) the more convinced I am that if it is
> war we must have a virtual dictator to be obeyed by everybody, military
> police, civil service etc., As it is we are a great sprawling hydra-headed monster

spending much of its time using one of its heads to abuse one or other of the others by minute, letter, telegram and good, hard, word of mouth. (PRO/30/59 Sir Mark Sturgis Diaries, 3/8/1920).

With compliance with the laws of Dublin Castle irrevocably lost, the chronic administrative and military disarray left little hope of a return of governability under a British administration. The breaking of the British regime left anarchy. The Cabinet embarked upon discontinuity by pursuing independence for Ireland through *detente*. Even Churchill, a noted hawk where Ireland was concerned, declared in Cabinet, 'It is of great public importance to get a respite in Ireland'. (Jones, 1971: 11c). For the British Government total war was out of the question because of the constraints imposed by the mood of international opinion in post-Versailles Europe, because of the lack of political resolve to pursue such a course and because of the strain upon military resources in the rest of the Empire which total war in Ireland would create. For Dail Eireann and the IRA, truce and a treaty debate would imply the tacit recognition of an *Irish* government. Noting this, both the British government and the already de facto government of Ireland sought a compromise. The Truce was signed on July 9th, 1921. The British Government in Ireland had been irreparably broken and substituted by alternative hierarchies of authority. The Truce was merely statutory recognition of that fact. In December, 1921, with His Majesty's recognition of a new Irish State discontinuity was complete.

CONCLUSIONS

The aim of this study of the Anglo-Irish struggle 1919-1921 has been to locate the critical factors involved in the decline of governability. The decline in governability involved a long-term downward trend in effective administration and control; there was no dramatic discontinuity prior to the de jure severance imposed by the Truce in 1921. Is it, however, possible to detect de facto discontinuity, a threshold somewhere along the exaggerated downward slide following the commencement of the war in 1919? What induced that discontinuity? Was it a discontinuity forced upon the British Government by external forces or did it arise from an inability to choose between two policy alternatives — conciliation or coercion?

(a) *The Threshold of Discontinuity*

The evidence suggests that there was a threshold of discontinuity on the downward slide into disorder, Bloody Sunday, November, 1920. (See Bowden, Elliot-Bateman and Ellis, 1974). The murder of key British intelligence officers broke the British counter-offensive and the policy of coercion nullified. The introduction of the special intelligence and reprisal unit in 1920 had marked the beginning of the British Government's swing toward coercion in the old coercion-conciliation cycle. Bloody Sunday not only destroyed the apparatus which it was hoped would consolidate that upswing but implied continued decline in the British position. So low were the powers of the British in Ireland in the aftermath of Bloody Sunday that the further downward slide of governability brought about discontinuity by putting the situation over the threshold.

The policy alternatives open to the British government were thereafter stark. There had to be a serious move towards effective conciliation. The other alternative, declaration of total war was, given the external constraints on the British Government, out of the question. After Bloody Sunday the latter policy was never more than a threat which Lloyd George could and did use as a bargaining weapon in the Treaty negotiations.

For the short-term resolution of conflict, the Royal Irish Constabulary and their Special Branch and then their replacements, the secret intelligence unit recruited in London during the summer of 1920, were the units with the potential for upholding the existing political regime. Brigadier Frank Kitson, regarded as the contemporary British Army's expert in low intensity operations against guerrilla forces, has observed, 'The problem of defeating the enemy consists very largely in finding him; it is easy to recognize the paramount importance of good information'. (Kitson 1972: 95). This is particularly true in rapidly moving and violent crisis situations. Information and feedback are vital for the development of an effective, flexible policy in police work even more than in other fields. In a crisis situation it is the prime task of the intelligence organs to ather and collate such information. Bloody Sunday wiped out the leading cadre of the British intelligence and counter-assassination group. Thereafter little or no 'hard' information, that is information as opposed to hearsay, came into British hands. Michael Collins, the Irish guerrilla leader, wrote,

> Without her spies England was helpless. It was only by means of their accumulated and accumulating knowledge that the British machine could

operate . . . Without her police throughout the country how could they find the men they 'wanted'? Without their criminal agents in the capital, how could they carry out that 'removal' of the leaders that they considered essential for their victory? Spies are not so ready to step into the shoes of their departed confederates as are soldiers to fill p the front line in honourable battle. And even when the new spy stepped into the shoes of the old one he could not step into the old one's knowledge. (Collins, 1970: 70).

The scene at Dublin Castle on the afternoon of Sunday November 21, bore out Collins' assessment, 'The Castle' we are told:

> . . . was in uproar. Intelligence officers – or their remnant – were crowding the gates with their families and possessions, their value as 'plants' among the ordinary citizens gone. Jostling them came the touts and spies whose little back-street lives had suddenly lost their comfortable anonymity. Michael Collins, they felt, in their panic, knew all about that widespread word, that discreet passing of money in a dingy pub. (Forester, 1971: 171).

It is as well to re-emphasize that this shattering blow to the control force built upon the longer-term inadequacy produced by years of governmental inactivity on the security front since the 1880s. Over the long term there had been a policy of covert disengagement characterized by one author as 'concealed abdication'. (Hawkins, 1968: 169). In 1916 Sir Neville Chamberlain, Inspector General of the Royal Irish Constabulary, giving evidence to the Royal Commission of Inquiry into the Easter Rising, stressed that,

> unquestionably, the policy of non-intervention which was practised, tended to discourage activity on the part of the police and induced them to turn a blind eye on what was going on. (Cd 8279: 48).

Bloody Sunday compounded that 'blindness'. After November, 1920, the British Government was forced to continue its Irish presence through the military, and the influx of Black and Tans and Auxiliary police. The Truce of 1921 was a formal recognition of a state of affairs which had existed at least from November, 1920. The underground Irish Government had by that time and on that particular day demonstrated its resolve, efficiency and ruthlessness.

However, the discontinuity confirmed by the Truce of 1921 was not induced solely by Bloody Sunday. Bloody Sunday can be taken as the threshold point on the downward slide. Financial stringency and political expediency helped start the slide. The Dublin Castle government became enfeebled. The law was not enforced. It is worth reiterating the verdict of the Royal Commission into the origins of the 1916 Easter Rising that,

> The main cause of rebellion appears to be that Ireland, for several years, had been administered on the principle that it was safer and more expedient to leave law in abeyance if collision with any faction of the Irish people could thereby be avoided. (Cd 8279: 12).

Bloody Sunday was the threshold of the passage to discontinuity: it did not mark the end of the pressures brought to bear, not just by the Irish on His Majesty's Government. The mansions of the remaining English landed gentry in Ireland were systematically burnt. Pressure was brought to bear on the Coalition Cabinet from the gentry's representatives in both the House of Commons and the Lords. The IRA extended the conflict to England at a time when the Cabinet was harrassed and preoccupied with public order problems stemming from escalating industrial strife in England. Reprisals such as the razing of Cork city by the Black and Tans, the systematic burning of Irish creameries, Co-operatives and farms and the random public floggings in the street by Auxiliary Police and Black and Tans led to the incessant urging of independent commissions of inquiry. For example, 'On March 21, 1921, the Lord Chancellor . . . received a distinguished deputation headed by the Archbishop of Canterbury to complain' (about Ireland). (Younger: 1968: 132). Even the *Times,* once opposed to conciliation, now came out hard against coercion, and the *Manchester Guardian,* under C. P. Scott, became the scourge of the Coalition Government's policy in Ireland. On April 21, 1921, Lloyd George affirmed that, 'It would take another twelve months to quell the trouble in Ireland but he doubted if the British people would allow it to go on for so long'. (Younger, 1968: 133). Cabinet papers make it evident too that Ministers were desperately worried about the availability of manpower to deal with the public order situation in the Empire, in Ireland and at home.

Clausewitz, that perceptive military theorist, stated the problem clearly in cost-benefit terms when he wrote, 'As soon . . . . as the required outlay becomes so great that the political object is no longer equal in value, the object must be given up, and peace will be the result'. (Clausewitz, 1966: 30).

Public order is an unusual type of policy, since it is concerned with the very existence of the regime. In Ireland 1919-21 public order was destroyed by the presence of organized, frustrated, and aggressive citizens, alienated and prepared to use force of arms to alleviate their perceived frustration. There was a lack of legitimacy of what was a superimposed colonial government; a weak consensus of support; a declining political will and, above all, an indeterminate policy regarding how to deal with the crisis. Operating in favour of the British Government was the sheer inertia or habit of obedience, the legal monopoly of armed forces and a police force capable of and experienced in locating and prosecuting opposition — at least until the beginning of the 20th century. It was the malaise within and the ultimate collapse of this police force which led to the downturn in governability. The terrorist's plan of campaign exacerbated that decline. Bloody Sunday dealt the final blow. Oscillating between coercion and conciliation, successive British governments allowed Ireland to drift into rebellion through being deficient in its own self-defence.

Rose has noted (1973: 81) that cyclical policies can only occur if governments have a good understanding of the processes that create pressures for change, and the technical knowledge and organizational capability to adopt and enforce requisite counter-cyclical policies. In Ireland it was possible for conciliation and coercion to work, but only so long as the British Government possessed sound knowledge on which to predicate policy, knowledge gained during the 19th century from the Royal Irish Constabulary but seldom gained thereafter; and the will to hold on to Ireland. When these elements became lacking, then the cycle could not be maintained; the forces pushing down the Government's authority were not balanced by the forces thrusting up. The result was the greatest discontinuity of all: the end of the regime. As Popper has observed (1964: 6) 'Institutions are like fortresses. They must be well designed and properly manned'.

NOTES

---

1. It is perhaps as well to indicate clearly here what is implicit throughout this study. That is that the deterministic theory which holds that the Irish rebellion was inevitably bound to work is rejected. Rather is it suggested here that the manner and the time in which the rebellion occurred reflected choices made by the British Government and Dublin Castle, as well as choices and forces favouring

the Irish Republican Army and Dail Eireann.

2. The British governed Ireland though the Irish office represented in Ireland by the Dublin Castle government. Dublin Castle was a centralized bureaucratic structure whose chief officers were appointed by the British government. The structure was headed by a Viceroy who supervised the work of the Chief Secretary and Under-Secretary, the bureaucrats in charge of daily business. The chief executive arms of the Castle government in the localities were the Royal Irish Constabulary and the local magistracy. The whole edifice was inflexible, suffered from inadequate resources, both financial and human, and seemed, since its inception to be a completely alien instrument of governance. Its problems were exacerbated in the 1880s by a reduction in its role. However, the Castle structure was neither rationalized nor reformed to meet the new policy posture. As a result, top-heavy with personnel, it simply deteriorated. Asquith had in fact felt in 1916 that the Castle Administration had irrevocably broken down. Yet, surprisingly, the old Castle was not reformed until 1920 — the aftermath of the Fisher Committee of Inquiry. The reforms then introduced merely heightened the Castle government's major problem — too many bureaucrats. The 1920 reforms were an extravagant and unsuccessful experiment enacted far too late when, since 1916, it had been apparent that the chief requisite to stabilize the Irish situation was a reassertion of British authority.

3. Interestingly both Rose (Governing with Consensus. An Irish perspective, 1971) and Mansergh (The Irish Question 1840-1921, 1965) make the point that the Irish are indeed more European than English and suggest that perhaps the English are less nice outside England.

4. It is important to note here that in Ulster 'ungovernability' took a different form. In Ulster two non-British armies, one the UVF and the other the IRA struggled against each other with limited intervention by the Royal Irish Constabulary and His Majesty's Government. Nevertheless Belfast was under martial law for approximately four years. The rebels were ultimately put down not by the government forces but by the ultras whose legality was minimal. For this see in particular Sir Arthur Hezlet, The B Specials (Pan Books, 1972) p. 10 ff.

5. The Black and Tans and Auxiliary police were para-military units, mainly recruited from British soldiery returning from World War I. They were dispatched to serve as shock-troops and give a stiffening of battle hardened men to the collapsing RIC. The notion of using such a force was Churchill's, based upon his Boer War adventures. The Black and Tans never assimilated into the RIC proper and in their operational ethics tended to resemble an undisciplined rabble. The Auxiliaries, an elite ex-officer unit, proved to be much more effective and their intelligence units especially effective. The Auxiliary Division was inaugurated on 27 July 1920. Its members were contracted to serve for six months with an option on a further six months. They were paid £1 a day all found but had no pension rights. The first Black and Tans arrived in Ireland in the Spring of 1920, 25 March 1920 to be precise. For a detailed treatment see R. Bennett, The Black and Tans (Edward Hutton, 1959) and Cmd 1618, The Royal Irish Constabulary Auxiliary Division, 1920.

6. Sir Mark Sturgis, Senior Dublin Castle Administrator notes in his diary that Smythe was hastily called to London to explain his remarks. See PRO 30/59 Vol. I 15 July 1920.

REFERENCES

BOWDEN, T. (1972) 'Bloody Sunday — A Reappraisal' *European Studies Review* Vol. 2 No. 1 (January).

———, (1973a) *The Breakdown of Public Security. The Case of Ireland 1916 — 1921 and Palestine 1936 — 1939* Unpublished Ph.D. thesis, University of Manchester.

———, (1973b) 'The Irish Underground and the War of Independence 1919-1921' *Journal of Contemporary History* Vol. 8 No. 3.

BOWDEN, T., ELLIOT-BATEMAN, M. and ELLIS, J. (1974) *Revolt to Revolution* Manchester University Press.

CALLWELL, MAJOR GENERAL SIR C. E. (1927) *Field Marshall Sir Henry Wilson His Life and Diaries* Vol. 2. Cassell, London.

CHAPMAN, B. (1970) *The Police State* Pall Mall, London.

CLAUSEWITZ, K. VON (1966) *On War* Vol. 1 translated by J. J. Graham, London.

COLLINS, M. (1970) *The Path to Freedom* Mercier Press, Cork.

CONSTABULARY GAZETTE (1916) Vol. 29 No. 7, 4 September.

CONSTABULARY GAZETTE (1918) Vol. 41 No. 2, 10 August.

CONSTABULARY GAZETTE (1919) Vol. 40 No. 47, 21 June.

CORFE, T. (1968) *The Phoenix Park Murders* Hodder and Staughton, London.

FORESTER, M. (1971) *Michael Collins — the Lost Leader* Sidgwick and Jackson, London.

HAWKINS, R. (1968) in Williams T. D. (Ed) *The Irish Struggle.* Routledge and Kegan Paul, London.

IRISH BULLETIN (1920) Vol. 3 No. 56, November 19.

IRISH BULLETIN (1921) Vol. 4 No. 92, May 20.

JONES, T. (1971) *Whitehall Diary* Vol. 3 Ireland. Cambridge University Press.

KITSON, F. (1972) *Low Intensity Operations* Faber and Faber, London 1972.

MACREADY, SIR NEVILLE (1924) *Annals of An Active Life* Vols. 1 and 2 Hutchinson, London.

MOODY, T. W. (1968) Editor. *The Fenian Movement* Mercier Press, Cork.

"PERISCOPE" (1922) "The Last Days of Dublin Castle" *Blackwoods Magazine* No. 212, 1922.

POPPER, K. (1964) *The Poverty of Historicism* Harper Torch Books, New York.

ROBINSON, SIR H. A. (1923) *Memories Wise and Otherwise* Cassell, London.

ROSE, R. and MILLER, W. (1972) 'What are the odds on justice?' Unpublished manuscript University of Strathclyde, Glasgow.

ROSE, R. (1973) 'Comparing Public Policy. An Overview' *European Journal of Political Research* Vol. 1 No. 1.

SUNDRY TRACTS ON IRELAND. No details. Central Reference Library, Manchester.

TYNAN, P. J. P. (1894) *The History of the Irish Nationalist Invincibles and their times* Chatham and Co. London.

WHEELER-BENNETT, J. (1963) *John Anderson, Viscount Waverley* Macmillan and Co. London.

WINTER, SIR O. (1955) *Winters Tale* Richmond Press, London.
YOUNGER, C. (1968) *Ireland's Civil War*, Fontana, London.

Government Publications and Documents:
in the order of appearance in the text.

Crime Special Branch ex. Green File 28, April 9, 1913. State Papers Office,
   Dublin Castle.
Crime Special Branch ex. Green File 28, March 6, 1913.
Cd 8279. Royal Commission on the Rebellion in Ireland 1916.
Colonial Office (after C.O.) 904/172/2 Establishment of Chief Secretaries Office,
   Public Record Office (After P.R.O.) London.
C.O. 904/174/1 October 20, 1895. P.R.O.
C.O. 904/174/2 Part 1 Military Status of Police, 1912-1915. P.R.O.
Judicial Statistics, Ireland. Cd 1746; Cd 2218, Cd 2632.
C.O. 904/19/5 Intelligence Notes W. Service, Judicial Division P.R.O.
C.O. 735/315 Secretary of State to High Commissioner, Palestine on Martial Law.
   State Archive, Prime Minister's Office, Jerusalem.
P.R.O. 30/59 August 3, 1920. Sir Mark Sturgis Diaries.
Cmd 1025 June 1920.
Hansard Vol. 129, 20 May 1920.
C.O. 904/188/97 Sir John Anderson's Papers P.R.O.
Ms 900 General Order, New Series. No. 9, 19 June, 1920. I.R.A. General
   Headquarters. Brigade Orders 1919-1921. National Library, Dublin.
C.O. 904/188/1 containing both Anderson's diary and additional papers P.R.O.
W.O. 35/70 War Office General File. H.Q. Dublin District. October 10 to Decem-
   ber 31, 1920. P.R.O.
C.O. 904/113 November 1920. Special Branch Reports P.R.O.

Chapter VIII

CRISIS MANAGEMENT AND POLICY-MAKING: AN EXPLORATION OF THEORY AND RESEARCH

Robert J. Jackson

Carleton University, Ottawa

INTRODUCTION

> Dog and man looked at each other in a dazed and distrustful silence for a moment. Mountolive struggled for words. He had always loathed sausage-dogs with legs so short that they appeared to flop along like toads rather than walk. Fluke was such an animal, always panting and slavering from its exertions. It sat down at last and, as if to express once and for all, its disenchantment with the whole sum of canine existence, delivered itself of a retromingent puddle on the beautiful Shiraz. (Durrell, 1958: 267).

David Mountolive's problem may appear somewhat low on a scale of crises to be resolved, but it illustrates that what commonly constitutes a crisis situation can range from the tragic to the absurd. The 1848 revolutions were triggered by a student dropping his cane into a Munich orchestra pit and the 1970 Kingston Penitentiary riots in Canada began when inmates were deprived of late-night television. The lesson is clear; practically every event is a crisis for someone.

Even at the level of the state, crises are ubiquitous. International crises are the essence of the study of foreign relations, and collective violence and disaster form a crucial part of the analysis of domestic politics. National crises occur regularly; the effectiveness with which they are managed may have major effects for system legitimacy and spill over into every area of policy-making. (Weber, 1949: 182-85). And, yet, while the handling of such crises may be the most critical form of policy-making which governments undertake, no studies exist on the dynamics of public policy in this area.

To place crisis management in a public policy perspective, however, we shall have to do more than illustrate its unique interest for the study of society. While the number and variety of crises could be considered infinite, some limitations must be imposed on the variations in order to recognize the phenomena when it appears. Since crises are recurrent, it should prove possible to examine their characteristics systematically. Then, we shall have to outline and assess the policies that have been employed in crises in order to determine the short-term sequence, the dynamics, and the consequence of government response.

DEFINITION OF CRISIS

Unfortunately, the universe of crises has not been sufficiently described to provide a contextual definition in the form of, 'If, and only if . . .'. The term's ambiguity may be handled best by a stipulated definition which characterizes 'crises' in erms of other words without violating common sense. With such definitions, tentative generalizations can be made which are at least confirmable and relevant about observable objects. (Caws, 1965). The problem of definition in this field has been confronted most generally by students of sociology and most explicitly by specialists in disaster research and international relations. Perhaps the broadest definition of a crisis is 'a large and unfavourable change in the inputs of some social system'. (Barton, 1963: 3). The narrower definitions equate disasters and crises. A disaster is:

> an event, concentrated in time and space, in which a society or a relatively self-sufficient sub-division of society undergoes severe danger and incurs such losses to its members and physical appurtenances that the social structure is disrupted and the fulfilment of all or some of the essential functions of society is not provided. (Fritz, 1971)

The definitions employed in international crises have been somewhat more restricted and the following tentative definition (which is intended for future comparative analysis across nation-states) is built on that foundation. (Hermann, 1972). For the purpose of relating crises and policy-making at this early stage of investigation it is most useful to define crises in terms of their situational determinants, rather than in the abstract as changes in the rate of change or as the psycho-social consequences of change. It is stipulated, therefore, that a crisis is an event or a series of events which occur in a system and which meet the following requirements:

1. *It must be related to an important human requirement for which national governments take some responsibility.* (Hermann, 1963: 64) One approach would be to determine if the event(s) would affect basic human needs such as those included in psychologists' lists. In practical terms governments in liberal democracies are apt to include as their minimum responsibility:
   (a) reacting to external challenges to sovereignty and interests,
   (b) preventing loss of, or restoring constitutional order,
   (c) preventing, ending or minimizing loss of life or damage to property. (Emergency Preparedness, 1973).
2. *It offers what policy-makers perceive as a limited amount of time in which a response can be made.* Decision time cannot be treated as an absolute because it 'varies with the intricacies of the decision and with the number of participants'. (Robinson, 1968: 510-514; Hamblin, 1958: 67).
3. *It is relatively unexpected or expectations are general to the problem and not related to a specific event.* Of course, predictability of future events varies enormously from case to case. (Simon, 1958: 49-58).

Many other concepts are used to discuss various aspects or types of crises — stress, anxiety, conflict, tension, panic, catastrophe and disaster. (Dynes, 1969). However, while these concepts are useful for depicting specific behaviour, the language of crises may be more helpful for comparison between states and for relating them to the dynamics of public policy. This definition may also be criticized because it is phrased in the negative mood. There are positive results to a crisis; it is well known, for example, that they often generate cohesion. In Chinese a crisis (wei-chi) means both danger and opportunity. (Wolin, 1960: 230). This paper assumes that crises arising in society are resolved by governments; government crises are not solved by societal action.

As well as conceptual difficulties in this field there are also measurement problems. The most serious is that no scales have been developed. James A. Robinson's (1970) distinction of 'most crisis-like' situations does not resolve this difficulty as no cut-off points have yet been delineated to determine which events are most crisis-like. While we can employ the above definition to distinguish, in a rough manner, a crisis from a non-crisis, one cannot measure degrees of 'crisisness'. Floods, for example, may on occasion fit our definition and yet clearly not every flood is a crisis.

POLICY-MAKING AND CRISES

Little attention has been paid by policy analysts to how governments cope with crises. Not one article in *Policy Sciences* or *Public Policy,* for example, discusses the problem. Theodore Lowi's (1964: 677-715) often repeated classification makes no reference to the non-routine in policy-making, and except in the field of international relations, Hugh Heclo's (1972: 83-108) survey of the literature in the field does not cite any studies of crises, violence, disaster or similar events. While passing reference is made to crises in the vast literature on organizations, they are treated as deviant cases or faults in a system. (Etzioni, 1961).

An attempt to link 'crisis management' to the study of policy-making may cause trouble for policy analysts. The difficulties do not arise from the definition of policy. No matter how it is defined – by Heclo (1972: 84-85) as purposive acts and their consequences; by Rose (1973: 84-85) as 'a generic symbol pointing toward a field of interest'; or by Jackson (1972) as a 'long-term perspective in a subject area' – crisis management fits the subject. But, at least four other difficulties are encountered in linking the study of crisis-management to that of policy-making.

First, the 'substance' of crises varies over time. Oil spills have only recently been elevated to the level of crisis because of societal concern for pollution. In the ebb and flow of crises, topics become routine and lose their importance for national decision-makers. These might include annual floods in the same location, perpetual mine disasters, and small riots in the Latin Quarter, eventually even the hijacking of aircraft may reach this list. In other words, those events which national decision-makers wish to identify and manage as crises are not constant.

Secondly, there is great difficulty in determining what is meant by management or control. Generally, management refers to the central government's efforts to bring the crisis under control by returning to the status quo. But, if crises are considered to have a permanent impact on the system, it will prove extraordinarily difficult to identify what the status quo might be in the wake of a crisis. In practical terms the list of government responsibilities enumerated under clause one of our definition might be helpful. But, how does one measure the success of the policy output? Even if the goal is to return to the 'status quo' as quickly as possible, this explains little about the alternatives of arriving at the objective. Whereas health policy effectiveness may be measured against (say) mortality rates of children or life expectancy statistics, there are no equivalent measures for crisis handling. That is, there are no obvious standards to compare government action to. Obviously, the number of deaths or injuries is a factor, but this must be weighed against such imponderables as the 'potential' or the 'magnitude of threat' of a crisis. At the extreme, crises consist of situations in which anything is possible – even the collapse of the regime itself. The multi-goaled nature of the policy process means that crisis management may involve an equation which consists of numbers of deaths and such values as freedom and law. These goals are likely to be incompatible in some crises.

Thirdly, it is difficult to determine which parts of the policy-making process are involved in crises. Of course, crisis management begins at home. The first individuals involved in a shipwreck are the sailors; in a mine disaster, miners; in a riot, rioters, etc. The actors involved expand by concentric circles to local, intermediary and central government authorities. While the collective behaviour of all these actors will affect crisis management, in this chapter we will be more concerned with the actions of governors than mass publics. In the short run the comparative study of crisis management can best be delineated by concentrating on central decision-makers – executives, sectors of the public service and especially such compliance forces as the military, security forces, and the ordinary police. This restricts the field of investigation, but the vantage point allows an examination of all crises that the government considers important. The focus is thus the central government management of crises, not an analysis of the crises as events. The crisis-event provides the situation or occasion for policy-making; central government's response is the result of the interaction of the occasion, the individual characteristics of decision-makers and the organizational context. (Robinson, 1970). While personality characteristics are important but difficult to handle in comparative cross-national research, (Barber, 1972) there is a somewhat greater possibility of indicating the effects of organizational behaviour. Yet even in this field we know little about the complex internal processes that crises provoke in central governments.

Fourthly, what can central governments do in response to crises? While Theodore Lowi's classification of policy output does not include crisis management the logic on which the classification is built may prove helpful. The political characteristics of distributive, redistributive, regulative and constituent policies are differentiated on one axis by the degree of directness or indirectness in the application of legitimate coercion. Common sense leads one to assume that governments will progress successively from the least coercive governing instruments to the most coercive. Over time all governing instruments will be employed. In Lowi's schema the executive's role will develop from 'passive' through 'co-ordinate' and 'supplicative' to 'legislative' output. (Lowi, 1972: 298-310). This hypothesis has proven useful for a tentative examination of normal policy-making in Canada. The sequence, however, appears to be incorrect for crises. The nature of crises is such that after symbolic output has been offered, governments are most likely to adopt the most coercive policies (legislate, employ compliance forces, etc.) and only after the crisis will they have time to allocate (spend) to anticipate and resolve future crises.

DYNAMICS OF POLICY-MAKING IN CRISES: CASES

Since there has been little or no literature about cross-national management of crises, some preliminary method must be found to obtain tentative generalizations or hypotheses for future examination. We might examine the literature on political development (usually institution-building) and the sequence of national problems (Binder, 1971); at this stage in our investigation this approach is probably too general to be useful for constructing hypotheses. This preliminary study, however, attempts to examine the pattern or configuration in government response to a number of non-representative (in the scientific sense) crises. With the exception of internal government crises (such as coups d'etat) the cases represent some of the major events that governments consider to be crises.

The cases include 15 events of civil violence and disaster which all meet the definitional requirements for a crisis. (see table 1) They provide possibilities for within nation and between nation comparisons over time. They were chosen both because there was a sufficient body of data and information on each case and because they differ from each other. That is, the research design was purposely constructed to study different types of crises rather than the 'most similar' cases. In the course of applying the steps in policy-making outlined in chapter one to the cases, however, we shall have to eliminate two events because they do not have the proper components to be considered here. At this stage in our investigation, it should be borne in mind that we are not attempting to unravel or explain the events themselves. John Fitzgerald Kennedy warned:

> The essence of ultimate decision remains impenetrable to the observer — often, indeed, to the decider himself . . . There will always be the dark and tangled stretches in the decision-making process — mysterious even to those who may be the most intimately involved.

TABLE 1
A Catalogue of Crises

Civil Violence		*Disasters*	
1. 2.	V.E. and V.J. Day Riots, Canada, 1945	8. 9. 10.	Manitoba Floods, Canada, 1950, 1966, 1969
3. 4.	Kingston Prison Riots, Canada, 1954, 1971	11.	Hurricane Hazel, Canada, 1954
5.	Montreal Police Strike, Canada, 1969	12.	Springhill Mine Disaster, Canada, 1958
6.	FLQ Kidnappings, Canada, 1970	13.	Torrey Canyon Pollution, Britain, 1967
7.	May Revolt, Paris, France, 1968	14.	Santa Barbara blob, USA, 1969
		15.	Arrow Pollution, Canada, 1970

SEQUENCE AND DYNAMICS OF POLICY-MAKING

1. *The Initial State*

In this period the normal life of the state is routinized. There is no crisis which requires a national response. From the point of view of 'crisis management' this is still a period of considerable importance. The ability of a government to handle a crisis depends considerably on what is done in 'normal' time. The ability to manage events depends greatly on the degree of anticipatibility.

In this pre-crisis stage, the effectiveness of later government response may be determined. (Powell and Royer, 1952). Warning of crises are determined by the quality of continuously monitoring, evaluating, forecasting and briefing the government about future difficulties. Indicators may be said to exist conceptually on a continuum from a simple forewarning to prediction. Forewarning consists of mere advance notice that a crisis is possibly, while prediction leads to projections of time, frequency, location, scope, intensity and duration of the event. Simple forewarning is presumably better than no indicator of a crisis, but it does not greatly aid the policy-maker because counter-arguments will normally be advanced asserting that no crisis will occur.

In this pre-crisis period, plans may be constructed to handle a future event. Such plans must be very carefully designed as organizations have difficulty adjusting to crises. In fact, adaptation must be built into the plan itself. Roberta Wohlstetter shows how the United States Army at Pearl Harbour was prepared to handle sabotage. When it was told to expect an attack *from without* it promptly activated its anti-sabotage activities. (Wohlstetter, 1962). Plans for crises may be classified as contingency schemes for specific emergencies and general plans for government response to any type of difficulty. Contingency plans *cannot* be drawn up for every *conceivable* crisis because this would require an infinite variety of responses. Consequently, contingency plans must be based on the most predictable crises. For example, detailed plans may be available for recurrent floods or hurricanes, but not for explosions, fires and transportation accidents.

Psychological literature indicates that if there is some form of warning in the pre-crisis period it will affect behavioural patterns. While some individuals will be blessed with what has been termed 'reflective fear' and become discriminately vigilant, others will act in a mal-adaptive fashion, over-reacting, or even developing psycho-neurotic symptoms. (Janis, 1962: 59). As usual, new events (even if ambiguous) will be interpreted by past experience – tornado victims often report having heard a loud train. (Beach, 1960). These considerations indicate that if crisis management is to be successful, there is a need to have the least possible ambiguous information and warning in the pre-crisis period.

In our fifteen cases the degree of predictability varied enormously. In each succeeding Manitoba flood from 1826 more information was available for prediction, so that the 1969 Manitoba flood was predicted with such precision that it would be said to have lost its crisis quality. Government indicators pointed to the location, extent, location, etc. of the flood and an automatic contingency plan, which did not involve the federal Canadian cabinet or politicians, was immediately put into effect. In every other case, some forewarning took place. The fore-warning consisted of event clues and did not emerge from any form of social science prediction. In the case of the VE day, VJ day and penitentiary riots, clues had been spotted, although they were in-accurate about the scope of the difficulties which followed. In the Springhill mines there had been 'bumps' every year (with an average death rate of ten) and a government team had been inspecting the 'bumps' shortly before the crisis. Hurrican Hazel came 24 hours after warnings from the Dominion Meteorological Offices at Malton Airport.

In the case of pollution, it had been known for some time that the chance of an oil tanker crashing off the shore of Britain, Canada or the United States was high. The possibility of a leak from an oil drilling rig had also been recognized, because drilling in any area of geologically unstable rock formation greatly increases the possibility of an oil leak. There had been legislative debates on the subject in all three countries, in the British case, the Cornish authorities had actually called a meeting on oil pollution before the disaster. But, in none of these cases was accurate prediction of the impending crisis thought possible.

In the three cases of collective violence — Montreal Police Strike, FLQ and May Revolt — prediction was impossible. Warnings took place before all three events, but there was no way for any of the govern-ments to evaluate the warnings. The press and other soothsayers con-tinually warn of such dangers but prophecies are rarely helpful to decision-makers.

In most of the events there were no plans to deal with the emer-gency situation. The norm can be represented by Hurricane Hazel. The first co-ordinating meeting which attempted to develop an organized plan for action did not occur until four days after the storm struck. The exceptions are military riots for which officers employed their normal plans for riot control, and the later Manitoba floods and the Santa Barbara Blob, both of which were resolved by putting into effect a contingency plan. Canadian governments had learned how to handle such floods and in the American crisis at Santa Barbara much had been learned from the oil leak of the Torrey Canyon in Britain. These cases imply that governments may be 'learning mechanisms', but, on the other hand, Canada did not learn from either the Torrey Canyon or the Santa Barbara Blob, although there was ample opportunity before the Arrow pollution case occurred.

2. *Placing a Condition on the Agenda of Political Controversy*

Once the status of crisis is awarded to an event, it is immediately placed on the agenda of political controversy. The event is a massive demand input. However, since the agenda of central decision-makers is always cluttered by competing policy demands, the ability to obtain crisis status for an issue or problem is most significant. The fact that an event meets the definitional requirements for a crisis does not automatically mean that the government will award it the status of a crisis. To some extent of course, Cabinet's recognition of an event implies some 'crisisness' has been awarded to the issue; a better test is whether the government reacts to the event.

In each of our cases crisis status was related to the identification and reaction of politicians to the situation. With the exception of the VJ day riots, political authorities upgraded the event from local demands to ask the central government to help resolve the issue. This would indicate that the VJ riots should be eliminated from the study, as a crisis without central government policy-making. In each of the remaining cases it was the extent of the crisis, not its presence, which caused the government's response. Riotous troop celebrations, prison upheavals, kidnappings and student riots in the Latin Quarter do not normally involve politicians directly. Manitoba floods occurred for a hundred years before the 1950 flood endangered the greatly grown city of Winnipeg. Massive damage and the 83 deaths made Hurricane Hazel into a crisis. In the case of the Springhill mine it was only when 174 individuals were buried (75 finally died) that a 'bump' finally became a crisis. The three pollution cases occurred during a period of growing concern for ecology.

Much crisis management occurs at the site of the event. The literature about participants' behaviour in crises is more extensive for disasters than for other types of crises. Contrary to popular (and often government) opinion, panic behaviour is rare; leadership is usually provided by those individuals with skills which are used in normal situations, and the behaviour of the affected population during the impact of a crisis is generally adaptive. (Tyhurst, 1951: 764-69). This means that even in the face of hardship the elevation of a local event to the national level is not too likely, and disaster victims often oppose government efforts during the height of the crisis. No research on this topic exists for civil violence.

3. *The Advancement of Demands*

Unlike non-crisis policy-making, there is by definition little time to evolve demands for government management for any particular crisis. The demands are placed on the agenda through the activities of the local authorities, press, police, or some other body. Even the liberal model of governing may have to be adjusted to account for the type of government response in crises since the members of the society usually play little, if any, role in the process. (Rose, 1973). In most cases placing a crisis on the agenda is equivalent to the advancement of the demand. For political authorities this crisis demand is overriding. Only in the long-run and especially for recurring crises, such as floods, can the normal demands of society be accommodated as in the liberal model.

With the exception of the French events of May, organized political demands were not made in these 15 cases. The crisis communication went from actors in the event to the national compliance forces; then the issue was placed on the agenda of the executive. The normal intermediary groups of a liberal society rarely have much of a role to play in such situations. The demand for police, troops, relief, subsidies, compensation, and other responses is not greatly related to political parties. Many politicians call for aid in a crisis; it is extremely rare to hear politicians arguing in a crisis that no central government policy is warranted.

Only in the case of the recurrent Manitoba floods and the Arrow disaster could one argue that there had been an advancement over time of demands. After the 1826 flood citizens had demanded special flood control plans and techniques, but only after the 1950 flood did such demands begin to be heard in provincial and federal politics. In the other cases the central government had an automatic responsibility because of statute or common law. In the VE day riots, it was Canadian troops which did the damage and therefore the federal government had to pay compensation. Prisons are a federal responsibility and the Kingston riots required a Cabinet decision in the form of an Order in Council before troops could be used. In the Montreal Police Strike and the FLQ crisis, the 'aid to civil power' sections of the National Defence Act were invoked by the Quebec Minister of Justice. When Section 233 is invoked a response by federal troops to a provincial Attorney General is mandatory.[1] No federal policy decision can be made about the use of the troops — although eventually the central decision-makers may play a role as the federal government did, for example, in the case of the FLQ when it finally enacted the War Measures Act. In the Paris May crisis, the French authorities were clearly responsible for public order. In contrast to Anglo-Saxon countries, French police are required to promote public order as well as to repress outbreaks against it. (Ridley and Blondel, 1964). The multitude of French events are well known and too intricate for repetition here. Possibly the most significant event was on May 3, when the rector of the University of Paris, Jean Roche, after consultations with Alain Peyrefitte, Minister of Education, called in the police to eject several hundred students from the Sorbonne. After that the trail of unrelated events would bewilder even a Sherlock Holmes of crises. The automatic elevation of the university crisis to the highest government level was spontaneous. There was no rise of demands in the singular sense after that event; a myriad of conflicting demands emerged from a deeply divided society. Students of collective violence have almost always concentrated on the causes of violence or the input side of these questions. Few social scientists have considered what governments do or ought to do in the face of social upheaval. It is thus not surprising that the social science literature on the May crisis is devoted entirely to the causation side of the equation.

In the disaster cases (except the floods discussed above) demands were localized in the disaster area. In Hurricane Hazel and Springhill, the demands were raised to a national public outcry because of the extent of the difficulties. The federal troops were called out automatically by the provincial authorities and therefore no political decision-making took place in the initial stages. The federal government was not the major participant until compensation was demanded.

In only one of the three pollution crises did public demand mount before government action took place. In Britain the government accepted responsibility for a response within two hours of the crash and in Santa Barbara within a matter of several hours. In both cases the disasters were outside the three-mile limit and were therefore either federal or international responsibilities. Theoretically, Britain committed piracy when it bombed the Torrey Canyon in international waters, but it was undertaken in 'defence of the realm'; in Santa Barbara the coastguard took control immediately. In the Canadian pollution case public demand was required before the government put the case on its agenda. Two weeks of local, provincial and media pressure finally provoked government response.

4. *Reviewing Resources and Constraints*

A favourite contemporary method used to explain government policies is through the examination of economic resources and expenditure patterns. However, such economic determininism is unlikely to help in the study of crisis management. The limited resources of a state get conveniently forgotten when there is pressure to resolve a crisis. While this position is consistent with the comparative work of Arnold J. Heidenheimer (1973: 315-40) Anthony King (1973: 219-313), and Richard M. Bird (1970), it does not accord with publications which find that political variables explain little of the variation in policies in the United States or Canada. (Hofferbert, 1970: 316-44). Even if spending on maintaining order is used as the policy output (unsatisfactorily, we believe), data from another study show that approximately the same percentage of the national budget has been allotted to the French Ministry of the Interior since the middle of the 19th century. Since the most extreme forms of crises have come and gone continually since then, it is surprising that there is little variability in relevant aspects of the budget. Crisis management is a field where the study of government expenditure patterns may prove to be of limited importance.

The canvassing of alternatives and the alternative chosen are not predetermined in crises by economic constraints. The manner in which governments survey the resources and constraints for a decision has been examined from a multitude of perspectives in social science. The decision-making literature is divided roughly into incrementalist, (Braybrooke and Lindblom, 1963), rationalist (Dror, 1968), and mixed scanning models (Etzioni, 1969). The rationalist models are based on various theories which include the classical theory of the firm, statistical decision theory and game theory. The theoretical arguments against the possible use of rational planning in central governments cannot be repeated here. (Jackson and Atkinson, 1974). In a crisis, rationality may be an ideal to aim at, but it cannot easily be realized. In real situations all options cannot be determined, especially for the long term. As one organizational theorist put it: all decisions are made under one of three sets of conditions —

a) certainty — 'alternatives in the choice to be made are known and each alternative is known invariably to lead to a specific outcome'.
b) risk — 'the alternatives are known and each alternative leads to one of a set of possible specific outcomes, each outcome occuring with a known probability'.
c) uncertainty — 'the probabilities of specific outcomes are unknown or perhaps not even meaningful'. (Taylor, 1955: 50).

At the time of the impact of crises the decision(s) are close to the uncertainty end of this scale making rational decision-making impossible. However, the government response to a crisis (as opposed to the crisis itself) takes place over time, and thus various forms of decision-making may take place.

Incrementalism is usually assumed to be the policy-making method of 'administrative' man. The administrator is thought to construct a simplified model of the world and to act only in relation to this model. He does not search out all alternatives (that would be too costly) but selects some minimum satisfactory conditions and chooses the first alternative he finds which satisfies his requirements for a decision. He 'satisfices'. Since he knows the status quo best, radical change is unlikely. Thus, policy-making progresses by slow disjointed incremental steps.

This type of policy-making theory is also consistent with the idea that organizations are not a single unit, and while sub-units may take actions which are perfectly rational for them, the result will be incremental policies. The goals of any one government sub-unit may be quite different from overall government goals. In the Cuban missile crisis, for example, all of the military men on the committee advising the President favoured direct military action. (Kennedy, 1969). Graham T. Allison (1971: 145) has summed up the inter-departmental conflict which even prevents the use of standing operating routines in a crisis:

> Choices by one player (e.g. to authorize action by his department, to make a speech or refrain from acquiring certain information), resultants of minor games (e.g. the wording of a cable or the decision on departmental action worked out among lower level players), resultants of central games (e.g. decisions, actions and speeches bargained out among central players), and 'foul-ups' (e.g. choices that are not made because they are not recognized or are raised too late, misunderstandings, etc.) – These pieces, when stuck to the same canvas, constitute government behaviour relevant to an issue.

The conclusion from this research is that the net behaviour of a government in a crisis is rarely the intended activity of any group, especially since during a crisis politicians may have to rely even more heavily on their advisors for a rapid answer than during routine policy-making.

The compromise to these two models of decision-making is found in 'mixed scanning'. (Etzioni, 1967: 385-92). In this model the executive engages in both rational policy-making and incrementalism. When the cabinet asks for alternatives, it is more than satisficing; it is employing rationalism to offset the conservative bias in incrementalism. Now when we apply this model to crises we find that both forms of policy-making may exist at different stages in the process of crisis-handling. At the onset of a crisis, central government organizations, since they dislike uncertainty, will search out the most obvious solutions in a search for certainty. Short-run considerations will be paramount, not long-range planning. The search for solutions in the impact stage will be in the realm of solutions which have been employed in the past. It is this behaviour which makes organizations appear to learn. Partial solutions are likely because the usual response to a crisis will be the least possible change to return to the status quo. Unfortunately two unsatisfactory results emerge from this form of policy-making. First, crisis responses are likely to be 'handled sluggishly or inappropriately'. (Allison, 1971: 89). And, secondly, while politicians will attempt to keep the options open rather than rely on old solutions, this will be difficult. 'With the onset of a crisis, the total number of communication channels [and decision-making groups] used for the collection and distribution of information will be reduced'. (Dynes and Quarantelli, 1948: 140). And, the number of alternative policies for handling the event will be narrowed. (Holsti, 1969: 226-48). But, after the impact stage more alternatives may be canvassed and basic objectives will be considered.

Our cases of crises bear out this thesis about policy-making. In the initial stage of each crisis the most obvious old solution was used. The organizations were divided, confusion ensued, and the result was only a partial solution to the problem. While specific laws governed the legal responsibilities in each Canadian case there was delay, confusion and inefficiency in the government's response. Communication between local authorities and central government officials was direct, inappropriate and often legally incorrect. Only in those cases where the hierarchy of command was clear — as in the troop and prison riots — was this not detrimental to the solution of the crisis. The best example of the problem was in the case of the sinking of the ship *Arrow*. For the first 16 days the Ministry of Transport left the operation to the oil company and merely acted as an observer. During that time the individual representing the Emergency Measures Organization was not accepted as having any authority, Cabinet did not regard the event as a crisis, and oil poured into Chedabucto Bay. As usual the easiest alternatives were chosen first — statements of intent, speeches and the like — and then immediately the compliance forces were used. In the long-run contingency plans were drawn up and something approaching rational policy-making may be said to have occurred. In the case of the American Santa Barbara Blob, the initial crisis was handled by a contingency plan, as was each succeeding flood in Manitoba. Planning can aid in the management of crises, but if the crises differ from what is expected (as is likely) the standing operating routines will restrict the handling of the event, make the initial response 'ad hoc', and rational approaches will only be possible in later stages of the crisis.

5. Shifting From No Decision to Decision

Once the crisis status has been awarded, there will automatically be decisions for the short-run. In every case governments will attempt to assure the public that someone is handling the crisis. In social crises, in particular, such symbolic outputs are important and will presumably determine to some extent how the public will regard the government. Symbolic outputs are relatively easy to dispense, but they are rarely sufficient. Coercive instruments will be required. In collective violence cases the use of troops, police and their equipment is rarely a subject for debate among central decision-makers. In all of our cases in federal countries the compliance forces were employed *without* a formal central government decision. The laws and precedents have evolved so that municipal officers can obtain the use of the compliance forces through the direct decision of provincial or state authorities. In the initial stages, then, federal political leaders were active more in a supporting than in a command role.

In the short run, it is unlikely that there will be much difference between the time of the ritual decision and the real moment of determining which policy to follow. The deadlines for governments to respond to disaster and collective violence provide special timetables unlike those for normal policy-making. In our seven cases of collective violence, compliance forces were used, and then a variety of long-term policies were enacted to pay compensation, improve prisons, increase policemen's pay, enhance the bilingual policy, inaugurate special financial schemes to aid Quebec, and in the case of France, to call a referendum, be forced into an election, agree to the Grenelle compromise for the highest percentage of raises for working men since 1945, and dismantle the Napoleonic educational system. In the disasters, the decisions first concerned co-ordination and later compensation, building prisons, passing new shipping laws, and contingency planning for future similar crises. All of these results were due to the spill-over effect and could be said to be opportunities resulting from the crises.

In the pollution cases, political control varied enormously. In Great Britain, Maurice Foley, Parliamentary Secretary for Defence (Royal

Navy) arrived on the scene the second day of the crisis, and immediately provided leadership for the operation. The Cabinet Committee in London was seized of the problem by the fifth day — before
the oil hit the beaches. In the Santa Barbara case the Department of
Interior pollution experts flew to the scene immediately and the Secretary of the Interior visited the scene shortly after the event occurred.
The exception was in Canada. When the Arrow crashed all the agencies,
such as the Coastguard, the Emergency Measures Organization (EMO)
and the Ministry of Transport were informed quickly on the first day,
but they did relatively little. Ottawa left the disaster to the oil company. In the second week the Ministry of Transport was given operational control over the organization, but their representative did not
have the authority to make decisions. Eventually federal leaders took
an interest and 16 days after the event a central government task force
began coordination.

With the possible exception of the FLQ crisis, jurisdictional disputes
between municipal, provincial or federal governments did not cause
significant difficulties in the early stages of central government
response. This was to be expected in the unitary governments of Britain
and France; the Santa Barbara Blob occurred first in waters under the
jurisdiction of the American federal administration. In most of the
Canadian cases the federal troops and the central government only
became involved because of the request of other political authorities. In
the American and British pollution cases, central government control
was exercised almost immediately. In the United Kingdom, the Prime
Minister and the Standing Emergency Committee of Cabinet exercised
control, and in the United States a federal contingency plan was put
into effect by a lieutenant and the federal Department of the Interior
automatically became the co-ordinating agency. In Canada confusion
about the seriousness of the Arrow disaster caused difficulty in establishing clear lines of authority. In all three cases, when the oil reached
the shore, other levels of government became involved. Co-ordination in
the British and American cases proceeded without difficulty. In
Canada, however, jurisdictional confusion helped the government delay
two weeks before taking action. When McTaggart-Cowan was finally
sent to lead the task force he was assigned specific responsibility for
co-ordination with the Nova Scotia government. While the federal
Ministry of Transport was initially responsible, this changed when the
oil washed on to the beaches. The administrative conflict has still not
been resolved, since two federal departments now have legal responsibility — the Ministry of Transport and the Department of the

Environment. The question of compensation was handled most easily in England. London simply informed the local authorities that they would receive 75 percent of their operating costs for handling the pollution, but that in no case were they to raise the rates more than two pennies in the pound to fight the disaster. The British government then sued the shipping line. In the Santa Barbara case, the California local authorities sued the federal government for half a billion dollars to recoup their losses.

At least in these cases explanations of governmental response to crises couched in terms of the federal or unitary nature of the government seem to contribute little to an understanding of crisis management. When contingency plans were present, federal governments were able to act with the same flexibility as unitary governments. This leads to the proposition that differences in crisis management may depend very little on differences in constitutional division of powers.

6. *The Determinants of Government Choice and Content*

This paper has been based on the hypothesis that variations in choices and responses to crises are little affected by national environment visualized in economic, cultural or institutional terms. (Groth, 1971). The cases — with the exception of May 1968, France — illustrate little significant variation in government management between cases or between the three countries. The sequence of government response in particular appears unaffected by national or crisis-specific characteristics. The leadership for each crisis came essentially from one minister until the crisis gained a highly volatile political significance. For example, Cabinet agreement was sought to pay compensation in every case and to use troops to storm the Kingston prison. In the FLQ affair Cabinet was involved but the Prime Minister took the lead. And in the flood disasters provincial control was dominant. Only in the Candian pollution case did Cabinet play no role; the minister and Ministry of Transport were the main actors. Legislative bodies had no functions in the crises until the main decisions and actions were taken. Afterwards, they had a role in debating the issue and reassuring the public.

The formal characteristics or content of responses vary with time; eventually all governing instruments are used. However, Lowi's hypothesis that governments will begin with the least coercive and move to the most coercive instrument is untrue in the case of crises. Symbolic outputs came first in every case; the government provided statements of intent, speeches, and encouraged dignitaries to visit the victims. There is a tendency for the most coercive instrument to be the second alternative because there is no time to allocate or spend. Moreover, a government will be prone to use the most coercive instruments as early as possible because it has control of these forces, and can be reasonably certain of what they can do. Politicians may begin with the feeling that they will get 'burned' in a crisis, but when they do face up to the necessity to act they will tend to want a 'quick fix' on the situation. It is this reaction that gives coercive organizations such power during crisis. In all of these cases compliance forces were employed secondly because there was no time to spend or legislate, and the military and police had established structure, equipment and standard operating procedures for reaction to crises. Moreover, the police and military could be activated by municipal or provincial authorities without consultation with the central government.

The only exception to this pattern of coercion before allocation occurred in the third Manitoba flood. Otherwise, all the cases show the same output pattern – symbolic, troops, and lastly legislation and allocation. The legislative phase and the use of troops may coincide, as for example when the Canadian government enacted the War Measures Act, or the final phase may be a constitutional act – e.g. the dissolution of Parliament – instead of a spending phase. On occasion a third phase of symbolic output occurred before the allocation phase – the best illustration of this is in the work of Royal Commissions or Advisory Committees which advise the government on the allocation of funds to alleviate crisis-stricken or crisis-prone areas.

7. Implementation

In order for policies to be implemented in a crisis, the field situation must be correctly understood. In the early stage the participants will be attempting to resolve their own problems. Symptoms of stress will be felt by most citizens, class barriers will decrease and public interaction with strangers will increase. (Drayer, 1957: 151-59). During the riots in the Latin Quarter in May, 1968 individuals would stop perfect strangers on the street and query them about society and their personal financial resources. In this period the uncoordinated nature of recovery activity at the local level leads to conflict and inefficiency, but at the same time the participants are usually hostile to government interference and prefer to receive help from organizations which are part of the community or well known to them. Then, as the recovery stage advances social solidarity deteriorates and social differentiation returns. Individuals begin to think about their future rather than about the crisis. The process of social differentiation returns and the standards of reference change from values of survival to values associated with continuity and stability.

If crisis management is viewed in terms of command and control functions – reacting to indicators in the pre-crisis state and taking decisions during the crisis – then it can be argued that, with the possible exception of the FLQ crisis, federal cabinet control in Canada has been somewhat ineffective. The least government disruption was in the Torrey Canyon disaster where the British junior ministerial system allowed a flexibility not found in the Canadian, American or French cases. Except for the use of the military (and symbolic output) central political involvement usually began *after* the crisis had passed. Setting up inquiries and providing financial assistance was the major activity. In general, the Canadian cases show that federal political handling of crises has been in the post-crisis stage. The pre-crisis stage seems to be considered insignificant[2] and in the actual crisis period politicians, to some extent, avoided involvement.

8. *The Production of Outputs and Evaluation*

While records of expenditure and manpower requirements are easily researched, a difficulty comes in measuring the outputs. How does one measure the output or evaluate the War Measures Act which suspended civil liberties in Canada, or the Gaullist decision to call an election to quell the May 1968 revolt. Even in disasters the potential deaths or property damage or polluted beaches must be evaluated, compensation to stores and flood victims determined against an abstract threat of possible difficulties. Moreover, the outputs are often in the form of 'positional' policy which defies statistical treatment. The most important government decisions in the aftermath of the FLQ crisis may have been to organize an analysis and planning secretariat in the Solicitor General's Office and organize a Crisis Management Study Group. In all 15 cases, however, new plans for future emergencies were constructed. The most successful, was the plan for the handling of the Manitoba floods and the provision of an $83,000,000 floodway so that future floods would by-pass Winnipeg.

9. *Feedback*

No means have yet been developed for systematically evaluating crisis handling in any of our four countries. All governments prepare post-incident analyses, create new plans and categorize what they have learned from a crisis. The difficulty in studying feedback is how to catalogue all the massive changes in structure and behaviour that occur because of a crisis. No equivalents of programming, planning and budgeting, cost-benefit analysis or management by objectives has been attempted in this field.

After a crisis the major actors normally conclude that there was to much 'ad hoc' behaviour. During the crisis, they will be subject to fear of a single catalytic event which create great political or social discontinuities. Thus, they respond to each event as a unique phenomenon. This is soon forgotten after the event. After the crisis, prescriptive forms of thought lead to assumptions of rationality and a new planning phase commences. Routine and standard operating procedures go back into effect. New structures are set up in parts of the policy-process. If the total package of reforms were ideal then there would be no more crises − at least not in those fields where crises had already occurred. Like revolutions, crises would carry the seeds of their own self-destruction even if different forms of crises emerge.

The most important consequences may be in the development of or the loss of diffuse support for the political system. Crisis responses rarely show up in election manifestos. But their results spill over into other substantive policy areas. In our cases they helped in decisions to provide new prison reforms, special considerations for Quebec, higher wages for police and firemen, education reforms, higher wages for workers, improved flood control, location of prisons, better mine legislation, new pollution regulations, etc. Therefore, the results of crises must also be judged by studying other policy areas.

FUTURE STUDIES OF CRISIS
MANAGEMENT AND POLICY-MAKING

Some hypotheses and conclusions from this paper warrant further empirical investigation.

1. There are similarities in most crises in what might be called the procedure of response, if not the substance of the response. The whole range of instruments can only be used if there is adequate time; this is not the case during the height of crises. In disasters and collective violence, the secondary forms of spending or allocating are used after all other instruments are attempted. During crises governments will search for certainty and the use of compliance forces will appear more certain than other forms of policy-making.

Legislation is usually enacted only in the aftermath of the crises.

2. In unfamiliar situations some degree of trial and error is likely. Consequently, incrementalism is the decision-making model which most approximates behaviour in the initial stages of crises. Afterwards, the degree of rational-planning modes is increased. However, the consequences of rational planning are determined by the degree of predictability of the crises; when they become highly predictable (especially when this extends to location, scope, intensity, duration and so on) then by definition the crisis disappears.

3. Governments do learn from handling crises; in a few cases this is helpful when the next case occurs. The United States government learned from the sinking of the Torrey Canyon. Canada did not: it had to experience its own crisis first. This illustrates clearly the need for more comparative policy studies, work that could have practical application.

4. The content of crises varies over time, but the procedures and government response do not. Thus, except for recurring crises, such as floods in the same location, the new rational policy-making structures set up to resolve crises are not often a complete success.

5. The behaviour of senior politicians in crises is badly understood. With rare exceptions personality characteristics have not been used to analyse crisis handling at the highest level. The role of politicians in assigning the status of crisis to events should be further explored. This is very difficult because one needs to determine if some objective or subjective conditions forced the status upon the issue, or whether the politicians raised the issue to crisis status because they thought it could be solved.

6. The termination of a crisis almost always brings with it new 'positional' policy; that is, new units are set up, departments reorganized, contingency plans organized, personnel re-assigned, etc. This positional policy affects future government behaviour both in crises (especially in defining them) and in normal policy-making. Thus the crisis spills over into other policy fields.

7. Aside from the normal psychological distortions in crises, our cases have now shown little cultural or national character differences in policy-making during crises. A further in-depth investigation, employing very similar circumstances would be required. But, the basic premise should be that crisis management will be determined more by the factors of normal organizational behaviour and the normal bargaining process than by between-nation differences per se.

8. The alternative policies for crisis handling are usually very narrow in the short run, but the constraints are not basically economic.

9. The type of crisis does not appear to structure the sequence of government policy-making.

10. The long-run consequences of crisis-handling have not been explored except slightly in political developmental literature. The solution to disruptive events has a profound effect on government and regime legitimacy, but no one has yet demonstrated how this process occurs. While students of collective behaviour have examined how violence or non-violence is related to degrees of legitimacy, they have not tried to calculate how the handling of crisis affects legitimacy. The governors have been left out of the models of social interaction and violence. To what extent is public order a function of the past handling of crisis events? If there is 'no significant correlation between economic and social standards and national levels of political violence' (Van der Mehden, 1973), is it not possible that the manner of responding to crises is an important determinant of conflict traditions and hence public order?

11. All types of policy output appear to result from crises: linear, static, cyclical and discontinuous. A new typology of crises must be developed before it will be clear why such variations in policy type emerge from crises. This should be the next step in what will be a long search for theory in this most relevant field.[3] Our analysis provides a beginning to this task. The relations between crises and policy-making are made meaningful by a four-fold table which employs the degree of predictability of crises (high-low) and the ability to know what the options are (certain-uncertain) as the major variables.

Table 2:

Crises & Policies
Knowledge of Options

Predicta- bility	Certain	Uncertain
High	floods	police strike
Low	hurricanes mine disasters pollution crashes	riots FLQ May Revolt

The·fifteen crises and the policy options studied in this chapter fit into the table easily. The next step is to develop this typology further.

NOTES

1. The Report of the Standing Committee on External Affairs and Defence, June 29, 1972 summarized the law as that 'Under section 233 of the National Defence Act the Canadian Armed Forces can be called out in aid of the civil power. The Canadian Forces or any unit or other element thereof, or any officer or man, with material, are liable to be called out for service in aid of civil power, in any case in which a riot or disturbance of the peace requiring such service occurs, or is, in the opinion of an Attorney General, considered as likely to occur, and that is beyond the powers of the civil authorities to suppress, prevent, or deal with'. Of course, the military leaders (and their political masters) decide how many troops are employed even if they cannot decide that no troops should be deployed.

2. In planning for crises there is usually an overestimate of how much control may be imposed by governments. Failure is then interpreted as bad planning and a new cycle of planning occurs.

3. Some general approaches to historical crises and development may be found in G. Almond, et al (1973) Crisis, Choice and Change. Boston: Little, Brown.

REFERENCES

ALLISON, G. T. (1971) Essence of Decision: Explaining the Cuban Missile Crisis. Boston: Little, Brown.
BARBER, J. D. (1972) The Presidential Character: Predicting Performance in The White House. Englewood Cliffs: Prentice-Hall.

BARTON, A. H. (1963) Social Organization Under Stress: A Sociological Review of Disaster Studies. Washington: NAS-NRC.

BEACH, H. D. (1960) Individual and Group Behaviour in a Coal Mine Disaster. Washington: National Research Council.

BETHELHEIM, B. (1943) 'Individual and Mass Behavior in Extreme Situations', *Journal of Abnormal and Social Psychology* 38: 417-52.

BINDER, L. (1971) Crises and Sequences in Political Development. Princeton: Princeton Univ. Press.

BIRD, R. M. (1970) The Growth of Government Spending in Canada. Toronto: Canadian Tax Foundation.

BOULDING, K. E. (1961) Conflict and defense. New York: Harper.

BRAYBROOKE, D. and C. LINDBLOM (1963) A Strategy of Decision. New York: Free Press.

CAWS, P. (1965) The Philosophy of Science. Princeton: Van Nostrand.

DRAYER, C. S. (1957) 'Psychological Factors and Problems, Emergency and Long Term', *Annals* 309: 151-59.

DROR, Y. (1968) Public Policy Making Re-Examined. San Francisco: Chandler.

DURRELL, L. (1958) Mountolive. London: Faber.

DYNES, R. R. (1969) Organized Behavior in Disaster: Analysis and Conceptualization. Mimeo. Contract OCD-PS-64-46, Work Unit 2651-A.

――― and E. L. QUARANTELLI (1948) 'Group Behavior Under Stress: A Required Convergence of Organizational and Collective Behavior Perspectives'. *Sociology and Social Research* 52: 420.

Emergency Preparedness in the Canadian Federal Government (1973) Ottawa: Information Canada.

ETZIONI, A. (1969) The Active Society. New York: Free Press.

――― (1961) Complex Organizations. New York: Free Press.

――― (1967) 'Mixed Scanning, A Third Approach to Policy Making', *Public Administration Review* 27: 385-92.

FEIERABEND, I. K. et al (1972) Anger, Violence and Politics: Theories and Research. Englewood Cliffs: Prentice-Hall.

FRITZ, C. E. (1971) 'Disaster', in R. K. Merton and R. Nisbet (eds.), Contemporary Social Problems. New York: Harcourt, Brace and World.

GAWTHROP, L. (1969) Bureaucratic Behaviour in the Executive Branch. New York: Free Press.

GROTH, A. J. (1971) Comparative Politics: A Distributive Approach. New York: Macmillan.

HAMBLIN, R. L. (1958) 'Group Integration During a Crisis', *Human Relations* II: 67.

HECLO, H. H. (1972) 'Policy Analysis', *British Journal of Political Science* II L: 83-108.

HEIDENHEIMER, A. J. (1973) 'The Politics of Public Education, Health and Welfare in the USA and Western Europe', *British Journal of Political Science* 3: 315-40.

HERMANN, C. F. (1972) International Crises. New York: Free Press.

――― (1963) 'Some Consequences of Crisis Which Limit the Viability of Organizations', *Administrative Science Quarterly* VIII: 64.

HOFFERBERT, R. (1970) 'Elite Influence in State Policy Formation: A Model for Comparative Inquiry', *Polity* 3: 316-44.

HOLSTI, O. R. (1972) Crisis, Escalation, War. Montreal: McGill – Queens Press.

––– (1969) 'The 1914 Case' in J. Mueller (ed.), Approaches to Measurement in International Relations. New York: Appleton Crafts.

JACKSON, R. (1972) 'Politicians, Parliament and Policy-Making'. Unpublished paper.

–––, and M. ATKINSON (1974) The Canadian Legislative System: Politicians and Policy-Making. Toronto: Macmillan.

––– and M. STEIN (1971) Issues in Comparative Politics. New York: St. Martins.

JANIS, I. L. (1962) 'Psychological Effects of Warnings', in G. W. Baker and D. W. Chapman (eds.), Man and Society in Disaster. New York: Basic Books.

KENNEDY, R. (1969) Thirteen Days. Chicago: W. W. Norton.

KING, A. (1973) 'Ideas, Institutions and the Policies of Governments: A Comparative Analysis', *British Journal of Political Science* 3: 291-313.

LA PALOMBARA, J. and M. WEINER (eds.) (1969) Political Parties and Political Development. Princeton, Princeton Univ. Press.

LINDBLOM, C. (1968) The Policy-Making Process. Englewood Cliffs: Prentice-Hall.

LIPSET, S. M. (1953) 'Opinion Formation in a Crisis Situation', *Public Opinion Quarterly* 17: 20-46.

LOWI, T. (1964) 'American Business, Public Policy, Case Studies and Political Theory', *World Politics* XVI: 4: 677-715.

––– (1972) 'Four Systems of Policy, Politics and Choice', *Public Administration Review* 32: 298-310.

MCCLELLAND, C. A. (1961) 'The Acute International Crisis', *World Politics* 14: 182-204.

MILLER, K. and Ira ISCOE (1963) 'The Concept of Crisis: Current Status and Mental Health Implications', *Human Organization* 22: 195-201.

NIXON, R. (1962) Six Crises. Garden City, N.Y.: Doubleday.

PAGE, G. D. (1968) The Korean Decision: June 24-30. New York: Free Press.

POWELL, J. W. and Jeanette ROYER (1952) Progress Notes: Disaster Investigation. Edgewood, Maryland: Army Chemical Centre.

RIDLEY, F. and J. BLONDEL (1964) Public Administration in France. London: Barnes and Noble.

ROBINSON, J. A. (1968) 'Crisis', International Encyclopedia of Social Sciences: 510-514. 1. New York: Free Press.

–––, (1970) 'The Concept of Crisis in Decision-Making', in N. Rosenbaum (ed.), Readings in The International Political System. Englewood Cliffs: Prentice-Hall.

––– and Richard SNYDER (1965) 'Decision-Making in International Politics', in H. C. Kelman (ed.), International Behaviour: A Socio-Psychological Analysis. New York: Holt.

ROSE, R. (1973) 'Comparing Public Policy', *European Journal of Political Research* 1: 84-5.

SIMON, H. A. (1958) 'The Role of Expectations in an Adaptive or Behavioriatic Model' in M. J. Bowman (ed.), Expectations, Uncertainty and Business Behaviour. New York: Social Science Research Council.

TAYLOR, D. W. (1955) 'Decision Making and Problem Solving', in J. G. March (ed.), Handbook of Organizations. Chicago: Rand McNally.

TYHURST, J. S. (1951) 'Individual Reactions to Community Disaster: The Natural History of Psychiatric Phenomena'. *American Journal of Psychiatry* 107: 764-69.

VAN DER MEHDEN, F. (1973) Comparative Political Violence. Englewood Cliffs: Prentice-Hall.

WEBER, M. (1949) The Methodology of Social Sciences. Glencoe: Free Press.

WIENER, A. J. and H. KAHN (1962) Crisis and Arms Control. New York: Hudson Institute.

WILLIAMS, H. B. (1957) 'Some Functions of Communication in Crisis Behaviour', *Human Organization* 16: 15-19.

WOHLSTETTER, R. (1962) Pearl Harbour: Warning and Decision. Stanford: Stanford Univ. Press.

WOLIN, S. S. (1960) Politics and Vision. Boston: Little, Brown.

Chapter IX

CONCLUSION:
POLICY DYNAMICS

Hugh Heclo

The Brookings Institution, Washington D.C.

The story is told of a circus dog who would bury bones under the ticket wagon in one town and spend the next day trying to dig them up under the same wagon in another town. Policy-makers and political scientists can appreciate the feeling. Dynamic changes in public policy seem so overwhelming that both actors and scholars are often left digging in barren ground as the show inexorably moves on. The growing attention to policy dynamics is an expression of both dissatisfaction and hope — dissatisfaction with the tendency for our understanding to be overtaken by events and hope for somehow doing better in the future.

The preceding eight chapters have offered a range of empirical illustrations of how changes have operated in a number of policy areas. The authors have done so with an explicitly comparative focus across nations, time, and subject matter. This final chapter will attempt to sift through these and other materials to delineate general features in the study of policy dynamics. In the first section dynamics is placed within a broader framework of stability and change. We then examine more closely the basic concepts likely to be associated with any dynamically changing policy. The final section speculates about political processes and institutions to cope with dynamic change.

These themes can be introduced by returning to the four models of change sketched in Chapter 1: statics, cycles, linear progress, and discontinuity. Two conclusions seem clear from the subsequent case studies. First, the four models overlap to such a considerable degree that they are probably best thought of as a continuum for ideal types.

Second, orienting ourselves to them depends less upon inherent qualities of the policy under study and more upon the particular aims and perspective of the analyst-observer. It is necessary to stress how far the type of change discovered is relative to the analyst's perspective. In the example of the circus dog, we see an essentially static picture from one view: certainly the dog is forever losing his bone. In terms of the dog's behavior, we can identify a cyclical alternation between possession, burying, search, and loss. From yet another viewpoint the system suggests linear progression from one town and bone to the next. Finally, a more dynamic picture emerges if we imagine interactions of the system over time; the dog's essential problem is to adapt to unfolding contingencies. Discontinuity will be introduced if, in time, the dog learns to consume bones as he acquires them or, better still, to hide them in rather than under the wagon.

The preceding authors show very well the perceptual relativity of policy change. For example, J. A. Brand concentrates on the cycle of local government reform (more precisely on the 'upswing' from disenchantment to reform); he also provides evidence of the need for cumulative functional changes, which gradually sharpen the symbolic significance of existing structures. Christopher Hood shows that by covering a longer time period cyclical policy developments can be associated with linear tendencies, such as the addition of different, somewhat inconsistent aims for fishing policy. Moreover, the cycles and externalities do not simply repeat themselves but also introduce discontinuities in the conception of what such policy is about; the effect of British entry into the EEC upon inshore and deepsea fishing is a good example of such change. Thomas Bowden shows that the 1921 discontinuity in Britain's Irish policy was in one sense an abrupt break, but in another sense the culmination of forty years of undermining Britain's security forces in Ireland. Irish partisans are more likely to see events from the perspective of a century of linear progress to independence.

In general, the four preliminary models help organize different aspects of change, not in terms of inherent subject matter qualities, but in terms of different facets of the same policy and of alternative analytic concerns. The interpretive character of this framework means that views will differ, but they need not do so arbitrarily. Rather than using mutually exclusive categories we can think of a continuum of more or less dynamic policy changes. One moves from the static to the dynamic end of this continuum the more that circumstances at time two are contingent on preceding events at time one. To say this is to speak of something more specific than causation in general, without reliance upon events in an unfolding strand of historical time. (In fact most laws of physical sciences apply regardless of whether time runs forward or backwards.)

A CONTINUUM OF CHANGE

Statics and dynamics can be thought of as two extremes in a continuum of change. The basic criteria for moving along this continuum is the extent to which we analyse events (processes, conditions, outputs and so forth) in terms of their dependence on the passage of historic time.[1] The more the analyst pays attention to the kind of cumulative interrelatedness and temporal irreversibility that might exist in policy, the more his analysis moves toward the dynamic end of the scale. This suggests that there are a number of waystations between the extremes of pure statics and pure dynamics. In this section we will describe and illustrate the continuum (Figure 1) in greater detail. While

FIGURE 1

A Continuum of Policy Change: Analytic Approaches and Orienting Questions

	Attribute Correlation	Steady State Processes	Comparative Statics	Sequence Analysis	Selective Reprogramming	Comprehensive Reprogramming	
STATICS							DYNAMICS
	What goes with what?	How do things work, get processed?	What difference does X make to the working of things?	What are the stages of change?	What are the elements of change?	What are the configurations of change?	

the term dynamic is often thought to indicate a superior and more interesting insight by its user, we should not denegrate less dynamic approaches. Statics has a quite respectable position in fields such as economics or engineering and so should it too in political studies. We are speaking of different analytic approaches, none of which is universally applicable to the many facets of policy processes and all of

---

[1] The term historic time is used to differentiate time as a past, present, and future with existential content from physicists' conception of time as a succession of abstract moments.

which may aid our understanding of stability and change. THE policy process does not exist.

Statics

Static conceptualizations treat policy events and interactions as if at some universal moment. The temporal succession of moments is taken to make no material difference to the structure of the situation. Probably the most common form of such analysis by political scientists interested in public policy is attribute correlation: attempts to find what goes with what. There is no need here to review the many studies testing statistical correlations among political/economic conditions and policy outputs (see, for example, Fry and Winters 1970; Jackman, 1974). One of the most important things they illustrate is that the results of such studies can be extremely sensitive to alternative ways of operationalizing variables, particularly policy outputs.

Quantified statistical correlations are not necessary. Traditionally, most political analyses have been at the verbal level and sought to identify conditions under which a certain type of policy tends to appear. At least since the days of the Federalist Papers, fragmentation has been a favorite touchstone; one of the central justifications of America's Constitution was the argument that more consensual, less oppressive policy would be associated with a federalized republic and divided branches operating in a heterogenous society. Similarly, a number of modern scholars have used the same theme in looking at the degree of correspondence between the coherence/fragmentation of inputs on the one hand and decision-making systems on the other. It is suggested, for example, that distributive policies tend to appear when both demands and decision-making are fragmented, regulative policies when only demands are fragmented, and so on. Or it may be thought that certain types of structures may, in certain varieties of contexts, lead to policies with certain qualities (Ripley et al., 1973).

Such static analysis is applicable to change as well as stability. The preceding article by Guy Peters shows how attribute correlation can illuminate changes that are linear or curvilinear depending on the time period in question. The issue is: what changes in the relationship of what independent variables go with what policy indicator, in this case budgetary expenditures. We learn that in Sweden social and political mobilization has been independently associated with higher expenditures, but that in later periods this association has weakened, and spending changes have become more directly associated with political institutionalization and economic resources. By using longitudinal data (rather than the cross-sectional data usually employed) Peters gives a sense not only of what goes with what, but also of how the answer changes through time. By and large, this case remains at the static end of the scale, because the values (but not the variables themselves) change over time. Cumulative interaction occurs only to the extent that there might be thresholds identifying the turning point from linearity to curvilinearity; presumably a country could also reverse the process.

Attribute correlation can also speak to issues by choosing 'change-oriented' variables for study. Innovativeness can constitute one attribute and then be associated with other characteristics to produce highly suggestive results. Consider, for example, policy innovation in American municipal government. Since the Rand Corporation in the 1960s broadened its interests to include domestic policy, a number of quasi-experiments have been set in train as a by-product of its recommendations. Some recommended innovations have succeeded in being introduced, while others have not. Do certain factors tend more often to be associated with the successful introduction of innovations? The first step is cataloguing possible factors — a reasonable list might include the nature of the organizations subject to innovation, the nature of the change, and the characteristics of the agent seeking to introduce the innovation. Assessing experience is the second step. Even on a rough judgmental basis, the results of such analysis may be far from trivial. Evidence from 10 innovations attempted since the 1960s suggests that the novelty of an innovation and the breadth of its application apparently did not matter much, but reversibility and testability of the change did. A high willingness in the agency to take risks seems less important than that it not be actively risk averse. The main barriers to successful urban innovations appear to rest not in inadequate authority or ignorance, but in a lack of mutual confidence and incentives (Szanton, 1973).

Correlating attributes attempts to associate given variables with each other, whether they are whole system qualities or attributes of only one subsystem. Models become increasingly complex as more factors are added, but the basic representation of policy processes is an array of paired regularities. When not disconfirmed such models may suggest, for example, that economic development but not political democracy is associated with increased social equality, or that redistributive policies are more prominent when demands and political institutions are not fragmented. Sometimes, these analyses indicate discontinuities (via change-oriented variables or different time-period correlations) and thus, become highly relevant for identifying change. The results do not, however, show why or how attributes and correlations themselves change through time.

Steady States

Although sometimes treated as synonymous with statics, steady state analysis here refers to models of a process maintaining a continuous cycle of throughput to execute established modes of input-output behavior. Much of economic theory, for example, is based on this form of analysis. Changes occur but these are by way of perturbances which lead to responses re-establishing stability. Supplies can increase and decrease but the supply/demand/price relationship persists; production functions do adapt (in terms of scale, substitution, etc.) but do so in accord with an established behavioral program; levels of savings may change, but the interdependence of savings/investment/full employment does not. It is precisely because values of given variables change that we can identify the nature of the basic equilibriating relationships.

Comparable ventures of political scientists have never managed to gain the specificity which characterizes economics, but this has not prevented an extremely widespread acceptance of steady state conceptualization of policy processes. In this regard all input/output models are much more alike than different from each other. Richard Rose, for example, has suggested six models of governing which very usefully alert us to distinctions in who or what makes demands and who or what reacts to these demands (Rose, 1973a). In process terms all six models share the same assumption, namely that policy outputs are created as a result of outside demands being acted and reacted upon. In addition, Rose has spelled out at least twelve stages of the policy process that could be applied to any input/output model. An initial state is transferred to a decision agenda, demands are advanced after a review of resources and constraints, decisions and choices emerge; once implemented the outputs are evaluated and produce a return flow of information, which may eventually deroutinize the previously stabilized end state. Taken as a whole the policy process is modeled along the lines of an individual problem solver and static in the sense that it is executing a largely invariate behavioral design. Like equilibrium models in economics, personality theory, or stimulus-response training, policy behavior is identified with:

> (1) the task of collecting and examining the evidence that reveals the states of the operating environment at input-output termini and that maintains the

organization of endogenous component behaviors, (2) interpreting the meaning of these signals in the light of system objectives, and (3) managing the component behaviors so as to reconcile the system objectives in the most efficient way with the operational environment. Such social behavior is absorbed in the service of maintaining a steady state system (Dunn, 1971; 208).

This 'system approach', which is explicitly or implicitly adopted in much political analysis, can be accurately identified as a machine system. It deserves that label because, while a very large number of behavioral options may be present, the system is characterized by a fixed range of such options, techniques, capabilities and criteria. In essence what policy making does — process demands — is fixed by its design. It is a system which processes but is not itself in process of change.

Although intellectually important and widely accepted by political scientists, the machine concept has seldom been pursued in much depth. The preceding articles on welfare and education are suggestive of the largely stable interaction patterns of interest groups and public bureaucracies. Probably the most rigorous application of the steady state concept is David Braybrooke's (1974) small and insightful book, *Traffic Congestion Goes through the Issue-Machine*. Using traffic policy in England, 1963-68, as his example, Braybrooke posits the political system to be an issue machine composed of a stable network of participating stations with stable programs of reaction to ranges of policy alternatives. These alternatives pass through the machine and are processed by being tested against each station's programs (program being used in the sense of computer instructions). Perhaps the most interesting thing is Braybrooke's demonstration that he can formalize the five years of discussion in this way while maintaining reasonably close touch with empirical reality. There appears to be an underlying stability in the contributions of stations and programs regardless of rather substantial changes in party control and government. In this fairly simple range of options, events seem economically represented by what Braybrooke terms *P-stability* — stable programs of response are brought forward and resonate with rather than substantively react to each other *S-stability*, the same stations acting in sequence in successive rounds, appears to be less important. Insofar as trial and error adaptations occur, they take the form of rather simple and direct extrapolation. His results are preliminary but Braybrooke has made a serious attempt to understand implications of the programming assumed in steady state approaches that extend far beyond notions of administrative busy-work.

Comparative Statics

The idea of programming is a suitable point of transition to more time-contingent analyses of variation. Within any considerable time span, programs — or operation codes — are likely to undergo some changes, as are the attributes of any policy within any conceivable typology of policy areas. There are approaches which can take some account of temporal adaptation without implying a fully dynamic model.

Whether we use the term elementary dynamics or, like the economists speak of comparative statics, the point is that steady state analysis can be extended by introducing the concept of reprogramming. In comparative statics, changes in behavioral modes are introduced from outside the system; the resulting equilibrium, once re-established, is compared with the stable situation prevailing before the variation was introduced. Econometric models, for example, typically operate by substituting programs that vary given parameters; the system is then solved and compared with the other equilibria produced by other variations. While none of our authors explicitly concentrate on this type of 'before and after' analysis, allusions to such change are common. At various points, fishing policy, for example, appears to have been affected by externalities (new technologies, international conflicts and economic integration) that have altered established programs and interactions. Robert Jackson's study draws the distinction between procedural responses which seem largely invariate in all crisis management (incremental and symbolic acts followed by coercion and a broader survey of options) and the creation of new 'positional' policy after the crisis episode (new units, reorganizations, contingency plans and so on).

Political scientists using the input/output model of systems analysis often unconsciously adopt a comparative statics approach by treating demand inputs as external interventions generated by socio-economic or other factors outside the political system. The impact of political variables is then identified as the difference between arrangements before and after the new demands were made (Holden and Dresang, 1975). Traditional power models typically approach policy through the comparative statics perspective, positing changes in the possession or relationships of power as the effective cause of reprogramming. Outright conquest from abroad or by revolutionary groups at home is an obvious instance. The 1921 Irish settlement, for example, represented a discontinuity, not because of violence, but because it involved a fundamental reprogramming of existing political processes and institutions.

The same comparative statics perspective has encouraged political scientists to attach intrinsic importance to the turnover of party control of government, administrative reorganization, passage of new suffrage laws, and so on. The tendency automatically to impute effects to institutional rearrangement is likely to exaggerate the amount of effective policy reprogramming which necessarily flows from changes in power relationships (Heclo, 1974).

Much less attention has been given to alternatives to power transfers in effecting exogenous reprogramming of policy processes. Diffusion, imitation, or exogenous surprise are three such alternatives which make little claim on power relationships but may have considerable importance for understanding changes in government programs. For example, the German introduction of social insurance in the 19th century was widely diffused and imitated internationally. In the process, contributory insurance principles rewrote a substantial portion of the pre-existing program for debating the poor law and conditions of the deserving poor. Surprises from areas normally considered outside a given policy system (education policy before and after Sputnik's launching, domestic effects of an abrupt foreign policy reverse, foreign effects of an assassination) may be so severe, widely known and universally interpreted as to yield significant shifts in pre-existing policy programming.

Enough has been said to indicate that different approaches at the static end of the continuum — attribute correlation, steady state models, comparative statics — can aid in understanding different aspects of change and stability. Attribute correlation offers a conceptual mapping of variables associated at given times. Steady state analysis emphasizes the large element of stability in the process of policy-making. Comparative statics recognizes a limited form of adaptation through exogenous reprogramming.

CONCEPTS IN THE DYNAMIC RANGE

Some aspects of variation are not adequately represented in abstract, interchangeable moments in time. A crucial analytic step occurs when different static descriptions are not only compared, but also made contingent upon each other's succession.

Sequence (or Stage) Analysis

While comparative statics emphasizes exogenous reprogramming, sequence analysis tends to concentrate on endogenous changes. Outcomes at (t plus 1) are wholly contingent on serial location relative to the previous period/stage/sequence at time (t). If, for example, at time (t), the values attached to political resources, expenditure of resources and creation of new resources are R, E, and C respectively, we might expect:

$$R(t \text{ plus } 1) \text{ equals } R(t) \text{ plus } C(t) \text{ minus } E(t)$$

It is much easier to write such difference equations than to operationalize them in any politically meaningful way. First order linear equations are obviously ruthless simplifiers of a complex world but they may suggest distinctions in time paths, that is, whether these paths are stable, explosive or oscillatory in some manner. Adding non-linearity can yield cycles of more constant amplitude, but any idea of a 'political trade cycle' remains difficult to justify except as a rough analogy (Kalecki, 1966). Moreover, any rigorous cyclical interpretation identifying given periods, amplitudes and frequencies could be more economically expressed, not as a sequence analysis but as an approximately static model with time-lagged variables. In practice, any close look even at supposedly obvious cyclical relationships – such as between economic performance and government popularity – is likely to show a very complex interaction, only a relatively small part of which seems due to cyclical determination (Miller and Mackie, 1973).

Studies of underdeveloped nations and political development have provided a natural testing ground for attempts at political sequence analysis. The term is used loosely inasmuch as the sequence in question often contains only paired statements about one stage; for example, a phase of political mobilization followed by political institutionalization. When more stages have been used they usually refer to institution-building – e.g., nation-states, parties, bureaucracies – and less often to public policy. Perhaps the most ambitious attempt is the 'crisis' interpretation of political development which has been used by the Committee on Comparative Politics. Sequences of national problems are described in terms of identity, penetration, participation, legitimacy and distribution (Binder et al., 1971; Almond et al., 1973). Unfortunately the closer such stage analysis is examined the more uncertain become its conceptual underpinnings. Whether there are one or many time paths to one or many, or any, end states is unknown. There is as much difficulty substantiating a probability that one stage follows another as a probability that one stage needs to be preceded by another.

Even assuming distinctive sequences can be identified, the most important issue is understanding the factors generating particular policy sequences. In the absence of explanations for the transformation between stages, sequence analysis risks either becoming only a device of convenience or sailing very close to the shoals of orthogenetic fallacy, i.e., presuming development to occur along a given line regardless of external conditions. The more reprogramming is assumed to be a purely endogenous operation, the more sequence analysis reverts to the strategy of comparative statics and leaves implicit the manner by which dynamic processes create adjustments. Thus, while rejecting Marxian determinism, social scientists may be tempted to use their analysis of past sequences as a kind of template for planning with extrapolations attempting to leapfrog over the immediate future from the past (though in doing so the planner implicitly destroys the template for future use). Some Committee on Comparative Politics authors conclude that planners armed with knowledge of crisis sequences might under certain circumstances be able to reschedule developmental crises or at least know about the consequences of (and presumably, anticipate) various sequences (Binder, 1971: 316). If the ultimate moral is that crises should be spaced to prevent demand overloads, then we should recognize that in the background lies, not a dynamic approach, but an implicit, self-maintaining steady state model which probably no one knows how to operate. Accepting this model, the policy-maker who did know how to delay a crisis would have to assume that doing so would not set in train dynamic forces creating a new sequence and possibly even worse crises.

Selective Reprogramming

An analytic focus on selective reprogramming presumes neither the exogenous interventions of comparative statics nor the endogenous time paths of sequence analysis but a mixture of both. Biological evolution is an appropriate analogue for suggesting the basic notion: an interplay between what Dunn (1971; 43) has termed, internally derived and externally encountered significances. Selectivity in reprogramming occurs through two sets of conditional probabilities, one attached to the behavioral options derived within the species' history and the second contingent on the environmental circumstances encountered. The result is a process involving variates at each moment in time. External information on current trials and internal information on previous experience are combined into successive, selective adjustments of behavior. Each step through time may or may not irrevocably foreclose other options, but the changes occurring are irreversible in the sense that, having moved through choice points one 'cannot go home again'. Both internal and external sets of conditional probabilities have been altered by preceding events and choices. To borrow the familiar illustration from Heraclitus, the philosopher cannot repeat his first step into the stream, not only because the stream is in flux but also because the philosopher himself has been changed by his previous experience.

As we move through this more dynamic end of the continuum, the challenge to adjust our normal conceptions of policy-making grows tremendously. Familiar conceptions of leads or lags in policy-making (e.g., ratios of demands to capabilities of government) blur; the system at some future time will not only be ahead or behind but in some sense a different system. Similarly, feedback becomes an ambiguous concept because effects internal to the policy system may make it to some extent a different system into which externally derived information feeds back. Robert Jackson's study of crisis, for example, suggests how spillovers and diffusions from handling a given crisis may produce changes in structure and behavior quite apart from the direct feedback of the crisis at hand.

Fortunately, many of these ambiguities are mitigated by concentrating on the selectiveness of selective reprogramming. Changes are likely to occur as adaptive specializations.[2] that is, refinements introduced into an otherwise unmodified behavioral design. In identifying adaptive specialization it is not the size (increment) of the change that matters but its contribution to a more precise, more narrowly efficient responsiveness to specific conditions — new categories of grants, revised regulations, adjustments in who consults whom, and so on. Insofar as incrementalism speaks to these features of dynamic change, it does so in terms of the *serial* nature of successive adaptation, not the conundrum of how big is an increment. The preceding case of Irish policy illustrates a progressively specialized adaptiveness after 1880. By gradually abandoning law enforcement, through curtailment and neglect. British officials found an extremely efficient means of avoiding immediate, overt trouble. While this selective reprogramming suited British needs, it was ill-fitted to deal with events developing in Ireland. Moreover, the very selectivity of this reprogramming meant that parts of the larger policy design, particularly British pretensions of responsi-

---

[2] As used here specialization does not necessarily mean a division of labor, since such division can just as readily facilitate adaptive generalization.

bility and control, were left unchanged. Later crises confirmed these growing contradictions.

Selective reprogramming carries us some but not all of the way toward the dynamic end of the continuum of change. It encompasses a range of limited reprogramming based on the interaction of policy-making systems and their environment. In the first place, we may discover little more than the stimulus-response type of interaction found in *classic conditioning* theory and steady state models. This, in effect, seems to be the thrust of much of the description of British and American attempts at welfare reform; interest groups have tended to respond to any new proposals as a threat to their customary indulgences (FAP and tax credits) or became so preoccupied with other issues as to miss the signals (FIS). Jack Brand's study shows similar features in local government reform, particularly as structural reform implicates established symbolic values.

In the second place, selective reprogramming is likely to extend to specialized adaptations introduced through *instrumental conditioning*. In such circumstances the policy-making system depends not only on the external stimulus and internal set but also on successive consequences of the policy-makers' own actions. What is learned depend to some extent on the preceding actions taken. Thus in Swedish and West Germany education policy, factors endogenous (memories of Nazification, continuity of social democratic power, etc.) and exogenous (social homogeneity) to the immediate policy system played their part. But so too did the unfolding consequences of policy-makers' own actions. By instituting an experimental design to counteract existing assumptions about the distribution of learning ability among children, Swedish policy-makers created a momentum that Heidenheimer terms rolling reform. By establishing ties with the bureaucracy, a strand of interaction was established capable of facilitating later policy reforms in related areas. Of course the reverse may also occur, as negative feedback from a series of actions leads to a rejection rather than reinforcement of the original response program.

Thirdly, the selective reprogramming of purely instrumental (or cybernetic) learning may be supplemented by *cognitive conditioning*. Particularly in circumstances where the environment is highly complex and thus not readily decomposed into fixed components, conceptual structures are likely to be a vital means of channeling the perception, interpretation and recall of signals for reprogramming. Accommodating as it does new ideas and inferences below the level of general structural adjustment, such constrained learning seems to be an extremely widespread mode of policy change (Steinbruner, 1974).

But the concept of selective reprogramming also has its limits in the study of dynamic change. Its adaptations occur on the basis of external and internal sets of conditional probabilities, but existing paradigms outside the area of reprogramming continue to provide rules of thumb for choosing promising paths through the undergrowth of complexity and uncertainty. Yet these general paradigms may themselves also change through time. As such shifts occur and are more than the mere summation of prior specialized adaptations, the boundary is crossed from selective to comprehensive reprogramming.

Comprehensive Reprogramming

The dynamic extreme of our continuum is reached with analysis of wholesale paradigm shifts. Obviously we are talking about big changes but it is important to emphasize that this does not necessarily imply big events, that is, occurrences arousing major political attention. In terms of dynamic change, a severe widely discussed international or economic crisis may represent little more than very selective reprogramming or a static routine with fixed programs. This was probably the case with many periodic provocations in Europe during the 1930s, most postwar recessions and many defense incidents in the 1950s and 1960s. Contrariwise, important paradigm shifts can occur through seemingly small, little-noticed steps. America's so-called welfare crisis of the 1960s, for example, led to no comprehensive reform; but almost as an afterthought, a limited program (Supplementary Security Income) grafted adult public assistance onto the Social Security Administration. This change, by nationalizing a portion of the American poor law into the contributory insurance system, could portend a major paradigm shift in future years.

If political attention and controversy are irrelevant, what are the basic issues involved in comprehensive reprogramming? In the preceding section we introduced the concept of adaptive specialization. To study comprehensive reprogramming is likely to require relatively greater attention to adaptive generalization. Rather than dealing more effectively with narrower, more specialized conditions, adaptive generalization means improving capacities to deal with a wider, more variable range of events. It is the difference between learning a technique versus a technology, a vocabulary versus a language, a melody versus harmony itself.

Analysis at this range of policy dynamics offers probably the greatest challenges to our normal conceptions of policy and change.

The major difficulty seems to be that adaptive generalization can only rarely be identified in the actions of one subsystem and its selective programs. Subunits actually capable of organizational self-evaluation occur infrequently and persist against great odds (Wildavsky, 1972). More commonly the reprogramming entailed by adaptive generalization appears in system-wide reinterpretations and accumulations. The very ubiquity of such dynamic change helps to account for its elusiveness. What does seem clear is that the more we are interested in analyzing the extreme dynamic end of the continuum, the more attention we must pay to the twin phenomena of interpretation and cumulation.

Analogies of physical evolution become strained in dynamic analysis of policy-making because of man's interpretive powers. In human policy-making, change can occur cognitively as well as physically. For biological dynamics to operate, generation must physically succeed generation if information and adaptations are to occur, be tested and become established or rejected. Political and other social processes can take shortcuts through thought. Policy-makers need not, like the unfortunate sea hare, produce 478 million offspring so that two may survive to carry adaptation forward. Information and changes are transmittable within as well as across generations, within many types of institutions rather than through only one species. Behavioral modes can be reprogrammed without one political party succeeding another. A policy may die as an operating hypothesis without ever having encountered the external world and without its host agency passing away. Thus if selective reprogramming emphasises the cognitive element in policy making as a learning constraint, comprehensive reprogramming accentuates its role as an opportunity for change through conceptualization and reconceptualization.

In addition to conditional probabilities associated with the system's inheritance and environmental encounters, there are important variations in an appreciative dimension — the ways we think about our situation.

> The situation to which the policy maker attends is not a datum but a construct, a mental artifact, a collective work of art. It has to be simplified, or it becomes unmanageable; yet if it is oversimplified, it will be no guide to action. It has to reflect present and future reality; yet if it departs too sharply from the familiar thinking of the past, it will not be sufficiently shared by those for whom it has to provide a common basis for discussion. It has to be not merely discovered but invented, not merely invented but chosen from among several alternative inventions, each a valid but differently selected view. Most difficult of all, it must not obscure the views which it supersedes. (Vickers, 1967: 66).

Over time, policy-relevant appreciations (Is X a problem requiring decision or is it only a condition? What alternatives are thinkable, and so on) may become diffused and shared so as to become 'ideas in good currency'. (Schon, 1973). There is some evidence that a particularly important feature in this process is likely to be the roles of bureaucracies, their circles of professionals and influential middlemen brokering ideas from outside the normal range of a given group's appreciations (Walker, 1974; Heclo, 1974).

The important shifts into comprehensive reprogramming occur as reinterpretations are applied not only to the internal system or external world but also to the sense of interrelatedness between the two. Through these dynamic changes in policy systems we reinterpret not just ourselves and/or the external situation but ourselves-in-the-situation. Our short cuts through thought envelope endogenous and exogenous boundaries into a realm of reflective self-awareness concerning the system's own role in its environment. Such changes in self-consciousness imply the most comprehensive paradigm shifts: where are we? why are we here? whither do we tend? Events of 1921 may represent not just issues of Irish policy but one piece of a larger transformation by which Britain's role in the world was being reinterpreted; a social reform may not only raise questions about aid to the poor but also be a force for reconceiving the meaning of social dependence and collective responsibility.

From the changeability of a policy system's sense of relation to the world springs much of the difficulty and richness in policy dynamics. Cues about success or failure in coping with the endogenous and exogenous tests of policy can be changed by reinterpreting what was wanted and what happened. Processes become not only multi-goaled but more indeterminate as through time experiences change both our goals and our sense of relation to them and the environment. To perceive these changing appreciations requires extending our frame of reference in historical time. In doing so we must take account of a second concept: cumulation.

Dynamic policy change is likely to emphasize not replacement as in pure evolutionary rivalry but accumulations of prior forms and processes whose co-existence and interaction at later times can lead to novel, holistic qualities. Something of this nature is suggested, for example, in Samuel Beer's description of the development of U.S. intergovernmental relations and centralization. The contemporary increase in centralization is seen to flow out of a cumulative series of political coalitions (porkbarrel, spillover, class, and technocratic alliances), each of which is conditioned by the socio-economic environment and by the forces set in train through its preceding history. Significantly, the increasingly interdependent and technical nature of this process strains, above all, the capacities for creating and maintaining any shared appreciative framework, or what Beer terms mobilization of consent (1973: 87).

Cumulative change is especially prominent because dynamic policy processes rarely concern an individual problem-solver — although most of our models seem to rely on images of an individual Decider reconciling his objectives and a troublesome environment. Rather we are likely to find a decomposable system in which components in the short run often seem independent and in the longer run depend on each other in only an indistinct, generalized way (Simon, 1965). This means that the institution most directly concerned in taking action may change little but reprogramming will gradually crop up elsewhere in a proximate institution, subunit or hitherto uninvolved actor. Little adaptation may be evident in concrete policy outputs but new behavioral rules of a process nature may lay the groundwork for substantial changes later. Unnoticed accretions of personnel, resources or ideas may increase subsystem overlap but the value of these new redundancies for reducing error may appear only later or never at all.

The cumulation of dynamic policy change implies something other than the addition of more factors. Its meaning also extends beyond the notion of a self-reinforcing sequence common in political activity, by which an unwillingness to run risks or take decisions at one time requires a willingness to run greater risks, make tougher decisions at subsequent stages. Dynamic cumulation suggests a continual accretion of factors whose later interplay presents unexpected constraints and opportunities. Accumulations may create a generalized agitation and response-readiness in policy. They may tax our analytic models by creating gradual changes in holistic configurations. In such cases:

> ... modifications of form will tend to manifest themselves not so much in small and *isolated* phenomena, in this part of the fabric or that, but rather in some slow, general and more or less uniform or graded modification, spread over a number of correlated parts, and at times extending over the whole. (Simon, 1965; 72).

Insofar as there is a structure to these modifications of comprehensive reprogramming, it does not seem well-represented by static, linear, cyclical or discontinuous conceptualizations. At the extreme range of dynamic change a model is required for dealing with the

cumulative movement and reinterpretations of policy, one applicable
both to the stream of observable events and to the equally powerful
stream of development in ideas, basic paradigms, dominent metaphors,
standard operating procedures, or whatever we choose to call the
systems of interpretation by which we attach meaning to events. The
essence of such a model seems dialectic, with its basic principle of
self-engendered opposition and transcendence. Dialectic change refers
to the tendency for both policy actions and ideas in good currency to
produce, from within their own line of development, reactions ques-
tioning the continuance of that line. Confrontation may then lead to a
new formulation reconciling these forces but also setting in train its
own eventual protests. Such change is cumulative and reinterpretive in
the sense of bringing into operation approaches (adaptive generalizations) that are derived from but wider than their forebears.

Historical determinism has undoubtedly given dialectics a bad name,
but it can be used without implying inevitability and without hearing
the footsteps of either Hegel's Universal Spirit or Marx's class struggle
marching through history. As used here, the dialectic of dynamic policy
change is problematic; it ay or may not be observed and supportable
through the reasoning and evidence of policy analysis. Imagine, for
example, thinking retrospectively about the key issues that might have
been settled, at least temporarily, by any given policy – what if any
non-profit criteria shall apply in urban planning? is public income
support a social right or a welfare dispensation? what are the pero-
gatives of central and local authority? and so on. If we ask ourselves
how this outcome came to be, we may find little more than the routine
of a steady state or another cycle of controversy alternating with
apathy on recurring issues. But why has this issue been accepted as
routine or been defined as comparable to the last recurrence? We may
find the usual bargaining and mutual adjustment of the political marketplace; but how is it that people come to be bargaining about these
issues and conceiving them in one way rather than another? We may
find that selective reprogramming has occurred, with its attendant
cognitive constraints, feedback from environmental encounters, and
communities of policy professionals. But there may also be larger
configurations that are dependent only very indirectly on each particular component or adaptation. We may discover that the broad issue
under study had been answered differently in the past; that it generated
its own contradictions and eventually produced a new synthesis producing new sets of difficulties, for example, the basic conception of
government as regulator aiding the allocation of resources to factors of

production while yielding increased dissatisfaction with the resulting distribution of income may be followed by an interpretation of government as distributors of benefits to compensate for social maldistributions. Yet our difficulties may then proliferate, not because we lack technical capabilities of meeting environmental, energy and economic problems, but because the existing configuration of policy actions and ideas is poorly suited to deal with the conscious distribution of costs. In this way the dialectic of policy dynamics calls into question not just our internal policy assessments or external responses and feedback but also the nature of the self-consciousness by which policy-makers link the two realms.

Clearly, given the elusiveness of the factors involved, we should not be surprised if our political institutions find it difficult to deal with much less anticipate dynamic policy change.

COPING WITH DYNAMIC CHANGE

Political institutions and processes do not exist to deal exclusively with dynamic change, nor would many people be satisfied if they did. Any policy-making apparatus has originated in an interplay of forces across the entire continuum of change. It is likewise expected to act across an equally broad range of change — to permit static self-defense by interests and recognize established associations among variables, to counteract cycles and to progress linearly toward goals, to absorb exogenous interventions and to act within the appropriate sequences, to acquire both more specialized and more generalized adaptations. In short, we probably expect as much from our political apparatus as life expects from each of us as individuals. Given that we want responsiveness not only to continuity and change but also to different types of change, it is idle to criticize policy systems because they possess some non-dynamic characteristics. More serious are the mounting criticisms that existing policy-making arrangements are relatively over-equipped for making static adjustments and relatively deficient for dealing with dynamic changes. What are these deficiencies and what seem promising strategies of political response?

Challenges

It is tempting to define the dynamic challenges to policy-making in terms of an ever-accelerating, destabilizing race into the future. Unfortunately, the doctrine of future shock tends to be comparable to

19th century predictions that the speed of motorized transport would seriously impair human physiology. As riders of old-style British omni-buses know, there is a considerable difference between stepping onto and walking in a moving vehicle. Existing policy-making procedures are not stationery fixtures that must somehow mount and brake various exponential trends. Rather, both policy systems and their subject matters are moving factors, forever in midpassage. The problem is not, then, to catch up with dynamic change but to maintain the capacity for continuously moving with it.

From the large number of recent critiques of post-industrial society, two fundamental challenges seem to stand out (Vickers, 1975; Lind-berg, 1975). One is a cumulative growth of interdependency and the other is a decline of shared appreciations in public policy.

Interdependency means not only the interpenetration of foreign and domestic policies. It refers more broadly to the fact that partitions which were previously assumed to separate all policy areas are more often being called into question. Supposedly external factors seem integral to the prospects of any particular policy, just as any given policy imposes externalities vitally affecting other areas. Public income maintenance programs, for example, now interact powerfully with general taxation measures and ostensibly private systems of wage settle-ment (Heclo, 1975). Minimum subsistence standards, which might ignore arrangements above any given minimum, have yielded to rela-tional standards and concerns with general income distribution – an expansion of perspective by which everyone becomes potentially impli-cated in government policy. Likewise, in energy, economic, environ-mental and a great many other policy areas, our awareness of the externalities and uncertain boundaries has expanded greatly in the last decade. Moreover, these interdependencies seem to depend not only on what impersonal economic and social forces do to us but also on man's own socio-economic interventions and changing conceptions.

Equally important is the tendency of our policy processes to generate appreciations that are shared only in the sense of expecting more solutions and requiring progressively higher thresholds for satis-faction. As boundaries of policy expand, government bureaucracies cannot mandate the cooperation required for effective programs. They must depend more and more on a mutual 'sense of the situation' among government authorities, private groups, and individual citizens – an ability to see the connections among things, expenditure and taxes, benefits and costs, personal claims and social side effects. Increasingly, policy problems stem not from policy-makers' inability to acquire or process information from an outside environment, modern capacities for which are immense, but from our difficulty in finding those shared appreciations which our common life requires. Vickers has summed up the basic dilemma well:

> All the peoples of the developed West in varying degrees have become dependent on external relations, political and economic, which span the world. All of them also, within their national societies have become dependent on political and economic relations involving central regulation, the provision of huge common services and the massive redistribution of income. Even these internal, still more the external relations far transcend the limits of direct experience.
>
> On the other hand these peoples are as dependent as their neolithic ancestors on *experienced* human relations to create the conditions of human life — the conditions which make possible effective common action, mutually understandable communication, assured personal identity and mutual trust. This realm of shared personal experience is today far too limited in extent and far too varied in its impact to generate the understanding or the consensus on which we in fact depend. (Vickers, 1975: 34).

This central dilemma of dynamic change is certainly not new. Early sociologists observed the paradox by which the social division of labor would create both more social interdependence and more individual autonomy (Durkheim, 1893). What modern liberal democracies now seem to be encountering is a much intensified version of this challenge, more intense because it has less chance of being relieved by recourse to previously powerful cognitive frameworks such as faith in economic growth, nationalism, free market doctrines, or religious tenets.

A reestablishment of common interpretations is possible, say, through a resurgence of nationalism or a moral ecumenism. If, however, responses to cumulative interdependency and appreciative fragmentation are to occur through liberal democratic politics, the type of responses called for seem clear. Adaptive specializations, such as more powerful government planning units, increased technical expertise, more precise regulations, etc., are of limited utility for meeting these challenges. Adaptive generalizations are necessary to cope with the wider varieties of interdependency and understandings. While not throwing overboard static functions, more flexible capacities need to be developed within and across policy systems. The remaining sections speculate on what seem two of the most promising directions of development.

Redundancies

Redundancy is used here to refer to overlap and duplication among policy systems. Its value as a means of increasing the reliability of systems operating amid uncertainty has been increasingly recognized. (Landau, 1969). Less well recognized is the fact that redundancy can be an important aid in coping with interdependencies and the absence of common appreciations. But it seems likely that only certain forms of redundancy is suitable for dealing with the dilemma of dynamic change.

The institutional pluralism of American government has traditionally been used as an example of how, by sharing powers among divided branches and levels of government, the reliability of a whole system may exceed that of any part. Historically, this design has worked extraordinarily well. Not the least of its advantages has been that, from a dynamic perspective, it has minimized the cumulative aspects of change and thus also minimized the build-up of unpredictable inter-actions. By and large each major policy change must be fought anew, coalitions and bargains struck anew, commitments traded anew and then only for the immediate purposes at hand. Welfare reform shows very well how little cumulative commitment had been generated after decades of experience with income support programs. (The Social Security program on the other hand remains an exception, made possible because it has been insulated from the normal policy process in Washington.)

The American form of redundancy may be less appropriate for dealing with the problems of interdependency and common under-standings. Despite a presumed sharing of powers, the redundancy of American policy systems is based largely upon the notion of sub-division. The often noted advantages for self-defense and veto are the reflection of a policy process which operates through a progressive narrowing of the decision stream through a finer and finer mesh of particular interests. Thus, in welfare, the entire issue of reform in income maintenance could eventually come to turn on very narrow technical and political considerations. In fishing policy, geographic concentration led to the under-representation of particular fishing in-terests in British policy, but would undoubtedly be an advantage in the American context. If the dynamic changes are such as we have described, what is needed is not further subdivision of interests and perspectives but more powerful means of aggregation. The fact of differentiation becomes less important than that differentiation should not be permanent or mutually exclusive. In particular, there is a need that those helping to make decisions should have to bear the consequences, and those bearing the consequences should be involved in the decisions.

Given that governments must continue to act throughout the continuum of policy change, there is little reason to look for a single fundamental reform for coping with dynamic change. Rather, redundancies are more likely to evolve throughout many different, seemingly disparate areas of activity. In labor relations, increased interpenetration of formerly separate employer/employee spheres is one such change. Worker participation in management (management's participation on the shopfloor is still rare but perhaps equally necessary) encompasses many emerging experiments in overlapping policy systems, the effect of which may be an increased recognition of interdependence between claims pressed by management or labor and the capacities to respond.

Government and interest group consultation are pervasive but forms of consultation may not be equally promising for coping with dynamic change. The more competitive, fragmented American tradition is likely to give access and adapt to changing groups and orientations; but access is likely to be to veto rather than collaborative positions and adaptability implies little ongoing commitment to sharing the costs of interdependency. American criticism of 'interest group liberalism' (Lowi, 1969) suggests the dangers of relying on a balkanized public authority to maintain its independence in these dealings. Comparison of local government reform in Britain and Sweden suggests the importance of proximate groups within a less veto-prone structure. But it also points up the limited capacities of Britain's more insulated, mutually exclusive group process. Perhaps the greatest aid in coping with policy interdependencies and mutual understanding may come from the kind of overlapping memberships, or at least close ties evident in Sweden, for example, in the case studies of local government and education reforms. Without internal organizational openness (not necessarily at each moment but through time), the dangers of creating an interlocking social directorate are profound. Yet this corporativist risk may have to be run if business, government, labor, and consumers are to take more realistic account of each other's mutual effects and needs.

Probably nowhere is the need for increased redundancy greater than in political, fiscal, and monetary policy spheres. Domestically and internationally the de facto interdependencies among these systems have grown immensely, so that only rarely can any nation or policy maker avoid the consequences of their interaction. Politicians are held accountable for the effects of fiscal and monetary decisions over which they usually have little control; at home and abroad, monetary decisions are taken by those who bear few of the consequences. The downside risk of more closely integrating these policy spheres is that political expediency may overshadow longer-term, technically 'expert' considerations. This too may have to be a risk or even a probability that has to be accepted; only hard experience may be able to teach the vices of expediency and virtues of more reasonable restraint. In any event these are not lessons likely to be taught by shielding those responsible for important decisions from public view.

Vastly increased emphasis will probably have to be given to the concept of social exchange. Within the government sphere, coping with dynamic change suggests a need for more interchange between normally separated bureaucratic, political and central/local personnel. Between government and public, greater interchange will probably also be required in referenda, hearings and consultations with transient 'cause' groups. Thus, paradoxically, not' faster decisions and heightened reaction time but more delay and advance preparation may be called for in dealing with policy dynamics. Political parties will probably have to become even more permeable, organizing the electorate around very general intentions and a succession of transient issues rather than concrete party programs. Most basic of all, educational policy systems will need to facilitate mutual understandings and interdependency through the conscious exchange of social and job roles. The aim will be to create, not renaissance men or cross-cutting cleavages, but an appreciation of the different stations in life among which individuals may choose without stigma and with possibilities for re-choosing at later times.

The redundancy needed for coping with dynamic change is not one of duplication and subdivision but of sharing and aggregation. The implication is that if modern policy systems are to move in this direction, our traditional overarching conceptions of political responsibility will have to adapt. What is involved is a shift away from notions of mechanistic accountability (identify and hold responsible the actor 'who did it') and toward conceptions of collective accountability (all are responsible by virtue of 'being in it together'). Such an emphasis may extend the capacities of policy systems to deal with a wider range of phenomenon from differing perspectives. It will provide less help in dealing with the uncertainty inherent in dynamic policy change. For this we will need a second type of adaptive generalization, one that helps make policy processes more responsive to contingencies.

Contingencies

Contingency refers to the fact that dynamically changing policies are dependent on uncertain events. Uncertainty is inherent. Even if policy-makers could accomplish the impossible and know everything about the present, they will still not know about unexpected spillover and new dynamic forces created by their present actions, much less be able to predict the impact of future events generated quite apart from their own decisions.

The troubles besetting economic thought suggest that political scientists are not alone in their difficulties in dealing with dynamic contingencies. In urban economics, planners have had to introduce drastic simplifications to find technical coefficients for the design of an efficiency optimum in activity and communication networks. Sub-optimized components adapt behavior, supposedly given external constraints change, and unpredicted modifications are set in train changing the already established coefficients. The general 'plan' typically becomes a formalization immobilized and made progressively obsolete by rearrangements at subsequent periods. In macro-economic analysis, Professor Joan Robinson has pointed out the problems produced by overlaying Keynes' original dynamic approach with a refurbished equilibrium model. Effective demand, Keynes argued, was a product of volatile, highly uncertain expectations. It was not just that factors of production and investment at any given time depended on complex probability calculations of risk. Expectations were governed not by calculable risks but by a fundamental uncertainty.

> On the plane of theory, the [Keynesian] revolution lay in the change from the conception of equilibrium to the conception of history; from the principles of rational choice to the problems of decisions based on guesswork or on convention .... For a world that is always in equilibrium there is no difference between the future and the past, there is no history and there is no need for Keynes (Robinson, 1973).

It now seems clear, for example, that inflation, unemployment and recessions can all grow together in ways not predicted by established models. Wage bargaining and other relationships adapt by taking into account the inflationary record, a given unemployment rate ceases to yield constant prices and the supposed policy trade-off between unemployment levels and wage rate changes is altered. The meaning of full employment itself blurs as the nature of labor market participation and notions of productive work change.

Politicians encounter comparable problems with avengeance because the ratio of uncertainty to calculable risks is much greater in politics than economics. Asked to define a price and its determinants, economists have a reasonably good idea. Asked to define a policy, political scientists are likely to create a typology. Translated into the economists' world, our situation is not like the marketplace actor with perfect information but more like an amnesic commodity trader trying to assess a current market price of claims against future assets. The May price of next December's wheat will depend both upon the later harvest (itself a function of the two conditional probabilities built up from accumulated harvesting techniques and environmental encounters) and current collective beliefs about the harvest. It is, therefore, not by accident that we have difficulty in using policy typologies to deal with dynamic processes. Characterizations based on allocation (distributive, redistributive, etc.) or structure (segmental, homogeneous, fragmented, etc.) or impact (frequency, severity, etc.) refer largely to intrinsic and static qualities. But policies can and do change in their qualities. They do so because conceptions of the qualities may differ considerably among the participants and because any given conception is likely to change in succeeding steps of the unfolding policy process. Every specific policy is a variable; its meanings are likely to vary among different people at different times.

The implication is that whatever the structure of redundancies, policy processes will need to take more explicit account of contingency. Structural overlaps will help because, as Arrow has observed (1974, 8), uncertainty in future markets can be somewhat mitigated by acquiring more information about those making claims; more overlap in policy systems should make such information more accessible and reliable. But uncertainty will remain and a number of specific devices may help increase capacities to act tentatively in relation to emerging events. There is the paradox that coping with dynamic change may require not faster, more decisive actions but more well-paced tentativeness.

Contingency contracts may be one such device. Policies could be bargained and commitments traded in terms of what will happen if specified circumstances occur. Clearly, some decisions are not amenable to such treatment, but many are. Building only half a school rarely makes sense, but it is possible to make the extent and rate of a general construction program contingent upon certain conditions. Results are also dependent on agreement whether a contingency has in fact occurred. Economic indicators are less ambiguous than social indicators, but some scope for agreement may be found. The general movement toward indexing, for example, depends on relatively unambiguous price or wage increases to activate the commitments; such contingency policies still remain fairly narrowly conceived, neglecting other contingencies such as overall economic performance or circumstances under which general budgetary overhaul may be required. Where agreement is unlikely, the contingency may be no more than an agreement to disagree and accommodate different bodies of opinion when they reach a certain threshold. A number of local American school systems, for example, offer both progressive and more disciplinary alternative curricula depending on parental choice.

A special form of contingency policy-making is the so-called social experimentation movement. (Rivlin, 1974). Rather than operating through fixed, authoritative proclamations, policy is expressed through a series of tentative experiments. These need not imply Orwellian attempts to change human behavior, but rather be self-conscious designs to describe likely behavior under alternative conditions. Pilot programs have long been used to test administrative feasibility, and 'showcase' projects have sometimes sought to create cooperation by demonstrating rather than mandating the virtues of change. Social experimentation adopts a more tentative attitude toward the future, seeking to discover contingencies before rather than after more far-reaching policy decisions are made.

Programming evaluation into the policy process is hardly new. Probably since the first bureaucracy, periodic reporting procedures have been used to maintain some check on forces previously set in motion. Most of these procedures seem to have degenerated into formalities (annual reports, laying regulations before the legislature, etc.) with little relevance to emerging contingencies of dynamic policy. In most countries, one can find hesitant efforts underway to discipline the momentum of existing policy through analysis and evaluation of what is being accomplished, and whether it is relevant to emerging conditions. A variety of techniques are being tried, with no consensus about how to relate ongoing evaluation to policy. Possibly only a continual ferment of approaches — cut-off dates and rejustification of appropriations, analysis as a weapon in budgetary bargaining, management by objectives, requirements for environmental and other types of impact statements, and so on — can deal with the tendency of each analytic device to be assimilated and de-sensitized to emerging contingencies.

The capacity to cope with dynamic contingencies seems likely to be strained under traditional conceptions of liberal democratic govern-ment, especially if political leaders are to be judged on the basis of achieving output objectives. While political contenders continue to promise to do more and better than each other, their ability to control events and contingencies may be less than ever before. Experience in many western democracies suggests an ominous situation in which the requisite for immediate success at the polls makes future survival less likely. The spiral of promises, failure, disbelief, rejection and more strident promises may become self-reenforcing. The means discussed for coping with dynamic change cannot substitute for some disengagement of political leadership from pledges of particular outputs. Too many contingencies may intervene to stake political success on achieving precise material outputs, such as full employment, stable prices, rapid growth, and so on. This is not to suggest an escape from political responsibility but a less exclusive reliance on often unobtainable out-puts as the test of responsibility. It suggests reducing expectations of doing everything better in favor of doing a few things well. Hence future political survival and policy change may require more emphasis on the qualities and performance of political leadership than on parti-cular policy outputs. Dynamic policy changes in the period ahead may indicate less not more attention to supposedly out-dated moral and ethical attitudes embedded deep in the western cultural heritage. A government that cannot survive by showing that it has hit every target may still create public support by engendering a sense that it has tried in good faith. In any event, there is a clear need throughout the western democracies to 'distance' the legitimacy of government from particular material outputs, much less from government responsibility for making people happy.

The results of coping with dynamic change will be problematic at best. A survey of our advanced techniques for forecasting dynamic situations shows a few small aids, an abundance of jargon and abstract models, and a 'system dynamics' literature that neglects political and other processes in favor of a few mechanistic relations between popula-tion, pollution, food and natural resources. The author's prescription for future progress in forecasting expresses very well the impossible task of those who would try to orchestrate dynamic change. What remains to be done is:

> ... the forecasting of human potentials and limitations, human relations,... modes of expression and communication, and modes of creativity .... Only then will a basis also become available to deal in a realistic way with the political processes implied by the systems approach .... (Jantsch, 1972; 498).

To assess the dynamic range of policy presumes no commitment to or model of self-maintaining forever adapting system that keeps its managers afloat. Through time, 'the' system is only one more variable. How the internal, external, and self-conscious appreciations of policy systems may alter in the future we do not know. We also do not know what novel situations may confront any policy-makers by virtue of the cumulative interaction of supposedly well-known factors. Nor, within a dynamic perspective, can we ever learn enough from the materials of the present to know these things. The show moves on.

REFERENCES

ALMOND, Gabriel A. et al (1973) Crisis, Choice and Change. Boston: Little, Brown.

ARROW, Kenneth (1974) 'Limited Knowledge', *American Economic Review,* March, 1974.

BEER, Samuel H. (1973) 'The Modernization of American Federalism', *Publius,* Fall, 1973.

BINDER, Leonard, et al (1971) Crises and Sequences of Political Development. Princeton: Princeton University Press.

BRAYBROOKE, David (1974) Traffic Congestion Goes Through the Issue Machine. London: Routledge and Kegan Paul.

DUNN, Edgar S. Jr. (1971) Economic and Social Development: A Process of Social Learning. Baltimore: Johns Hopkins University Press.

DURKHEIM, Emile (1893) The Division of Labor in Society. Translated by George Simpson, Glencoe, Ill.: The Free Press, 1947. First published in 1893 as De la division du travail social.

FRY, Brian and Richard WINTERS (1970) 'The Politics of Redistribution', *American Political Science Review* 64.

HECLO, Hugh (1974) Modern Social Politics in Britain and Sweden. New Haven: Yale University Press.

———, (1975) 'Frontiers of Social Policy in Europe and America', *Policy Sciences* 6.

HOLDEN, Matthew, Jr. and Dennis DRESANG (eds), (1975) What Government Does. Beverly Hills: Sage Publications.

JACKMAN, Robert W. (1974) 'Political Democracy and Social Equality', *American Sociological Review* 39.

JANTSCH, Erich (1972) 'Forecasting and the Systems Approach: A Critical Survey', *Policy Sciences* **3.**

KALECKI, Michal (1966) Studies in the Theory of Business Cycles. New York: Kelley.

LANDAU, Martin (1969) 'Redundancy, Rationality, and the Problem of Duplication and Overlap', *Public Administration Review* **29.**

LINDBERG, Leon (1975) 'Strategies and Priorities for Comparative Research', in Lucian Pye (ed) Social Change and Policy Response (tentative title) Bloomington: University of Indiana Press.

LOWI, Theodore (1969) The End of Liberalism. New York: Norton.

MILLER, W. L. and M. MACKIE, (1973) 'The Electoral Cycle and the Asymmetry of Government and Opposition Popularity', *Political Studies,* **21.**

RIPLEY, Randall et al, (1973) 'Policy-Making: A Conceptual Scheme', *American Politics Quarterly,* **1.**

RIVLIN, Alice, (1974) 'How can Experiments be more Useful?' *American Economic Review,* **May 1974.**

ROBINSON, Joan (ed) (1973) After Keynes. London: Barnes and Noble.

ROSE, Richard (1973a) 'Models of Governing', *Comparative Politics,* **5.**

———, (1973b) 'Comparing Public Policy', *European Journal of Political Research,* **1.**

SCHON, Donald A. (1973) Beyond the Stable State.. New York: Norton.

SIMON, Herbert A. (1965) 'The Architecture of Complexity', *General Systems,* **10.**

STEINBRUNER, John (1974) The Cybernetic Theory of Decision. Princeton: Princeton University Press.

SZANTON, Peter (1973) 'Innovation in U.S. Urban Public Services: Ten Case Studies', mimeographed paper from Rand Corporation to the OECD.

VICKERS, Geoffrey (1967) 'The Regulation of Political Systems', *General Systems,* **12.**

———, (1975) 'Social and Institutional Reality', unpublished paper, reproduced.

WALKER, Jack L. (1974) 'The Diffusion of Knowledge and Policy Change: Toward a Theory of Agenda Setting', paper delivered to the 1974 Annual meeting of the American Political Science Association, 29 August — 2 September 1974, Chicago, Illinois.

WILDAVSKY, Aaron (1972) 'The Self-Evaluating Organization', *Public Administration Review,* **32.**

NOTES ON CONTRIBUTORS

Tom Bowden is Senior Lecturer in Politics at Manchester Polytechnic, England. He is the joint author of *Revolt to Revolution* (1974), and the author of *Community and Change* (1974), and *Beyond the Limits of the Law* (forthcoming Penguin special). He has contributed to numerous journals and to the volume POLICE FORCES IN HISTORY (SAGE, 1975).

Jack Brand was born in Aberdeen, Scotland, and studied in Aberdeen, Stockholm, and London. He has been Senior Lecturer in Politics at the University of Strathclyde, and is now director of the Strathclyde Area Survey. He publishes primarily in the field of public policy and Scottish politics.

Ernst Gehmacher is Director of the Institute for Empirical Social Reserch in Vienna. His publications include *Methoden der Prognostik* (1971), and *Psychologie und Soziologie der Umweltplanung* (1972).

Hugh Heclo is a staff member of the Brookings Institution, Washington D.C. He is the author of *Modern Social Politics in Britain and Sweden* (Yale, 1974) and articles on politics and social policy and co-author of *The Private Government of Public Money* (Macmillan, 1974).

Arnold J. Heidenheimer is Professor of Political Science at Washington University, St Louis, Missouri, USA. He has published books on German party politics and comparative political finance, and is senior author of *Comparative Public Policy* (St. Martins, 1975).

Christopher Hood is Lecturer in Politics at Glasgow University. He has worked on an Anglo/American Carnegie Corporation Project on Accountability and Independence in the Contract State.

Robert Jackson is Professor of Political Science at Carleton University, Ottawa. In addition to authoring *Rebels and Whips* and co-authoring *The Canadian Legislative System,* he has been director of research for the privy council office of the Canadian government.

B. Guy Peters is Associate Professor in the Department of Political Science at the University of Delaware. During 1975-76 he is a Fulbright Lecturer in the Department of Politics at the University of Strathclyde, Glasgow. He holds his Ph.D. from Michigan State University, and has written a number of articles on comparative public policy.

Richard Rose has been Professor of Politics at the University of Strathclyde, Glasgow since 1966, and is Secretary of the Committee on Political Sociology, IPSA/ISA. He has written or edited more than a dozen books in the field of comparative politics, including *Politics in England; Governing Without Consensus: An Irish Perspective;* and *Electoral Behavior: A Comparative Handbook.* In 1974 he held a Guggenheim Fellowship to study the implications of new techniques of policy analysis for models of governing, and was resident in Washington.

Publications of the Committee
on Political Sociology

1. "Approaches to the Study of Political Participation", a special issue of *Acta Sociologica* VI: 1-2 (1962).

2. E. Allardt and Y. Littunen, editors, *Cleavages, Ideologies and Party Systems:* Helsinki: Westermarck Society, 1964.

3. S. M. Lipset and Stein Rokkan, eds., *Party Systems and Voter Alignments.* New York: Free Press, 1967.

4. Otto Stammer, ed., *Party Systems, Party Organizations and the Politics of New Masses,* Berlin: Free University, 1968.

5. Stein Rokkan et al., *Citizens, Elections, Parties.* Oslo: Universitetsforlaget; New York: D. McKay, (1970).

6. Richard Rose and Derek Urwin, eds., "Social Structure, Party Systems and Voting Behaviour", a special issue of *Comparative Political Studies* II: 1 (1969).

7. Erik Allardt and Stein Rokkan eds., *Mass Politics.* New York: Free Press, 1970.

8. Allan Barton, Bogdan Denitch and Charles Kadushin, editors, *Opinion-Making Elites in Yugoslavia.* New York: Praeger, 1973.

9. Richard Rose, editor, *Electoral Behavior: a Comparative Handbook.* New York: Free Press, 1974.

10. Thomas T. Mackie and Richard Rose, *International Almanack of Electoral History.* New York: Free Press, 1974.

11. Richard Rose, editor, *The Management of Urban Change in Britain and Germany.* Beverly Hills & London: SAGE Publications, 1974.

12. *Contemporary Political Sociology,* SAGE Professional Papers Series 06, (Beverly Hills & London) Vol. I (1974) *et seq.*

13. Charles Kadushin, *The American Intellectual Elite* (Boston: Little, Brown, 1974).

14. Richard Rose, editor, *The Dynamics of Public Policy.* Beverly Hills & London: SAGE Publications, 1976.